EMBRACING THE UNKNOWN
Experiences of Studying for a PhD in the Social Sciences

Edited by
Sarah Jones, Mikahil Azad,
Liam Miles, and Adam Lynes

Foreword by
Sarah Pemberton

First published in Great Britain in 2025 by

Policy Press, an imprint of
Bristol University Press
University of Bristol
1–9 Old Park Hill
Bristol
BS2 8BB
UK
t: +44 (0)117 374 6645
e: bup-info@bristol.ac.uk

Details of international sales and distribution partners are available at policy.bristoluniversitypress.co.uk

© Bristol University Press 2025

British Library Cataloguing in Publication Data
A catalogue record for this book is available from the British Library

ISBN 978-1-4473-7388-9 hardcover
ISBN 978-1-4473-7389-6 paperback
ISBN 978-1-4473-7390-2 ePub
ISBN 978-1-4473-7391-9 ePdf

The right of Sarah Jones, Mikahil Azad, Liam Miles, and Adam Lynes to be identified as editors of this work has been asserted by them in accordance with the Copyright, Designs and Patents Act 1988.

All rights reserved: no part of this publication may be reproduced, stored in a retrieval system, or transmitted in any form or by any means, electronic, mechanical, photocopying, recording, or otherwise without the prior permission of Bristol University Press.

Every reasonable effort has been made to obtain permission to reproduce copyrighted material. If, however, anyone knows of an oversight, please contact the publisher.

The statements and opinions contained within this publication are solely those of the editors and contributors and not of the University of Bristol or Bristol University Press. The University of Bristol and Bristol University Press disclaim responsibility for any injury to persons or property resulting from any material published in this publication.

Bristol University Press and Policy Press work to counter discrimination on grounds of gender, race, disability, age and sexuality.

Cover design: Andrew Corbett
Front cover image: Getty/shunli zhao

Contents

Notes on contributors	v
Foreword by Sarah Pemberton	x
Introduction	1
Sarah Jones, Mikahil Azad, Liam Miles, and Adam Lynes	

PART I

1	Re-entering academia: the unexpected journey *Sarah Jones*	15
2	Entering the fray: the hyper-competitive PhD environment *Alexander Black*	26
3	Conceptualising a PhD topic: navigating my way through academia *Mikahil Azad*	35
4	New horizons: moving countries to start the PhD *Eliska Suchomel Duskova*	45
5	From home to the unknown: applying for postgraduate study in the UK from the global south *Manikandan Soundararajan*	57
	Editors' reflections: Part I	69

PART II

6	Navigating the depths of grief: a journey through grief while pursuing a PhD *Rio Waldock*	73
7	Double duty: undertaking PhD research while being a full-time lecturer *Charlotte Rigby*	83
8	Balancing act: balancing family life with the PhD *Suzanne Baggs*	93
9	Managing the mind and PhD'ing *Abigail Shaw*	105
	Editors' reflections: Part II	117

PART III

10	Safety in cultures of precarity: complex trauma and the value of 'trauma-informed' PhD supervision *Lisa Edge*	123
11	Working for nothing: the exploitation of postgraduate students *Kyla Bavin*	135

12	How close is too close? Ethical tensions and reflections in the Breddon Centre *Kavya Padmanabhan*	145
13	Methodology unravelled: safely crossing the research minefield *Liam Miles*	156
Editors' reflections: Part III		169

PART IV

14	'Light at the end of the tunnel': the Viva and beyond *Nick Gibbs*	175
15	The whispers of doubt: ten years after the PhD and pervasive imposter syndrome *Adam Lynes*	185
16	Fifteen years later, at the moral crossroads: retaining purpose and direction in the face of academic capitalism *Daniel Briggs*	196
17	Mentoring moments: a collaborative reflection on supervision *Chelsea Braithwaite, Owen Hodgkinson, and James Treadwell*	210
Editors' reflections: Part IV		222

Conclusion — 225
Sarah Jones, Mikahil Azad, Liam Miles, and Adam Lynes

References — 227
Index — 243

Notes on contributors

Mikahil Azad is Lecturer in Criminology at the University of Worcester. Mikahil completed his PhD at Birmingham City University, which studied the experiences of safety in and around the space of mosques, by applying ethnographic methodologies. This involved making sense of the global nature of Islamophobia and structural inequalities. Mikahil sits on the British Society of Criminology Hate Crime Network as Deputy Chair, which involves working toward tackling hate crime in a national and international capacity.

Suzanne Baggs is currently Portfolio Lead for Criminology and Professional Policing at the University of Plymouth. She started at Plymouth as a Doctoral Teaching Assistant in 2017 teaching on various theory and research methods modules, and now mainly teaches on modules that take a harm-based approach to criminological issues. Her second-year module on addiction industries (for example alcohol, gambling, tobacco and so on) developed from her PhD research into how the design and marketing of gambling products negatively impacts women who play bingo and slots online.

Kyla Bavin is Lecturer of Criminology at Birmingham City University and a current PhD candidate at Staffordshire University. Her PhD looks at tribalism and social media. Her broader research interests include crimes of the powerful and the social harms of new technologies. Most recently, she wrote a book with Dr Adam Lynes and Professor James Treadwell, *Crimes of the Powerful: The Democratic Republic of Capitalism*. Kyla is a mature student who fell into academia because of her love of reading and her distaste for late-stage capitalism.

Alexander Black is Visiting Lecturer in Sociology and Criminology at Birmingham City University. He has been in this role since January 2021 and has taught subjects surrounding popular culture; the sociological gaze upon the media; self, identity, and society; city, community, and culture; alongside gender and crime, specifically masculinities and sexual violence. Alexander has been a research assistant, where he supported the investigation into Birmingham's 'Gay Village'. He has also developed a module within the 'Psychology of Gender and Sexuality' at Arden university. Alongside these roles, Alexander has also been a mixed methods interviewer for NatCen since April 2021. Alexander is currently undertaking his doctoral research at Birmingham City University, which examines his coined term of Western hetero-hegemonic masculinity, alongside victimisation and offending of sexually and/or gendered minoritised men and non-binary individuals, together with the police's responses to these social agents.

Chelsea Braithwaite is Part-Time Lecturer at Staffordshire University, where she has taught topics including criminological theory, youth crime, and contemporary issues in criminology. Chelsea is also a PhD candidate at Staffordshire University. Her PhD research focuses on the experiences of emerging adults in Stoke-on-Trent and the harms they face as a result of the COVID-19 pandemic. Chelsea's research interests include social harm, ultra-realist criminological theory, the COVID-19 pandemic, retail violence, youth justice, and emerging adulthood. Chelsea has also published research focusing on the impact of the pandemic on violence against retail workers.

Daniel Briggs, PhD, is Professor of Criminology and Sociology at Northumbria University. As a researcher, writer, and inter-disciplinary academic who studies social problems, he has undertaken ethnographic research into social issues from street drug users to terminally ill patients; from refugees to prostitutes; and from gypsies to gangs and deviant youth behaviours. More recently, he has published extensively around the harms of the COVID-19 lockdowns and the Ukrainian refugee exodus.

Lisa Edge is a PhD researcher at Birmingham City University whose research applies trauma theory to explore the context and motivation behind criminal justice-involved women's use of violence. Lisa is passionate about drawing on her own life experiences to help support and improve the lives of vulnerable women. She co-chairs an expert-by-experience participation group for her local county council and volunteers her spare time to the women's centre where she conducts her research. Lisa's research interests include social harm, violence and abuse, and the impact of trauma on the lives of disadvantaged and marginalised populations.

Nick Gibbs is Assistant Professor in Criminology at Northumbria University. Nick's research can be situated within the sub-discipline of critical sports criminology and spans the areas of masculinity, illicit markets, gym and physical culture, the football industry, novel and digital methods, and drug use and supply. His PhD, and subsequent monograph, concerned the use and supply of image and performance enhancing drugs and he has published widely in journals and books in the disciplines of criminology, sociology, public health, and drug studies. Nick's most recent research focuses on youth academy football and social harm.

Owen Hodgkinson is Associate Lecturer in Criminology at the University of Derby and has recently submitted his PhD in Criminology at Staffordshire

University. Owen has published on topical areas in relation to the social sciences, such as the COVID-19 pandemic and Black Lives Matter movement, and his PhD was an ethnographic study of the decaying night-time-economy of Stoke-on-Trent. Owen's main research interests are violence and masculinities, ultra-realist theory, post-industrialism, and consumer culture.

Sarah Jones is Visiting Lecturer in Criminology at Birmingham City University, where she has taught since 2021, covering a multitude of topics, such as Making Sense of Homicide, Human Rights: Theory and Practice, Key Debates in Criminological Theory, Youth Crime and Justice, Understanding Crime and Criminal Behaviour and Crime and the Media. Sarah is also undertaking her PhD research at Birmingham City University, which explores the post-homicide experiences of the family members of child and youth homicide offenders. Sarah has also published research exploring female participation in high-level drug distribution networks and has contributed towards published edited collections with chapters exploring our understanding of the changing nature of violence and internal misogyny and sexual misconduct within the police.

Adam Lynes is Associate Professor of Criminology at Birmingham City University, where he has taught since 2012, covering topics such as criminological theory, homicide, online crime, transnational organised crime, and corporate crime. Adam's primary research interest is in violence, with a focus on physical and more systemic manifestations. He has published research on such areas as serial murder, family annihilation and organised crime. He has most recently published an edited collection on the phenomenon of dark tourism, and his latest monograph is centred on the crimes of the powerful – both published with Policy Press.

Liam Miles is Lecturer in Criminology at the University of Northampton. Liam is undertaking his PhD at Birmingham City University where his community-based research focuses on the Cost-of-Living Crisis and its effects on young people. Liam's other research interests involve the political economy-based perspectives of crime and injustice, youth, community, and social harm-based perspectives.

Kavya Padmanabhan is a scholar-activist and Lecturer in the Sociology Department at Rice University in Houston, Texas where she teaches on the intersections between law, punishment, and society. She completed her PhD from the University of Cambridge, where she conducted an ethnographic study analysing the relationships between punishment and care in a women's centre in England. Her research takes an intersectional approach to interrogating marginalised women's experiences with punishment and explores the efficacy of gender-responsive, community-based models of care. Her work is informed by the principles of abolition feminism.

Charlotte Rigby is Lecturer in Criminology at Arden University in Birmingham, where she has taught since May 2023. She began reading for a PhD in Sociology in September 2020 at Staffordshire University. Her thesis, titled '"Looking for a Man's Job?": A Historiography of Policewomen's Experiences Throughout the Nineteen Seventies, Eighties and Nineties', adopts a life course approach to analyse the lived experiences of 35 former policewomen. As a cultural sociologist, Charlotte is primarily interested in social histories, and particularly the changing role of working-class women throughout the twentieth century.

Abigail Shaw is Research Fellow at the University of Nottingham and is also pursuing her PhD research at Birmingham City University. With years of dedicated advocacy for Black women within the criminal justice system, firsthand expertise in the field and as a survivor of the criminal justice system herself, Abigail has leveraged her lived experiences to influence both policy and procedure changes and has collaborated with organisations to integrate holistic and culturally appropriate approaches into their operations. She has also partnered with non-profit organisations within her local community to address child imprisonment and support initiatives for women involved in the criminal justice system.

Manikandan Soundararajan is a fully funded PhD scholar at Staffordshire University and holds an MPhil in Criminology from Raksha Shakti University and a Masters in Criminology and Criminal Justice from the University of Madras. He has previously worked as a research assistant at the Centre for Criminology and Victimology, National Law University Delhi, India and as an analyst at Parantapa Sciences, India. His primary research interests are Crime Prevention, Policing and Refugee issues.

Eliska Suchomel Duskova is a PhD student at the Institute of Criminology, University of Cambridge and she is a member of the Justice and Society Research Centre. Her doctoral research focuses on the experiences of Czech children with incarcerated parents, with an emphasis on how children of prisoners are informed about parental incarceration. Eliska is in ongoing contact with various NGOs which help prisoners and their families in the Czech Republic. She is a part-time social worker and consultant for one of the Czech NGOs and an Undergraduate Supervisor.

James Treadwell has been Professor in Criminology at Staffordshire University since 2017, having started his career as a lecturer in Criminology in 2003 at the University of Central England. He has recently been researching prison and criminal drug markets, examining the cultivation of cannabis in economically deprived areas and prison-based drug supply as a larger project on bullying, violence, and victimisation in prison. He is currently involved with a number of ongoing research projects and has recently published a monograph exploring new perspectives on crimes of the powerful. He is also a member of the executive of the British Society of Criminology and was academic advisor on the Howard League Commission into ex-military personnel in prison.

Rio Waldock is Crime Prevention Officer for the Youth Justice Team at Walsall Council, completing intervention work with young people to try and help them stay away from crime. She also works with children in residential care. Alongside these roles, Rio is also undertaking her PhD at Birmingham City University which explores the impacts of the now abolished Imprisonment for Public Protection (IPP) sentencing.

Foreword

Sarah Pemberton
Birmingham City University

Twenty years ago, in sunny Brighton, I found myself at a crossroads and seeking advice from the late, great Dr Sandra Winn, my undergraduate lecturer and an instrumental figure in my early academic journey. Sandra had not only taught me research methods but she recruited me into my first research post while at my graduation. When I asked her whether I should pursue a PhD, she reassured me with what I now realise was a deceptively simple truth: 'It's just about being organised'.

Fast forward a few research posts and universities later, I embarked on my PhD, which was a discursive exploration of how men convicted of rape accounted for their offences. A light-hearted topic? Not quite! Looking back, Sandra's words gave me the confidence to start my PhD journey, as my superpower was in the writing of a good to-do list. But let's be honest, it turns out there's a bit more to it than being organised!

The PhD experience, while unique, is also profoundly universal in its challenges. As you will discover in this book, there are shared experiences which will resonate with anyone who has undertaken a PhD. Imposter syndrome (spoiler alert: it never fully goes away), loneliness, and persistent uncertainty are familiar companions. Explaining what you do to others who haven't been on the journey ... whether it is your well-meaning granny who assumes you're avoiding a 'proper job' or your mates down the pub who don't quite get what you are doing, only adds to the complexity.

But let us not dwell solely on the struggles! The PhD journey is also a time of immense growth. It creates a community, a huge sense of achievement, and, of course, an original contribution to knowledge. Furthermore, nothing quite beats that moment when you get to change those bank cards to say Dr, even though you don't quite have the bank balance to go with it! These moments, while hard-earned, are some of the things that make doing a PhD worthwhile.

Embracing the Unknown is a unique contribution to the field whereby the editors have curated a range of diverse voices and nurtured an open, honest discussion about what it really means to 'do a PhD'. You will hear first-hand from the PhD researchers who are deep in the trenches, offering insights that go beyond your standard academic advice. This is not your typical guide to methodologies and theories; it is a raw, uncensored exploration of the real-life challenges that come with pursuing a PhD. From navigating research setbacks that feel HUGE at the time to balancing work and the curveballs that life can throw your way, including trauma, grief, financial stress, and systemic inequalities, this book beautifully captures the messy reality of the PhD process.

The brutally honest reflections of the authors provide the reader with encouragement, camaraderie, and wisdom that will inevitably leave you feeling less alone in this process. But this book isn't just suitable for those in the middle of a PhD or about the embark on the PhD process, it has utility to those who have just come out of the other side and want to sense check their experiences, but PhD supervisors too as the book serves as a really useful reminder that the PhD does not exist in isolation for our students; it intertwines with life in all its unpredictability and at the very least us PhD supervisors need to be mindful of this within our interactions with our students.

Grab yourself a cuppa and dive into these tales with an open heart and mind and remember that while the journey may be challenging, it is also deeply rewarding. *Embracing the Unknown* will provide you with community, inspiration, and a roadmap through the unpredictable path of a PhD.

To my younger self, I would tell you it was much more than being organised (but that is ok!) and that the PhD is not the culmination of your work, it is just the beginning. You have got this!

Introduction

Sarah Jones, Mikahil Azad, Liam Miles, and Adam Lynes

Where to begin?

To begin this book, we would like to take a moment to explain how and why it was written. Unlike some of the previous books in which members of the editing team have been involved, there was no initial grand plan or design for this collection. As PhD students in the social sciences and, in the case of one of the editors, a PhD supervisor, we are taught to consider each of our research projects carefully, to meticulously design and plan our methodology, our theoretical framework and, of course, our impact. This can, of course, be seen in the multitude of 'how to' books and guides written for new and aspiring PhD students as they embark on their journey, along with those more seasoned and battle-hardened researchers who may need a source of inspiration as they face, for example, a methodological barrier here or ethical quandary there. For instance, there are texts such as Duleavy's (2003) *Authoring a PhD: How to plan, draft, write & finish a doctoral thesis or dissertation*, Hockey and Gupta's (2019) book, *PhD 101. The manual to academic*, and Harrison's (2010) *How to write a PhD in less than three years*. While we acknowledge the practical significance and utility of such books, it was over a coffee and a catch-up on campus one morning that we stumbled upon a discussion about there being little to no texts that discuss placing the student's experiences at the centre, a book that is less a guide written by someone far removed from their own experiences of undertaking a PhD and one in which the realities, obstacles and reflections by those in the 'now' are at the heart. In essence, while there are plenty of books relating to the *process* of doing a PhD, there was little to nothing available that spoke to the *experience*. So, to reassure you, the reader, this is NOT your typical 'how to' guide or conventional academic textbook written by some professor imparting their wisdom and knowledge. Instead, this collection is one concerned with providing an eclectic assortment of voices from the PhD community, providing their thoughts, experiences and 'in the moment' accounts of what life as a doctoral candidate is really like within the higher education (HE) environment.

It is worth highlighting here that, out of the four editors, three are still undertaking their own PhDs at the time of writing. One of these editors highlighted how, while these aforementioned books did a splendid job in walking through the procedure of conducting a PhD, what was missing was an acknowledgement of the emotional, personal, and unique realities that go unseen or addressed. All the editors kept referring to the process of doctoral study as entering the *unknown*, and while these books helped to some degree regarding the overt and thus expected practices that constitute the PhD process, they did little to elucidate the more obscure and consequently unforeseeable experiences that each individual will ultimately face within their journey. It is not just these books we are referring to here but how, within the confines of academia, such experiences are often omitted, with students routinely judged on their progress by way of 'tick box' exercises in the form of annual reviews, monthly meetings (if they are lucky), and formal feedback. In essence, their progress is, as reflected by the editors currently enrolled on a PhD, judged on, and reduced to, how many words have been written and if the required bureaucratic 'hoops' have been jumped through. This discussion progressed to what, ideally, we would have liked to have seen in a book centred on the PhD process – one that shared stories and experiences from the 'trenches', so to speak, and one that connects with the internal dialogue of the PhD experience. It quickly dawned upon us that if there is currently no book out there to cater to this, then perhaps we would have to be the ones to offer a reinvigorated approach to 'navigating the field'. This was, obviously, a nerve-wracking proposition. As previously mentioned, three of the editors were enrolled and deeply involved in their own PhD journey and for the other, a plethora of other research projects, administration responsibilities, and teaching commitments were at the forefront of their minds. However, as days turned to weeks, this germ of an idea began to grow, and within each subsequent conversation and brief exchange along the corridors of Birmingham City University, the book took on a life of its own. Eventually, we all came to the same, inevitable conclusion: we needed to write the book that some of us would have benefited from while undertaking our PhD and, for others, about to embark on their journey. We wanted to create a text that would serve as a source of comfort and support for others, one that will help others as they navigate and, ultimately, *embrace the unknown*.

Observing the current landscape of higher education

This collection is, in many ways, the antithesis of all that we have learned and experienced within higher education. It is a unique resource that aims to place the student's experiences at the centre of the PhD journey, offering a perspective often overlooked in traditional academic texts. While we may have decided to write a book centred on PhD experiences given its inherent uniqueness, it was not until we mapped out the current state of higher education that we realised just how important this book is when we consider this is a sector underpinned by economic precarity, ontological insecurity and hyper-competition (Bone, 2021). This is reflected in a study conducted by Hazel and Berry (2022), who surveyed 3,300 UK PhD students, in which 42 per cent of them reflected that they faced significant mental health issues throughout their PhD. Milicev et al (2023) echoed such damning findings only one year later, noting the notable prevalence of mental health symptoms in Post Graduate Researchers in the UK, implying that institutional efforts to improve PGR well-being should include strategies to promote equality, diversity, resilience, integration, social support, and work-life balance of PGRs. Beasy, Emery, and Crawford (2019) stress that doctoral students experience 'poor well-being outcomes during candidature' (p 602). In particular, their study – consisting of 222 PhD students – determined that many of the participants encountered a range of obstacles, including inadequate support from both their supervisors and institutions. While this specific study was conducted in Australia, it echoes some of the similar themes outlined by studies in the UK, speaking to the universal nature of the PhD experience and the need to bring such students' voices to the fore.

Taking all of this into account, it is worth noting that the road to a PhD, given its prestigious status, is intentionally thwarted by challenges. It is estimated that only 2 per cent of the population in Britain holds a PhD, with 104,965 students enrolled in such programmes and 21,000 doctoral candidates graduating in the period between 2020 and 2021 (Higher Education Statistics Agency, 2023). Not only is a PhD incredibly rare but, as alluded to in the previous statistics, the actual pass rate is also relatively low compared to other levels of study, with 30 to 50 per cent of PhD candidates dropping out of their studies globally. More specifically, in the UK, where this book primarily focuses on, approximately 25 per cent of PhD students do not finish their studies (Firth, 2022). If we zoom in closer, we must also consider systemic and institutional barriers relating to class, age, ethnicity, and gender identity. To illustrate, class has always been a barrier to entry, with 26 per cent of 25- to 29-year-olds from the top socio-economic background in the UK having achieved a master's or a PhD – compared with just 7 per cent from the most disadvantaged group (Jack, 2023). Regarding age and doctoral research, over a third are aged 25 and under, but over 20 per cent are in their thirties, and 15 per cent are over 40. The profile for part-time students is significantly different, with 40 per cent over 40. Conversely, about half of full-time doctoral researchers are 25 or under (Gov.UK, 2013). If we examine ethnicity, Lynam, Lafarge, and Milani (2024) paint a rather bleak picture, too:

> The findings indicate that ethnic minority PGRs faced multiple challenges during their doctoral journey, which were often triggered and amplified by circumstances specific to their ethnicity. The results suggest that HE environments are still dominated by White norms as

well as oppressive systems and attitudes that disempower EM PGRs and stifle their sense of belonging and ability to thrive. Female and international EM PGRs were particularly marginalised. Participants made recommendations for change, including proactive outreach support for EM PGRs and creating culturally sensitive environments to foster positive doctoral experiences for all. (Lynam, Lafarge, and Milani, 2024: 1)

Focusing on gender identity within the context of the PhD and higher education more broadly, there has yet to be any national data examining such characteristics, which, in itself, speaks volumes.

Things also do not look promising for those fortunate enough to successfully complete and defend their thesis, with a report by Cornell (2020a) stating that, out of the 67 per cent of PhD students who wanted a career in academic research, only 30 per cent stayed in academia three years after. Another study by Cornell conducted in the same year (2020b) also determined that, out of 1,069 PhD students enrolled in a UK institution, 80 per cent reported that a career in research is lonely and isolating, with over one-third (37 per cent) of PhD students having sought help for anxiety or depression caused by PhD study.

We also have to consider the broader economic and cultural transformations happening within the higher education settings. In 2010, the then-coalition party, led by the Conservatives, increased student fees from £3,290 per year to approximately £9,000 per year of study (Hillman, 2016). While such decisions were met with almost instant outrage and opposition in the form of student protests (Webster, 2018), it is in the last few years that the ripple effect of these decisions has begun to be felt acutely by the PhD student, early career academic, and Senior Professor alike. The increase in student fees heralded by the increasing neo-liberalisation of English universities has spurred detrimental changes in higher education. With universities operating under marketisation pressure, their focus has shifted from educational quality to profit-making, mirroring corporate models which, as critical criminologists, we would often critique and deplore (Lynes, Treadwell, and Bavin, 2024). This shift is exacerbated by the financial strain imposed by heightened fees, burdening students with substantial debt and compelling institutions to prioritise revenue-generating ventures over academic pursuits (Meredith, 2024). Consequently, academic labour has become increasingly precarious, marked by job insecurity due to casualisation and limited benefits, something that is now more and more common when it comes to PhD scholarships offering to wipe out student loans in exchange for labour (Johnstone, 2004). Moreover, the pressure to secure research funding has skewed priorities, diverting attention from teaching quality to research outputs to score that bit better in the next Research Excellence Framework (REF) audit. Furthermore, the impact on diversity is notable, with funding cuts disproportionately affecting marginalised disciplines and scholars in the arts and humanities, which has also come under increasing attack by the Conservative party (Davies, 2020). The cumulative effects of these changes manifest in the deterioration of mental health among academics, driven by heightened workloads, publication pressures, and job instability, resulting in pervasive stress and burnout within the academic community (Kolomitro, Kenny, and Le-May Sheffield, 2019). This, as will become clear through the subsequent chapters, each written by current PhD students, is being felt, absorbed, and internalised within the next generation of social science scholars. Thomas Raymen, in his book, the *Enigma of Social Harm* (2023), discusses the need to return to Aristotelian ethics in the form of the Telos – the end, goal, or purpose for which an act is done, or at which a profession or institution aims. While his central thesis is one regarding a current lack of ontological cohesion in the term 'social harm', his discussions pertaining to the current state of higher education with regard to the Telos are pertinent to these discussions. Raymen notes that the university, 'as its traditional grand ideals and raison d'être have faded into ghostly traces amidst processes of marketisation and the commercialisation of knowledge, which encourages factionalism, careerism, and careful homogeneity' (p 43). As such, like many institutions and social roles once guided by notions of the Good, they have since devolved to, at best, hollow corporate PR tactics and, at worst, relegated to the trash heap of history.

In their own words: chronicling the PhD journey

The picture painted thus far is certainly not pretty and indeed worrying. However, with that being said, this book, hopefully, will be seen as a step in the right direction: a book that attempts to capture personal depictions and, importantly, the *experiences* of what life as a PhD student is actually like within the contemporary landscape of higher education. In order to achieve this, the editors set about the daunting task of compiling a series of contributors – most currently in the throes of their own PhD journey – to share with us, and now you, the reader, their unique stories. We were acutely aware of what we were asking for. Not only did our initial research outline the sheer scale of challenges in higher education, but we were also asking for relatively inexperienced researchers to share potentially emotive and personal reflections in an industry plagued by a sense of imposter syndrome. While imposter syndrome is by no means unique to academia, the competitiveness, high standards, and common experiences of rejection only serve to amplify such feelings. With that in mind, we, the editors, carefully considered our approach to selecting and working with the contributors. Our approach to editing was one of collaboration, mindfulness, and support. We ensured that regular meetings and catch-ups with contributors were held to support each stage of the writing process and to maintain a constant dialogue and source of support. This, as it would turn out, would yield some unexpected results, such as new friendships, a renewed sense of community across multiple universities, and, as one editor pointed out, a deeper appreciation for the diverse circumstances other PhD students are facing. We wanted to try to capture a multifaceted tapestry of individual experiences that, we hope, will speak to current and future PhD students. Furthermore, we also wanted to speak to those who currently and, in the future, will support such individuals.

The contributors to this collection come from diverse backgrounds within both sociology and criminology, reflecting a broad spectrum of academic perspectives. However, this book is less about the specificities of each contributor's research topics, theoretical approaches, or specific methodologies and more about the universal experiences encountered during the PhD journey. Criminology, in particular, serves as a rendezvous discipline drawing from the social sciences and beyond (Wilson, Yardley, and Lynes, 2015: 69). This intersectionality makes criminology an ideal framework through which to explore and articulate these shared experiences. So, whether your research interests lie in organised crime, prisons, the cost-of-living crisis, housing, cybercrime, social justice, or policy reform, the narratives contained within this book hold relevance. They transcend the confines of specific research topics, offering insights that resonate on a more personal and emotional level. The utility of these stories lies in their ability to speak to the commonalities of the PhD experience – stress, doubt, perseverance, and the search for meaning – regardless of the particular academic focus. Thus, this collection is designed not only for those immersed in criminology or sociology but for anyone navigating the complexities of academic life within the vast tapestry of the social sciences. It offers a candid portrayal of what it truly means to undertake a PhD in today's challenging higher education landscape.

This book is, therefore, intentionally crafted to resonate with individuals at every stage of the PhD journey in the social sciences, offering unique insights and reflections tailored to the varying needs and challenges faced throughout this potentially demanding process. For those contemplating the start of a PhD, the book provides an honest glimpse into the realities of doctoral life, helping to set realistic expectations and prepare them for what lies ahead. For those who have just begun, it offers validation and reassurance through the shared experiences of others, highlighting that the struggles they face are common and indeed surmountable. As students progress to the mid-point of their PhD, this book serves as a crucial source of motivation and guidance, reminding them that they are not alone in their journey. The stories within will, we hope, help them navigate the often-overwhelming complexities of research, writing, and academic life. For those nearing the end, the book offers reflections on the culmination of their hard work and strategies for coping with the stress and uncertainty of finishing. It also touches on the transition to post-PhD life, addressing concerns about future career paths and identity. For those who have completed their PhDs and may now be in supervisory roles, the book offers a chance to revisit their own experiences and gain deeper empathy for the challenges their students face. The narratives within can serve as a reminder of the diverse struggles and triumphs PhD students encounter, helping supervisors to offer more personalised and supportive guidance. In this way, the book transcends a single purpose, acting as both a mirror and a guide for readers at different stages of the PhD process and evolving with them as they progress from PhD candidate to PhD holder and, potentially, supervisor. As such, the following presents a brief overview of the following chapters and their respective contributors. As you will likely see, we have intentionally structured the book, in a general sense, to parallel the chronology of the PhD journey. We say generally because, as we started to compile the myriad of subsequent chapters, we began to gain a deeper appreciation of just how unique each PhD experience actually is, and we do not wish for the aspiring PhD student who may have picked this book up, to be in any way disheartened if their own experiences do not exactly marry up with what they expect their journey to be.

The stories in this collection weave together reflections and, where relevant, advice, offering a varied tapestry of experiences. Each contributor brings a unique perspective, shaped by the particular stage of their PhD journey and the focus of their chapter. However, we recognise that the line between advice and reflection is often blurred. Depending on your own current position, experiences, and stage in your PhD journey, the reflective elements of these stories may serve as valuable guidance. As you interpret and relate these accounts to your own experiences, you may find insights that resonate and offer direction in unexpected ways. Moreover, as you progress further in your PhD journey, the more specific advice and personal reflections may take on new meanings and utility. Stories that once seemed distant or unrelated may suddenly resonate deeply, offering fresh perspectives and guidance that align with the evolving challenges and milestones of your academic path.

Nevertheless, we will start this odyssey into PhD life where most, if not all, journeys will begin – considering even enrolling on a PhD programme in the first place. With that in mind, Chapters 1 to 5 provide a diverse array of voices and experiences that chart the path towards enrolling on a doctoral research degree, highlighting that no one route into academia is the same. Chapter 1, written by one of the editors and current PhD student, Sarah Jones, charts their path into higher education and how, importantly, there is no perfect route into doctoral research. It discusses how the decision to undertake a PhD is not one undertaken in a vacuum but rather one encompassed by personal experiences and unforeseen circumstances. Specifically, Sarah recounts their experiences of childhood bereavement and subsequent challenges. However, they do so to ultimately demonstrate that the traditional pathways into higher education are not the only route available to pursue your academic aspirations and that, no matter what you may have been through, you can prevail. Chapter 2 thematically picks up where Sarah's chapter ends. Alexander Black, a PhD student at Birmingham City University, describes their experiences writing a PhD proposal and applying for a funded scholarship within an increasingly competitive industry. Not only do they provide encouragement and advice on such important processes at the start of the PhD, but they also discuss their identity as a gay man both within the context of their PhD that examines instances of violence against non-binary and sexually and gender minoritised individuals, but also within the wider HE environment. It is here that they discuss important themes, including the sense of isolation, imposter syndrome, and the importance of self-reflection. Chapter 3, written by one of the editors and current PhD student, Mikahil Azad, presents their story of conceptualising their PhD topic but within the context of a self-funded PhD – something which is increasingly common. Similar to the previous chapter, the importance of identity within doctoral research is considered as they chart their own experiences of Islamophobia as a British Muslim and how this informed their conceptualisation of their PhD topic. Chapter 4, written by Eliska Suchomel Duskova from the University of Cambridge, and Chapter 5, written by Manikandan Soundararajan from Staffordshire University, explore the often-overlooked theme of moving abroad to commence doctoral study. Eliska charts their journey from central Europe while Manikandan recounts their experiences moving from India. Both chapters ultimately discuss how such drastic culture shocks within HE, along with a plethora of other challenges, have shaped their experiences regarding the PhD process and impacted their journeys.

Chapters 6 to 9 present a plethora of examples relating to how life outside of the PhD can impact one's experiences but ultimately provide the reader with solace and guidance as to how to navigate even the most seemingly insurmountable challenges. Chapter 6, written by Birmingham City University student Rio Waldock, narrates their story of the loss of their father just as they began to settle into life as a PhD student. Not only do they convey the sheer magnitude of their loss, but also how this impacted their desire to study. Rio walks through how they balanced dealing with the personal aftermath of losing their father while also making the important decision to change their mode of study from full-time to part-time. Chapter 7 introduces the reader to Charlotte Rigby – a lecturer at Arden University and a PhD researcher at Staffordshire University – who is further down the road of the PhD yet still encounters various challenges such as sustaining a work-life balance, the importance of a strong support network, and balancing numerous important responsibilities. Chapter 8, written by PhD student Suzanne Baggs, continues the theme of balancing work life with that of the PhD but also adds the importance of maintaining one's personal life. Suzanne, through their discussions of what they have sacrificed to pursue their doctoral dreams, highlights the importance of recognising our own limitations and what is ultimately important. Chapter 9, composed by Birmingham City University student Abigail Shaw, focuses on the often overlooked yet evidently prolific theme of mental health and, more specifically, neurodiversity within the PhD experience. In doing so, they trace their story back to their childhood and their journey into adulthood, intertwined with the institutional, structural and cultural barriers to learning.

Chapters 10 through 13 highlight some of the various barriers faced within the process of the PhD itself that many may not be familiar with as they enter the unknown world of doctoral study. These chapters provide accounts ranging from institutional hurdles, methodological quandaries and exploitative work environments. While these are all seemingly disparate themes, they emphasise the multitude of ways such barriers, or challenges, may manifest within the treacherous and murky waters of HE. Chapter 10, by Birmingham City University student Lisa Edge, discusses the much-needed importance of a more trauma-informed approach to PhD supervision. This chapter, written in the third person due to its sensitive nature, provides reassurance to students and practical advice for supervisors and the wider HE environment. Chapter 11 highlights the exploitative industry of some PhD scholarships, as conveyed by current Staffordshire PhD student Kyla Bavin. In this chapter, Kyla outlines how such practices – indicative of the wider sector – significantly impacted both their academic and personal lives, yet, through all the adversity, they prevail. Chapter 12 switches gear and draws attention to the importance of ethics and reflexivity throughout the PhD. Kavya Padmanabhan, from the University of Cambridge, reflects on the ethical tensions within their own PhD, discussing such themes as access, positionality, the navigation of space, and the relationship between researcher and participants. Chapter 13 continues some of these previous themes, including access, but frames them within the context of wider methodological complexities underpinned by broader structural conditions. Liam Miles, one of the editors and current PhD student at Birmingham City University, guides us through the methodological minefield of undertaking participatory methods within the current cost-of-living crises, reflecting upon themes such as risk and insecurity within a neo-liberal landscape.

Chapters 14 through 17 address a deficit that the editors – upon their initial discussions and reflections – feel is currently lacking when we consider the current provision of texts and guides on the PhD process: voices from those who have completed their doctoral journey. With that in mind, we chronologically planned these chapters to commence by providing an overview from someone who only recently passed their viva and gradually progresses to include more senior academics who, in their own words, express that their own experiences seem like a lifetime ago. With that in mind, Chapter 14 picks up with Dr Nick Gibbs – a lecturer at Northumbria University – who not only recalls in intricate detail their preparation and experience of the viva voce but also paints an optimistic picture of the final throes of the PhD journey and the inevitable options we all must consider once the experience does come to an end. Chapter 15 fast forwards to ten years post-PhD, with Dr Adam Lynes, Associate Professor at Birmingham City University and one of this book's editors. This chapter reflects on how, despite the years of experience acquired since gaining their doctorate, they are still plagued by the pervasive feeling of imposter syndrome. While this may concern some readers at the prospect of never fully vanquishing their inner feelings of doubt, capability and insecurity – even when finally gaining the coveted title of doctor – the premise of this chapter is that no matter your experience or level of qualification, it is okay to feel this way and talk about it. The penultimate chapter jumps to 15 years post-PhD with Professor Daniel Briggs at Northumbria University. This chapter reflects on the moral crossroads within the contemporary context of 'academic capitalism', by which we mean the increasing bureaucracy, hyper-competition, and metric-driven nature of HE. While Professor Briggs paints a somewhat dire picture of the world many reading this will enter, their ultimate message is one of hope and that, despite it all, he wants to remind us that the PhD was worth it for them and is for you. The final chapter in this odyssey ends with Professor James Treadwell and two of their current PhD students, Chelsea Braithwaite and Owen Hodgkinson, based at Staffordshire University. Professor Treadwell completed his own PhD 20 years ago and has since helped supervise many others to completion. This chapter is unique in its narrative in that it ebbs and flows between reflections of both supervisor and supervisee, cumulating in a reciprocal interplay between the two. In the end, both parties conclude that this important relationship is by no means one-way and that there needs to be a mutual understanding on both a personal level and in a professional capacity.

Why this book is needed and now

Hopefully, the way in which we have outlined this book provides a source of comfort to you, the reader, no matter what challenges you have faced or are currently going through. Or whatever stage of the PhD you are currently at. While this book is concerned with the PhD process, we are acutely aware of how the PhD can impact your life, and vice-versa. No matter if you are unsure of whether you are capable of undertaking a PhD;

struggling to compose your proposal; deciding whether funded or self-funded; navigating the supervisor/supervisee relationship; manoeuvring through the methodological minefield; wrestling with the ethical tensions of doctoral research; balancing on the tightrope of work life and personal life; dealing with burnout due to unforeseen increasing workloads or simply feeling like an imposter, we see you, we understand.

Despite these myriad of challenges that, for many, feel like a game of whack-a-mole that you may feel like you are constantly playing throughout your journey, we promise you, there is hope. One of the prevailing themes that emerged from the many contributors ranging from first-year PhD students to those with 20+ years' experience in academia was the cathartic nature of reflection and how many surprised themselves with how they overcame their various struggles and setbacks. We hope that this catharsis, experienced by our contributors through reflecting on their journeys, will also resonate with you, offering a shared sense of affirmation and understanding as you engage with each story. As you immerse yourself in these personal accounts, we hope that you find, if and when needed, solace and connection, knowing that you are not alone in your struggles and triumphs. Another interesting theme that arose was the importance of community. Through writing their chapters and subsequent discussions with the editors, there was a realisation that by coming together as a community, we could help change the status quo of the current state of HE. By reading this book, we hope you will also feel a sense of belonging to this growing community, finding strength and solidarity in the shared experiences presented. We invite you to join us in this collective effort to challenge and transform the current state of higher education, knowing that together, our voices are more powerful.

As you read and absorb each author's personal reflections, you will hopefully discover that while seemingly insurmountable in the moment, each challenge can be faced knowing that you are not on your own as you continue to *embrace the unknown*.

PART I

1

Re-entering academia: the unexpected journey

Sarah Jones
Birmingham City University

Sarah's PhD focuses on the experiences of the adult family members of child and youth homicide offenders. The experiences of this 'hidden population' are explored to investigate the impact that these uniquely distressing events have on differing aspects of their lives. Her research also aims to critically analyse the diverse nature of concepts such as victimhood, indirect victimisation, and disenfranchised grief.

Introduction

My story begins 23 years ago. This may seem unusual as this section of the book focuses more on the beginnings or early stages of the PhD journey and the many choices that must be considered. However, I must take you back to my past for my present journey to make sense. This is, however, challenging, as reflecting on a time when my whole world came crashing down around me is something that I scarcely do. Whether that be a response to childhood trauma or a coping mechanism of grief, the recollection of adversity for anybody is overwhelming. My chapter discusses some sensitive topics and experiences, yet I hope that my story can offer others a sense of confidence in themselves, especially when considering taking on the daunting yet profound task of a PhD.

The moment that changed everything

At 13 years old, I was a quiet, inquisitive, clever young girl. I was in Year 8 at secondary school and didn't have many friends as I had started at a senior school that none of my friends from junior school had progressed to. When I heard that a week-long school summer trip to the South of France was being organised, I jumped at the chance, as I thought this would be a great opportunity to make new friends, experience new things and have fun. My parents were supportive of me going, especially as it was a water sports holiday, and I thoroughly enjoyed these types of activities. Summer came around, and my bag was already packed. I was so excited to make new friends, windsurf in the Mediterranean Sea, and have my first slice of independence. On the morning of the day that I was leaving for the trip, my dad told me that he couldn't drop me off as he had to go to work. I remember being upset as we had a very strong father-daughter relationship; we did everything together, and I idolised him. However, he told me he would be there to pick me up when I returned, with a Kinder Surprise (my favourite chocolate snack!). So off I went, filled with excitement and enthusiasm, on an adventure of a lifetime.

The weeks on holiday went by so quickly, from what I can remember. I made new friends, one of whom is still my best friend and constant support system to this day. I swam, surfed, laughed, and had so much fun. Pulling into the school gates on the coach upon our return, I could not wait to see my family, especially my dad, and tell him all about my holiday. I knew he would be excited to hear about my adventures. When I eagerly looked out of the coach window for him, he wasn't there. I spotted my mum and my sister standing in the car park, hugging each other tightly. Maybe he had to work or was waiting for me back at home. As I got off the coach on to the school playground, they came walking up to me with their arms reaching out and tears streaming down their faces. Here, unfortunately, or maybe fortunately, is where my memory goes blank. The next thing I remember is lying on a bench in my back garden back home, with my head on my nan's lap. Her hands gripping me so tightly. I felt uncontrollable emotional pain, sadness, and confusion. My dad had been killed in a motorbike accident on his way to work while I was on holiday. He died instantly. At 13-years-old, my world had forever changed.

The death of a parent or primary caregiver before the age of 18 is known to be one of the most traumatic and challenging experiences for children and adolescents and is now commonly recognised as an adverse childhood experience (Woodward et al, 2023). Bereaved children, therefore, may have increased vulnerability when facing the developing psychological, physical, and social challenges in life (McLaughlin, Lytje, and Holliday, 2019). As the years went by, I changed from a quiet, clever young girl into an angry, grief-stricken monster. At this time, I lost all interest in learning at school; I rebelled; I had absolutely no interest in trying, and I didn't care about anything. I was getting into a lot of trouble for being disruptive and difficult, from being internally and externally suspended to receiving threats of expulsion. My mum constantly received phone calls from my school, telling her how 'awful' I was, divulging all of the 'terrible' things that I was doing at school. Thinking about it now, I know that my behaviour was a way of trying to disconnect from and harness the unbearable pain and life-changing grief that I was experiencing. As highlighted by Dyregro, Lytje, and Rex Christensen (2022), there are diverse aspects that are greatly affected by the loss of a parent in childhood, such as mental well-being in school, educational attainment, grades, and educational level. Unfortunately, I had no emotional support from my school, and my attendance dropped considerably. When I did attend, I was seen and treated as a disruptive troublemaker, not a grieving child – no wonder I didn't want to go. Alongside the lack of emotional support at school was the lack of educational support, which in turn greatly affected my performance. It has been suggested that childhood bereavement is a key factor in underachievement at secondary school (Abdelnoor and Hollins, 2004). I was placed in the bottom 'sets', with all the other troublemakers and underachievers. I was told over and over again that I was not smart enough to achieve anything, especially with my attitude. My circumstances were completely ignored – no wonder I had no desire to try. Around the time of studying for my GCSEs, it seemed as though all the attention was placed on my 'terrible behaviour' and 'poor educational performance' rather than my broken heart. The feelings of inadequacy and powerlessness that emerged from this narrative still pay me a visit to this day – I question whether these feelings of inferiority from my past are a manifestation of the ever-present imposter syndrome that haunts me now.

Later, when I received my GCSE results, I felt dejected but not at all surprised. I masked this with an 'I don't care – I'm fine' attitude. Of course, I failed most of my GCSEs, but this disappointment was nothing compared to the grief that encompassed me. This 'I don't care – I'm fine' attitude stayed with me for a very long time. It was my safety blanket. I thought that if I seemed like I was ok, then I wouldn't need to talk about my dad, and I could mask the excruciating pain that I was feeling – like a survival skill. Throughout the next ten years, I continued to suppress my grief. I buried it deep, deep down inside. Lytje and Dyregrov (2019) suggest that there is an increasing level of consensus among researchers that the loss of a parent in childhood can have all-encompassing consequences. I didn't want to talk about my dad or his passing – in any respect. I couldn't (and to this day, I still struggle to). I found it too difficult and could not bear to think about how he just disappeared, so suddenly. I conditioned myself not to think about him and the reality of not having him in my life, as I knew that if I did, I would completely fall apart.

The suppression of grief

In my late teens/early 20s, I had a mundane job, living away from my mum and sister and was in an unhealthy relationship. I was 'fine' on the outside, getting on with it, but desperately unhappy on the inside. As a young woman, I suppose that I had come to terms with the fact that this was my life, and that's just how it was. I didn't have any dreams, goals, or aspirations – why would I? My life had been shrouded in negativity for as long as I could remember. I was made redundant around this time and had the chance to change certain aspects of my life. I had gotten to the point where I could no longer stay in the relationship that I was in and moved back home to live with my mum. I began to feel like I could finally open up and express my emotions, and with her support, I started to acknowledge how I really felt. This was the starting point of me taking control of my life and finding the courage to deal with the grief that I had buried for so long. Although this may seem like a positive turn in my story, unfortunately, my life went into a downward spiral in the years that followed. The most well-documented consequence of parental loss in childhood is depression (Lytje and Dyregrov, 2019), and very suddenly, as I began to let my guard down, I began to experience severe panic attacks and intense waves of depression and anxiety. I threw away my mobile phone and very rarely left my house. I didn't want to see or speak to anyone because when I did, I broke down, and every time I broke down, I became more and more fragile. It was so difficult to explain this sudden but all-encompassing nightmare that I was living in, and so, in my mind, it was easier to shut myself away rather than share how I was feeling. I abruptly stopped all contact with my very close group of friends for fear of being misunderstood (the performance of my 'I don't care – I'm fine' attitude had been somewhat consistent up until this point). As I didn't understand what was happening to me, mentally and emotionally, or understand my own thoughts and feelings, I had convinced myself that they wouldn't either. Yet, they showed me so much love and compassion. I realise now how unbelievably lucky I am to have friends who supported me when I was at rock bottom, and for their unwavering love, I am eternally grateful. Through my reclusion, however, I began to have intense irrational thoughts. I became highly dissociated from 'normal' life and became paralysed by social anxiety and fear; I felt hopeless and was in constant emotional confusion and pain. My trauma thrived in the silence that I had chosen to be in. Sadly, I found myself contemplating taking my own life as I could not cope with the thought of feeling like this any longer. Sitting here now, writing this chapter and reflecting upon this time of my life is very painful, but relevant. While I will not dwell on this part of my story, it is, nonetheless, a significant aspect that highlights the impact of childhood trauma and grief. During this dark time, with the ever-present support of my mum, who was also still grieving, I started to see a psychotherapist (and continued to see for a number of years). This, slowly but surely, became something that allowed me to start to figure out and understand 'me'. I finally started to deal with the suppressed grief that lay dormant for so long and I started to understand the multifaceted impact of childhood trauma. I started to rebuild my life, little by little, and started to search for a sense of self that was absent for so long.

Finding 'me'

It took a while, but I was able to see a dim light at the end of a very long and challenging tunnel. I found that I was able to start thinking about my future and consider things that would make me happy. One day, when talking with my mum about what I would want to do with my life in a 'hypothetical' and 'perfect world', I mentioned how I would really like to go to university to study criminology. But straight away, I dismissed this passing thought because, in my head, this was never an option, especially as my anxiety burdened me so overwhelmingly. The thought of going out into the world and having to talk to people I didn't know absolutely petrified me. I incessantly envisioned people asking me what I have been doing over the last ten years and it scared me – I didn't want to have to disclose my trauma as I was humiliated by it. I was convinced that I would be judged, or that my anxiety would prevent me from being a 'normal person' in a 'normal environment'. I was also convinced that I was not smart enough, as I was told all those years ago at secondary school. I didn't have any GCSEs or A Levels or the capacity to think that I could achieve any kind of educational or academic qualifications. But this is where it all changed for me. Although I did not have any qualifications, what I did have was a role model. Someone who told me and showed me that I could achieve these things, even as a 27-year-old woman who was so doubtful of herself. My mum helped me believe I could do anything I put my mind to. She had been lecturing and doing her PhD research full time when my dad passed away, and understandingly put it all on hold when everything changed so intensely. However, she strived to continue and years later, received her doctorate. After looking into my options and realising that it did not matter how old I was and that there was, in fact, the opportunity for me to go to university. It took some convincing, but I plucked up the courage to enrol on to an Access to Higher Education Course in Social Sciences at my local college. This was a huge learning curve for me, which had its ups and downs, both socially and academically. A year later, after passing my Access to HE Course (which in itself was a shock to me!), I enrolled on to Birmingham City University's (BCU) Criminology Undergraduate Degree Course. I will not lie and say this experience was free from any difficulty either. I was still suffering terribly with anxiety and self-doubt. I had no experience of higher education, apart from my year-long college access course and had been far removed from full-time education for over 10 years. Starting university as a socially anxious, insecure 28-year-old woman, who had shut herself away for so long, was unbelievably daunting. Being labelled as a 'mature' student, either by myself or others, was and is still to this day, something that looms over me in a negative light. I fight a constant feeling of inadequacy in that I have not followed the traditional, or conditioned path that most university students usually do. This internal struggle, especially when starting at university, affected the little confidence that I had. The adverse challenges that I had faced in the previous years had greatly affected my self-esteem, and I felt like this magnified it. In turn, I constantly felt like a failure compared to the young, carefree students I was surrounded by. However, when I started my undergraduate degree, I found myself enjoying learning, reading, and writing, and little by little, I became more confident in my abilities, abilities that I did not know I had. Although this realisation was groundbreaking for me, especially after all the time that had passed, there were always whispers of uncertainty from that little voice of self-doubt. This followed me throughout my undergraduate degree and taunted me while I was undertaking my master's degree. I was fortunate, however, to have a group of friends that I had made on my undergraduate and master's courses who experienced this, too. We had a mutual understanding of the self-sabotage we were all individually experiencing. Although we were all so different in our personal circumstances, we shared a common way of thinking. We all doubted ourselves and our abilities. Although we were all thriving in our studies, we all feared failure. At this time, maybe I should have realised that this feeling was more common than I thought. Still, its overwhelming presence didn't allow me to put it into perspective, regardless of the personal achievements that I had made, especially as I was still trying to navigate and overcome what felt like a lifetime of grief. Even back then, when the thought of a career in academia or pursuing a PhD was never an attainable prospect, I did not allow for recognition of my personal or academic achievements.

Turning over a new leaf

In all honesty, pursuing a PhD was not something I thought I would ever undertake, or frankly, had the ability to undertake. After finishing my master's degree, although I had gained confidence in my academic abilities, I came to the sombre realisation that my educational and academic journey was over. The four years I spent studying were life-changing for me; I learnt so much about myself and the discipline I was so passionate about. Yes, I was now a more positive and more assured version of myself, and yes, I saw myself as a somewhat confident, educated woman, which I was proud of. However, I was, or I thought I was, being rational in my expectations of myself. I had an undergraduate degree and a master's degree in criminology, qualifications that I did not ever expect to achieve. Yet I did not have any idea of how to utilise these achievements and was still downplaying them in my mind. Shortly after I graduated, the COVID-19 pandemic struck, and everything came to a standstill. During this time, my nan fell down the stairs in her home. For me, this was what I now understand to be a trigger. I could not bear the thought of losing someone else who I loved so much – this feeling became all-encompassing and affected me greatly. After being in hospital for some time, she recovered well; however, the realisation that both of my grandparents needed extra support became clear, and I began taking on various caring responsibilities. As life started to get back to normal after the pandemic, I was given the opportunity to become a visiting lecturer in criminology at BCU. This is something that changed my whole outlook. Thinking back to my first teaching experiences fills me with happiness, as this is when I realised that this is what I wanted to do with my life. I felt like I had a sense of purpose for the first time. As someone who constantly thinks negatively about themselves and about, well, everything, this was a very emotional and defining time for me. I had always felt that I was not deserving of happiness and had a distorted view of myself, but here I was, teaching at Birmingham City University, the place which had enabled me to transform from an anxiety-ridden 28-year-old with little educational experience to a proud, educated 35-year-old woman whose hard work was starting to pay off both personally and professionally.

Within my first year as a visiting lecturer, I had already gained so much experience. I designed and delivered seminars and workshops to undergraduate students on differing modules, marking assessments, and supporting students on their educational journey. I was also still taking on various caring responsibilities for my grandparents, but thankfully, around this time, they had moved to a 'retirement village' where it was much safer for them, but they could still keep their independence. They always ask me, 'What would we do without you?' and I always reply, 'You never need to worry about that'. My grandparents are unbelievably important to me, and I am aware but deeply fearful of the inevitable. My nan was a pillar of strength when my mum, sister, and I lost my dad and is the matriarch of the family. She was also the only person I feared getting in trouble with when I was in my 'monster' phase. My grandad was the only male role model I had from the age of 13, and he showed me so much love and offered me so much wisdom (I know exactly how to wallpaper an entire room thanks to him!). For these reasons and many more, I dedicate myself to ensuring that life is easy for them and that they are happy, as healthy as possible and worry-free. I found it difficult at this time to internally balance my priorities. What is more important – my potential career or caring for my grandparents? This is something that still lingers over me, and I often contemplate the thought of having to choose one over the other. Thankfully, I have never been in a position where I have had to do this, and I am extremely grateful for that.

I had no plans or was not even considering studying for a PhD, partly due to the worry of not being able to put my all into such a mammoth task, a task surrounded by so many unknowns – but also because of the sheer lack of confidence that I had in my ability to undertake something so significant. I had been teaching for 12 months and was finding my feet as a visiting lecturer, re-connecting with and gaining knowledge and experience from lecturers and mentors who had taught me and supported me as a student. One such lecturer, Dr Adam Lynes, who had offered me immeasurable support and endless encouragement throughout my time as an undergraduate and postgraduate student, asked me if I had any plans to undertake a PhD. My immediate response was no, and honestly, the thought terrified me. Although I had gained academic qualifications and now knew that I wanted to continue to develop professionally within a HE environment, there it was, yet again, that self-doubt, that voice that tells you 'There is no way that YOU can do that'. I remember bringing it up to my mum in a passing conversation, telling her I had been asked if I had considered doing a PhD. She, of course, being an academic enthusiast and the biggest supporter of my progression, thought this was a brilliant idea. Yet, guided by feelings of fear and insecurity, I had decided that this was something that I was not competent enough to consider and removed it from thought.

Overcoming and re-defining personal barriers

Months passed and I was thriving in my newfound sense of purpose. I think one of the most valuable aspects of teaching for me is having the opportunity to support students in their academic journey and help them realise and achieve their potential. I see myself in many of them. I know the difference it can make to have someone in your corner, supporting you in the journey of understanding and valuing your own academic self-confidence. I look back on this time now, and I realise that although in my mind, undertaking a PhD was not something I thought I could achieve due to a huge lack of self-confidence and an abundance of self-doubt, I also had someone in my corner supporting me and helping me realise that this was, in fact, something that I could, and should do. Adam reassured me of my capabilities and reminded me of how far I had come. To have someone so accomplished tell you that you have what it takes to do a PhD and that they see your potential when you don't see it yourself is quite literally transformative. My mindset started to change here, and I started to consider undertaking a PhD. Instead of defining it as a daunting task that I, the self-doubting 35-year-old, could not achieve, I started to redefine it as something that would enable me to be an even stronger version of the person that I had become after all the hardship that I had experienced in my past. For me, giving new meaning to what it meant to undertake a PhD and muffling those negative, self-critical voices and thoughts by listening to those who saw my potential, changed everything. I started to get excited about the prospect of becoming a PhD researcher. Although the self-critical voices were still very much in existence, little by little, I was able to learn how to balance the internal contradiction between the belief I should have in myself and the doubt surrounding my abilities and fear of failure.

Around this time, I was seeking advice from colleagues and mentors, those who were studying for their PhDs and those who had completed their PhDs, to reinforce my decision. This was unbelievably helpful as I was offered invaluable advice about applying for a PhD and the PhD journey. This is where I started to understand and appreciate that everybody's journey was and is so unique and highly personal. Each story that I was told was so distinct in nature (and in topic!). I found these reflections and first-hand experiences to be so beneficial in solidifying my decision. I was also given meaningful and positive support when I revealed that I was seriously considering undertaking my PhD. This gave me confidence in myself and my capabilities. Yet, alongside the anticipation that I was feeling, I knew I had to make difficult decisions surrounding full-time/part-time study and finance. Did I want to take the plunge and 'go all in' as a full-time PhD student and potentially limit my teaching/lecturing opportunities? Or take it at a steadier pace as a part-time student and have the opportunity to continue to thrive in my position as a visiting lecturer and potentially work towards being a full-time lecturer? Did I want to apply for a funded PhD, which can arguably be a lengthy process, and the competition can be fierce but also financially beneficial, or be a self-funded researcher, which may allow for more flexibility but not necessarily be financially viable? These kinds of decisions, for anyone who is considering undertaking a PhD, should not be taken lightly. Motivations and intentions must be considered, alongside commitments. The passion that I had for teaching and lecturing made me worry that, if I were to go full time as a PhD student, my career path would be restricted for the duration of my studies as my priority would have to be my research. Yet, I also felt that if I were to take on my PhD research part-time, I would limit my research/PhD progression due to the hyper-competitive nature of academia (Weinstein et al, 2023). The consideration of these decisions was all interwoven with the thought of my grandparents and my commitment to their well-being. Ultimately, I had to think about what was best for me, in my circumstances. And so, with encouragement, support and anticipation, I put together a proposal and applied to become a part-time, self-funded PhD researcher. I could not help but smile!

Soon after I had applied, I reached out to two senior lecturers within the criminology department whose research interests aligned with my own and who I knew would be supportive in my journey as potential supervisors, one being Dr Adam Lynes, who had already shown me unwavering support in my decision to pursue a PhD. I was also very fortunate to have another senior lecturer within the psychology department see my PhD proposal after submission and became interested in supervising me and my potential research. Usually, at times like this, my anxiety would start to take over, and

I would begin to doubt myself or regret my decisions, as I'm sure many people do. Still, I kept reminding myself of how I have to contextualise and see undertaking a PhD as something that enables me to be an even stronger version of the person that I have become – this is something that I often still do when I have new hurdles to face within my PhD journey. I found that this helped with the self-doubt or worry that came with making the decision to undertake a PhD and in the times following my initial decision. Once I had my interview and received an unconditional offer, I knew that I had made the right decision, and I was overjoyed. I was excited for what was to come. I was proud of myself for stepping outside of my comfort zone and believing in myself. I was aware that the entirety of this journey would be somewhat outside of 'my' comfort zone (and it definitely is!); however, I had also come to the realisation that most of the people who I had spoken to felt the same. With being something so unique in nature, I would find it quite strange if you didn't feel outside of your comfort zone at some point in the PhD journey!

Embracing new beginnings

Being a year and a half into my PhD journey at this point, I can say that I am very content with my decision to become a part-time, self-funded PhD researcher. I have been able to concentrate on my PhD, teaching, and career progression equally while making sure that my grandparents are happy and as healthy as they can be. I am very lucky to have unbelievably supportive PhD supervisors and am so grateful be surrounded by a highly encouraging group of people who I cannot thank enough for their support and the advice that they continually offer. My career is progressing, and I have been given some fantastic teaching and publication opportunities as an early career academic. I also have the most loving and supportive family and group of best friends, who cheer me on and always remind me of how far I have come. The most important aspect of my life at this time, which I must reflect on, however, is that I finally feel happy. My journey from being in the depths of sadness and despair throughout my childhood and young adulthood to where I am today at 36 years old, has been a difficult one. But I am finally happy with my life, happy with who I have become and happy with where I am going.

After re-living and reflecting on the most harrowing times of my life, to be able to sit here while writing this chapter and express this sentiment to you is my proudest and most significant achievement of all. Don't get me wrong, though, I (very) often feel the heavy burden of grief, self-doubt, insecurity, and anxiety. Still, I try to remind myself that within the new journey that I am on, the existence of negativity is heightened by the unknown, but the unknown does not have to be encompassed by negativity.

Every now and again, I think about that young girl whose life was so abruptly torn apart by the death of her dad while she was on holiday, who lay on that bench in her back garden, paralysed by emotional pain. I reflect on her loss, her grief, and her vulnerability. I want her to know that although it may not seem like it, she will become someone who will be able to take the negative experiences that she will endure and use them to transform herself into a proud woman who will achieve things that were once perceived as unachievable. I (still) deal with the consequences of childhood trauma, which tore my entire life apart all those years ago, and the many ways in which it has subsequently manifested into my adult life. I (still) cannot think about my dad without my heart breaking and feeling the deep, unrelenting pain of loss. Losing my dad at a young age has allowed me to realise that grief has no timeline. It alters every aspect of your life. Twenty-three years later, grief still haunts me, and his absence still affects me greatly, especially when I think about the fact that I have been without him for longer than I had him in my life. But hopefully, by taking you back to my past, my present now makes sense.

Summary of reflections

Reflecting on the painful and difficult times of your life doesn't come without its challenges. In all honesty, writing this chapter has been unbelievably arduous, especially because since writing and editing my chapter and this book, my nan has passed away. I have had to re-live my nightmare both on and off the page, the nightmare that, for so long, I tried to wake up from but could not. But here is where I share with you the reason why I chose to recount my journey so far to you – because while myself and the other editors were in the process of dreaming up the idea for this book and having eye-opening conversations with the contributors, I realised that I was not alone. I was not alone in my self-doubt; I was not alone in my grief or anxiety, and I was not alone in my PhD journey. What I hope you take from my reflection is that no matter what life throws at you, you are not alone in this journey. My realisations are my reassurance to you. Hopefully, I have assisted, in some small way, in encouraging those who may have experienced the extreme pain of loss or empowered those who might doubt themselves or have something holding them back from realising that they CAN achieve what they think is unachievable.

2

Entering the fray: the hyper-competitive PhD environment

Alexander Black
Birmingham City University

Alex's PhD examines sexual violence from the narratives of victims/survivors and offenders who identify as sexually and/or gendered minoritised men and/or non-binary individuals. It draws upon the singularised normality of masculinity and how this influences survivors when reporting, offenders when perpetrating, and the police's responses to survivors and offenders within cases of sexual violence.

Introduction

This chapter will provide an overview of my experiences in applying for doctoral research funding. Initially, I will explore the necessity of reflective writing when discussing my experiences of attaining funds for my PhD research. I will also examine the competition I faced when applying for my PhD's research funding. This will be complemented by discussions on applying for research funding and the importance of research proposals having both originality and innovation (Baptista et al, 2015). I will also discuss the process of constructing my research proposal, centrally around imposter syndrome and my identity as a gay man. This chapter hopes to reveal the three key processes to attaining doctoral research funding, including developing a personal statement, presenting research to a potential doctoral supervisory team, and how to hopefully obtain funding for the PhD itself. I will follow this with deliberations around how I secured a Visiting Lecturer role and the intrinsic conflicts I faced as a young academic. It is important to acknowledge that this chapter examines sensitive issues, where I expose my lived realities of bullying, sexual violence, victimisation, and dysphoria with both my sexuality and gender.

Competitiveness, originality, and innovation

When I first applied for my PhD, I always hoped to obtain some form of funding. Receiving funding was an essential goal for me due to the UK's competitive economic climate. It would have made it unattainable for me to sustain my external jobs, live near my university, pay for my PhD, and, most importantly, have time to study. On a more personal note, I dreamt about having my PhD funded to illustrate to my mother that the work she had put in for me to stay focused on my education was worth it. Even when I would not do my homework, or I would get critiqued for my persona, or how my brain takes in information, even the way that I pronounce words, these all put me at a disadvantage in school. I went through years of bullying, contemplating suicide, and, unfortunately, attempting suicide because of my sexuality and gender dysphoria. However, my mother always tried to support me throughout my personal growth in my identity as a gay male and within my battles in education. So, the completion of my master's, in my eyes, was not enough to show how much my mother has helped me develop within my academic positioning. And I will be frank: I will probably not feel like my PhD will be enough to demonstrate to my mother how much she has guided me. From encountering economic battles within the PhD funding process, and even much earlier within my childhood and adolescence, the ability to gain funding was a love letter of appreciation for the younger me surviving and to my mother for her support.

Because I received funding, people assume that I immediately received it. I did not! Applying for PhD funding is a strenuous process. To contextualise, I initially applied for funding in 2020, where I constructed my first-ever PhD research proposal. I went against many students who all desired (and deserved) a funded PhD. Luckily, only 20 students were put forward, and I was one of them. I was filled with joy. I felt that for someone who had not always done so well in primary and secondary education, I could now prove to myself more than ever that my work was worth funding. Unfortunately, only four out of the 20 students would receive places. Unfortunately, I came fifth in the selection process, which resulted in my proposal not receiving funding. This initial rejection put me in a place of self-doubt, where I would question my self-worth within academia. I realised here that I had hit a mental and emotional wall, repositioning me back into my primary and secondary school mindset, where I would get doubted by nearly every teacher for my academic abilities. Soon after, I was given the opportunity to apply for funding again, which unfortunately resulted in me getting rejected yet again. After my second attempt to attain funding for my PhD research, the feeling of rejection became overwhelming. So, I decided that I would have to secure a non-funded PhD. But, just before the ball started rolling with this, my research was put forward to the staff board, and again, I was given the opportunity to be interviewed and apply for my own research proposal. After experiencing such loneliness at this time, alongside the reality of the health risks throughout the COVID-19 pandemic and my sister being diagnosed with cancer, I decided that risk-taking had been internalised into my mindset. On a socio-economic level, the realities of a competitive economy within a Western capitalist society (Hall and Winlow, 2018) further pushed me to take a risk, so I decided to go for it!

I want to acknowledge here the importance of trying to make your proposal stand out from the crowd. I decided that I wanted my potential research to be something that gave younger Alex a voice. After growing up in a domestically violent household, being bullied throughout my school years, and experiencing intimate partner violence in two consecutive relationships, I have always experienced some type of interpersonal violence (Waters et al, 2005). It was very important to me when planning my proposed research that my inquiry came from my personal lived realities. I wanted my research to tell my story (Etherington, 2004). Drawing upon my personal experiences has allowed my research to have originality. In relation to my identity, the one thing I experienced throughout my life was the recurring issue with people wanting me to be so-called 'masculine' and 'heterosexual'. This is problematic, as it can result in an individual internalising these labels as their identity (Becker, 1963). This was no different for me, as I embedded the idea that I was not masculine or heterosexual. Even if I felt like I was embodying both labels, I had been conditioned to feel like they were not 'me'. With such labels being attached to my gender (Garlick, 2003), yet being detached from my sexuality (Pollitt et al, 2021), I designed my doctoral research proposal to be reflective of my personal identity trauma and society's version of my identity. Ironically, these potentially self-deprecating experiences innovated my research from undergraduate sociological explorations of bullying towards criminological investigations of sexual violence. Ultimately, these pieces of research resulted in me developing my doctorate proposal while providing both originality and innovation for my research proposal on two levels. First, I drew upon my experiences as a gay man and how this constricts me from embodying heteronormative and hegemonic values of masculinity, which led to me coining my own theoretical compass around masculinities. Second, where I decided to come from my personal narrative as a gay male and survivor of sexual violence, subsequently, this resulted in me grounding my research around social agents who identify as sexually and/or gendered minoritised men and/or non-binary individuals who have either been victimised by or have perpetrated sexual violence.

Writing the personal statement

When writing my personal statement, I was lucky enough to have recently completed my master's dissertation, which was the grounding for my PhD application proposal. However, if you have not had prior experience writing a master's dissertation or doing a master's degree, that is completely okay! My advice is to write your personal statement around an area that reflects your identity. On the contrary, you could choose any area of intrigue or something you love, like a particular book collection or television series. Alternatively, you could also investigate an area where you feel like a potential individual or a certain group's narrative has not been listened to, and you want to use your research to challenge this. To contextualise, from my investigations in my master's research into the training that the police receive in England and Wales, my semi-structured interviews with participants, and my media content analysis around cases of male-on-male sexual violence, I developed an understanding that the police are not simply marginalising agents of minorities. Crucially, I concluded that the police have a lack of understanding around the traumatisation of sexual violence, significantly in cases of male-on-male sexual violence. As recognised before, it was essential for me as a researcher to interlink with theories and concepts and have my personal identity and, more broadly, my personal narrative in the research proposal. As with other researchers, it was also crucial for me to follow my passions and interests. For me, this was writing in the field of sexual violence and for my research to provide voices to non-binary, alongside gendered and/or sexually minoritised male identities. And yet, the one contribution that I, as a researcher, was not sufficiently informed about prior to doing my PhD was the importance of impact. Drawing on my master's dissertation data, I was able to present a series of various forms of impact that could be offered before my potential research had even started. Therefore, this has been vital for my journey, and this has truly helped during the PhD itself to have a grounding in how my PhD proposal cannot simply result in a funded PhD project. Still, it is necessary to idealise and bring reality to what results can be produced from the doctoral research's completion.

Constructing a research proposal: being gay and a victim

When formulating my research proposal, I experienced a high level of imposter syndrome (Joshi and Mangette, 2018). Despite structuring my undergraduate dissertation on the sociological gaze around bullying and masculinity for cisgender, male-identifying individuals and my master's dissertation centring on a criminological gaze towards cisgender males and non-binary individuals' perceptions around male-on-male sexual violence, I still doubted my PhD research proposal, even though this connected both research exemplars. This self-doubt, notwithstanding my prior knowledge and experience, exemplifies my lived reality of imposter syndrome. It is necessary to recognise that the development of my doctoral proposal can be reflective of my desire to challenge the realities of violence and imposter syndrome that I have faced during my childhood, adolescence, and continuing into my adulthood (Robertson, 2022).

I knew when applying for my PhD funding that my sexual orientation interconnected with my research proposal; and from the proposal requiring a theoretical gaze of feminism, masculinities studies, and ultra-realism, I knew that my identity and experiences of sexual violence could fit into each theoretical positioning. This theoretical positioning sustained the reality of my work having originality while I was simultaneously innovating from normalised theoretical climates, as I had not seen any academic intertwining of these theoretical groundings. Accordingly, as a gay male who has been judged by Western heteronormative value systems, binaries, and identity violence, each of these theoretical positionings provided me with a voice. From these interconnections, I was able to have self-belief not simply in my identity and realities of sexual violence victimisation being recognisable within the research proposal's conceptualisations, but within the theory that supports these deliberations. Here, I want to reinstate the importance of me as a PhD researcher having interrelations with my research proposal within every lane possible. This resulted in my research proposal no longer being an idea or a theory but becoming my personal narrative. However, it is important to recognise that not every researcher will have this form of self-identification with their research and that every researcher will experience a different journey. From establishing this, I knew this research project was for me, and this is my central recommendation when either applying for a research proposal written by other academics or when you have designed the research proposal yourself.

My research, my reality: mental preparation

It is essential to see how you relate with the community that you are researching and, yet, understand your positioning as a researcher while remaining objective (O'Brien, 2010). This was no different for me, as I furthered my emotional connections with my study throughout the funding application process. I doubted whether I could even provide a voice for so many individuals from my communities, whether this be my participants' identities or any individual who feels like they have not had their voice heard from their encounter/s with sexual violence. I want to make sure people feel safe when participating in my research or that victims have some time to read narratives from other survivors and feel like they are not alone. This has been a truly emotional process of self-reflection while also battling constrained emotions within my mind and body, which I did not even know were there until writing my MA dissertation and my PhD research proposal. I want to state this here, as I want you to know that no matter what sensitive topic/s you investigate, you will find yourself in your writing, and emotional recognition will follow. Due to sexual violence victimisation being a traumatising experience (Miller, 2018), it is pivotal for me to acknowledge other sexual violence researchers and reiterate to you that trauma is at the crux of sexual violence, so traumatising realities re-emerging from your past are completely understandable, and you are never alone. From these emotional and trauma-based interlinks, it is fundamental for you as a researcher to tackle the restrictions of information, resources, and what your institutions provide for your personal needs and ensure that you have the support mechanisms in these three instances, especially when dealing with emotional topics, significantly, sexual violence. Sexual violence victims face realities of post-traumatic stress disorder (PTSD), depression, anxiety, fear, and self-blame, alongside issues surrounding the survivor's social and work adjustment, together with their sexual functioning (Regehr et al, 2013: 9). Therefore, as a researcher exploring this sensitive area of investigation, alongside me being a survivor of sexual violence, it is essential for me to understand the sensitivity of my research participants and the research itself. And more significantly, to acknowledge the sensitivity of my positioning as a sexual violence survivor. The sensitive researcher faces the realities of being vulnerable, reflective, reciprocal, and emotionally fatigued when researching vulnerable communities and, more broadly, sensitive topics (Sherry, 2013: 282–286). Ultimately, each sexual violence researcher, or those investigating complex areas of research, should have the emotional, mental, and economic support from such exemplars as their institutions, as the researcher will experience emotional responses when investigating such sensitive issues.

Bringing it all together: presenting the PhD proposal

As I have acknowledged previously, if you see yourself within the theoretical positioning and the conceptualisations of your potential research, and you see your personal identity and lived experience narratives being notable within your research proposal, I believe you have a higher likelihood of succeeding within your application for PhD funding. When you draw upon these personal interconnections, you will be able to express your passion, which is pivotal for any researcher who wants to maintain both their motivation and excitement for the research. Whether funded or unfunded, this can be transferrable to your personal statement, your interview, and your presentation for the PhD research itself. However, one battle that I constantly faced during the period prior to my interview and presentation was the feeling of nervousness. A juxtaposition for this feeling is the reality of people constantly telling me that I am 'extremely confident'. When internalising both nervousness and confidence simultaneously, I felt like I was unsure of where to place myself, and I believe that these contradictory feelings exemplify my lived experiences of imposter syndrome again. It is hard to decipher how you can draw upon nervousness when presenting.

Yet, it is important to remember that most students experience public speaking anxiety (LeFebvre et al, 2019). There are many ways in which you can prepare for your presentation to mitigate feelings of nervousness alongside imposter syndrome and transform these feelings into a release of passion and confidence. To exemplify this, ensure initially that you have your aims and objectives developed and have a personal understanding of how these interrelate with your identity, concepts, and theories. Following this, I believe it is essential to rehearse your presentation. From doing drama GCSE, I treated my presentation rehearsal as if it were a performance rehearsal. Try to think of your favourite person in the world being in front of you and as if you are having a conversation with them; it really helps. This has worked for me and may or may not work for you! Everyone is different, and that is ok!

Lecturing: ageism and homophobia

In July 2022, I received the news that I was successful, and I received my conditional PhD offer. I cannot put into words how happy I felt, after fighting so hard for this dream to finally come true! I then, upon meeting the criteria, started my PhD in September 2022. I was also privileged enough to be offered a Visiting Lecturer position in tandem with my research. Along with receiving my funded PhD offer, I think that this was one of the best moments of my life to date. I screamed, sprinted around the room, laughed hysterically, and called my mum with happy tears running down my face. I genuinely cannot express how incredibly lucky I felt at this time. I am so privileged to have received this after only turning 22 years old. When people speak about your dreams coming true, I would always deny these statements but since working in this role, I have never enjoyed a form of employment more. Therefore, I want to inform you of the unspoken necessity of gaining teaching experience when applying for a PhD and when doing the PhD itself and the competitiveness of doctoral students being required to have teaching experiences within a university. Interestingly, research has demonstrated that there is a limited acknowledgement of doctoral candidates needing teaching experience. Such institutions provide minimal information about teacher training opportunities within their universities, and students feel like their teaching responsibilities are not valued by colleagues who are further into their academic careers (Jepsen, Varhegyi, and Edwards, 2012). This latter element is notable within my teaching experiences, where I have faced consistent ageism as a Visiting Lecturer.

These encounters have unfortunately heightened my imposter syndrome and had me doubting whether I can pursue my PhD or be a lecturer in higher education. Not simply because I am a young academic, but the fact that I look a lot younger than I am, together with being a gay male who can confidently express his femininity. These features have always made me feel like I should watch how I act within the university setting. Despite these experiences, I always try to ensure that I am confident and eloquent in how I express my values towards life and academia. But, at 22 years old, I encountered an overload of teaching goals to achieve, the battles between my professional and personal lives, and feeling isolated within a colleague environment that should allow you to feel supported. This is conjoined with my identifying as a gay male student, where I believe that being a younger-aged academic and being gay may place me at a disadvantage in comparison to other students and staff. This is expected, as 22 per cent of lesbian, gay, and bisexual (LGB) students do not feel comfortable reporting any form of homophobic or biphobic bullying to their retrospective university staff (Bachmann and Gooch, 2018: 10). Unfortunately, this reveals that as a student from the LGBTQIA+ community, I am predicted to experience a non-inclusive university environment. This may also be reiterated within my academic career in higher education, where LGBTQIA+ staff's sexual orientations are presented as a barrier to specific forms of training and progression (AdvanceHE, 2024).

When concluding my experiences of obtaining funding for my doctoral research, I can honestly express that it is not an easy experience, but it is worth it. I personally experienced lots of potential routes that seemed credible, but most of these offers resulted in rejections. If you choose to apply for funding, ensure that you are prepared for potential rejections and that you feel passionate and enthusiastic enough to carry on applying. My advice would be to draw on an area that excites you and that you know you can repetitively read and research, no matter your feelings that day. If you are fuelled with excitement for your project, then nobody can stop you from believing in the fact that you will receive the funding and complete your PhD.

Summary of reflections

In my chapter, I have delved into the practical yet extremely personal and emotional realities of my PhD journey so far. I have discussed my journey of doctoral research funding; this is not a simple process. I have reflected on the construction of the personal statement, the design of the doctoral research proposal, and the necessity of having both originality and innovation within your research ideas. I have tried to shine a light on the internal dialogue that has accompanied me as a doctoral research candidate. What accompanies this is my personal narrative surrounding the sense of imposter syndrome that I still face and grapple with. I truly believe that embracing this internal dialogue can be harnessed in a positive way to enable me to pursue my passion. I also wanted to provide narratives from my positionality from an intersectional lens and the influence my identity has had on my PhD journey. From my experience of working on the PhD proposal, I believe it can be beneficial to draw from yourself and your life experiences. I believe that your experiences can empower you. Just remember, surviving is thriving.

3

Conceptualising a PhD topic: navigating my way through academia

Mikahil Azad
University of Worcester

Mikahil's PhD research, undertaken at Birmingham City University, involved completing a nine-month ethnography of Birmingham mosques to understand the lived experiences of Muslim communities, identify threats, and the improvement of safety. This involved being immersed in and around mosques and speaking with worshippers, staff and volunteers.

Introduction

Completing a doctorate involves overcoming several inter-related trials and tribulations; however, little has been written about the experiences of starting the PhD, in this instance, the forming of a topic. This chapter will provide my experiences of conceptualising a PhD topic and reflect upon the various issues which affected my entry into academia. It is hoped that you will gain a detailed understanding of what should be considered when conceptualising a topic for a doctorate. This chapter will take you on the journey of how I was initially unsure of whether I should undertake a PhD to ultimately conceptualising my research topic, while referring to the challenges faced along the way. Although everyone's experiences will differ, it can be said that the process is not as straightforward as I was led to believe.

Context of the PhD

The PhD, regardless of the chosen discipline, upon completion, will consist of between 60,000–80,000 words (excluding references and appendices), which can be compared to authoring a book. Upon realising the extensive word count of a doctoral thesis, I was in disbelief this qualification could be achieved due to the magnitude of the task. At this point, I did not consider the breakdown of a doctoral thesis, such as the literature review, methodology, findings, and discussion chapters. I have realised that a doctoral thesis's word count should not be given this level of intimidation. Instead, the focus should be on conceptualising a strong, robust research question, which this chapter ultimately addresses. Arguably, reaching the word count is simply an inevitability. Undertaking a PhD differs from an undergraduate and taught master's degree, as these qualifications have a safety net in which structure, pre-defined questions, and learning objectives are embedded. Upon completion, the PhD means that you have enhanced a specific area of study by providing your input, which stems from at least three years of independent research. One may assume that because the PhD is a lengthy submission, the topic chosen must be broad to reach the word count. As found with my experiences, the process of conceptualising a PhD topic involves going through the steps of having a broad topic and refining it to the point that is focused and precise. However, this chapter will acknowledge that the specific focus on the PhD can and will likely change during the early months of the PhD.

Conceptualising a PhD topic

In March 2019, I was approaching the end of my undergraduate degree in criminology at Birmingham City University (BCU) and almost ready to submit my dissertation. During supervision meetings, my supervisor and I would often digress by discussing his PhD, which fascinated me. My supervisor highlighted that although the level of detail, pressure, and work is vastly higher for a PhD compared to an undergraduate dissertation, they require following a similar process in terms of conceptualising a question, completing a literature review, and displaying and analysing findings. This discussion eliminated several misconceptions that I had about the PhD as I realised that the building blocks resembled the undergraduate dissertation process. Before enrolling at university, I did not engage well with secondary school and sixth form, and teachers often discouraged me from considering going to university. I recall the words spoken by my former law teacher during a tutor meeting: 'Mikahil, for you, going to university would be a complete waste of time. You should think of something else.'

These words echoed throughout the remainder of sixth form and during the important time students needed to decide which path to follow post-sixth forms such as university, apprenticeship, or employment. Despite my tutor's 'words of wisdom', I decided to enrol on an undergraduate degree in criminology at Birmingham City University, as I envisioned joining the police service following graduation. For a long time, I thought completing an undergraduate degree would be the end of my academic journey. At this point in my studies, I was familiar with and had built professional relationships with the criminology teaching team. I was deeply inspired by their commitment to complete research alongside their teaching responsibilities. I received kind feedback from lecturers to consider undertaking a PhD as

I developed a deep fascination with criminology as a discipline; however, the prospect of completing a doctorate was daunting as a series of questions began to conjure in my mind, such as, can I do a PhD? What should I study? Who will supervise me? How do I apply? At this point in my academic journey, I made significant progress in eliminating the echoing voice of self-doubt; at least, that is what I thought at the time, but these questions gave rise to new insecurities. As I pondered these questions, I realised that I was perhaps not quite ready to tackle the PhD just yet. So, to enhance my understanding of the vast and diverse discipline of criminology and find my specific area of interest, in September 2019, following the award of my BA(Hons), I enrolled on a master's degree in criminology at BCU.

In September 2019, as I embarked on the next stage of my academic journey, my intention was clear: I wanted to pursue a PhD. During this time, I asked numerous members of staff for their advice, which I was grateful for, but I felt close to information overload. I received insight into a 'pre-defined' PhD scholarship, which involves completing a study following the guidelines provided by the university, supervisors, and funding body. Although there are several appealing factors, namely having a pre-defined structure, this felt like I was constrained, as I desired explorative freedom despite not yet forming a question or locating a specific research area. This was compounded further when I asked a handful of PhD students who received funding and were undertaking pre-defined research. They expressed how they felt frustrated at times and wanted the freedom to explore new and exciting concepts and theories but could not do so given their PhD prerequisites. However, they did acknowledge that for themselves and many others, pre-defined questions and aims are the only opportunities to complete a PhD due to the support of a financial stipend. After considering their advice, I ultimately decided to pursue the freedom of a self-funded PhD.

During the early stages of my master's degree, I developed a strong connection with a senior lecturer in criminology, who then became a reliable, incredibly supportive mentor. I confided in them over coffee in October 2019, explaining that I intended to pursue a PhD. I began to list a series of potential research topics, which ranged from organised crime to domestic abuse and knife crime. It was clear to my mentor that I was not allowing myself to go through the organic procedure of conceptualising a topic. Instead, it was pointed out that I was rushing the process and not developing academic rigour. It was almost like I was competing with myself to reach the finish line of locating a topic, which was negatively impacting me from reaching my goal. At this point, I was driven by the desire to complete the process as quickly as possible to move on to the next stage of submitting the proposal and enrolling on the course. Although I knew where I wanted to go, I felt a mixture of anxiety and insecurity, as I was acutely aware that some of my MA peers were also actively considering and pursuing their own PhDs. While I tried to be supportive and offer my own thoughts on this endeavour, I felt like I was competing with them – like I was in a race to the finish line. These feelings were only intensified because, at this point in my academic journey, I knew I wanted to become a lecturer in criminology. To be appointed, I was aware I must possess or be working towards a PhD; therefore, to reach the next stage, I needed to enrol on a doctorate. Consequently, I felt pressured to conceptualise a topic as soon as possible. On reflection, the source of this pressure did not come from my peers; I was, in fact, my own competition. However, this race towards the finish line revealed my naivety surrounding the research process. I initially thought I was able to construct a topic quickly. I was advised to allow myself to go through a specific procedure and to keep a series of factors in mind.

Although the PhD consists of 80,000 words, the topic must be specific in focus. A doctoral thesis may draw upon several concepts, theories, and arguments; however, the core focus must be clear and precise. In addition, the journey can be an exhilarating and fun process. However, there will be guaranteed trials, tribulations, and falls; therefore, you will need to be constantly picking yourself up, and the only way you can do so is to be dedicated to meeting the research aims. In other words, you must have a genuine passion, dedication, and belief in your topic, as this will be the driving force to ensure you complete the study. My driving force was to make a real-world impact in supporting Muslim communities surrounding mosque safety. Upon the realisation that there was a much bigger picture, with much more importance than just 'completing' a PhD, I was enthused with a greater sense of passion and, consequently, purpose. As I established this motivation, I began to conceptualise my PhD slowly. I finally felt like the justification to undertake a PhD extended beyond myself and my personal goals. The purpose of completing a PhD is to contribute to knowledge and input your findings in the sphere of pre-existing literature. However, as explained, in terms of criminology and broader social sciences, to complete a PhD must be more. When undertaking empirical criminological research, we often learn about sensitive and traumatic experiences, and that research must mean something to participants. In other words, besides supporting the development of scholarship, the underpinning focus should be on impact. Taking the consideration of real-world impact became the driving force of my journey, not just for conceptualising the topic/question, but for the entire PhD.

Finalising the PhD topic

As a Muslim who has been impacted by various forms of Islamophobia – overtly, verbally, and physically – I wanted to understand why people hold such views toward Muslims and where misconceptions come from.

Therefore, I engaged with as much academic literature as possible. I could say there was a personal, motivating reason underpinning it. As mentioned, Islamophobia has impacted me and my family. This aligned with the advice provided, which was that I should focus on a topic which I deeply and personally care about. I came across a monograph written by a notable scholar on Islamophobia based in Britain. I reached out to this individual via email, which led to having a phone call regarding my plan to pursue a PhD following the master's degree. I was pleasantly surprised by the welcoming nature of a prominent academic figure and his enthusiasm to have a discussion. I initially thought my email would get lost in his inbox to which I would not receive a reply. On the contrary, in hindsight, my experiences of reaching out and asking for advice were positive. His advice to me was, when forming a topic, to keep in mind that I am unlikely to change the world. However, through research and dissemination of knowledge, I can change the lives of a few. Initially, I was disheartened by this advice. At first, I admittedly interpreted these words as negative, that they perhaps thought that I did not have the potential, or that my research ideas were valid, or of consequence. However, it soon became clear to me that this was, in fact, sage advice. Through discussion with other academics, I soon realised that change and impact do not happen overnight; it is a gradual, slow process. This realisation gave me insight into the connection between academic scholarship and real-world impact.

During my deep dive into the academic literature of Islamophobia and British Muslim communities, I gathered and recorded the key themes and topical areas in contemporary scholarships, such as definitional disputes, the persistence of oriental discourses, and the impact of political actors (Green, 2015; Zempi and Awan, 2016; Jackson, 2018). I then began to draft research proposals about the experiences of Islamophobia following 'trigger events'. Trigger events, in the context of Islamophobia, are considered notable, internationally recognised events, often terror-related, which are used as justification for political figures and far-right groups to harm Muslim communities (Awan and Zempi, 2020). My initial idea was to assess the impact on Muslim communities following a trigger event, to which the feedback from lecturers was that this topic was vague and needed a specific focus. At first, I thought I was reverting to rushed tactics of wanting to skip to the end and find a topic. However, upon reflection, this was part of the process which I needed to draft, reflect, and implement.

Locating the gap in the literature

During my research, I read quotes from victims who lost loved ones in the Christchurch terrorist attack in New Zealand in March 2019. In early 2020, news broke about an Imam (Islamic religious leader) who was attacked inside the space of a mosque in London (Quinn and Khalaf, 2020). I found the news of this deeply concerning. A mosque, regardless of architectural typology, is meant to be a space where Muslims of all backgrounds can unite, find peace, pray, unite, and strengthen their faith. However, as found, this is a total contradiction. It was concerning how there is an absence of literature exploring the experiences of mosque members regarding experiences of Islamophobia, especially in the context of Britain. In addition, I inspected guidelines published by third-party organisations currently in place to keep mosques safe. Upon examination of these sources, I was shocked that there was an absence of guidelines and recommendations in place to keep mosques and worshippers safe despite this apparent. Instead, there were a series of documents that provided vague, underdeveloped suggestions stemming from questionable, unidentifiable methods. As a result, this meant that I found a gap in the literature. However, identifying this gap did not mean I had found the question, but this was a significant start to the process.

Refining the topic

Despite finding the gap in the literature, it was 'rough around the edges'. In other words, although I was able to narrow down a topic, I needed to consider several factors, such as methods, including sampling, locations, and ethical considerations. I wanted to avoid falling down the metaphorical 'rabbit hole' of making my research topic too broad. I realised to avoid the rabbit hole, you sometimes need to fall inside it first.

At this point, I wanted to focus on mosques in terms of safety experiences of threats and dangers. I referred this idea to my mentor, to which he expressed with joy that I had found the focus of my research, which aligned with public impact. This now needed to be refined with a clear structure and rationale. I then began drafting a research proposal in which the focus was on understanding the experiences of mosque worshippers across several cities in Britain, including Birmingham, London, and Leicester – these locations were considered due to the influence of the literature in terms of vulnerabilities of Muslim communities (Zempi and Chakraborti, 2014; Awan and Zempi, 2020). During this part of the process, I aimed to conceptualise a PhD topic which can make a supportive difference to Muslim communities about mosque safety from differing cities.

However, I can now see that at the time, I was overloading my PhD research with different methodologies. I aimed to apply as many streams of data collection as I could, to gather as many insights, opinions, and experiences as possible. However, I have come to realise that I was approaching the methodology similarly to my research topic. I was clearly in a rush, and my desire to quickly establish a methodology to help me reach my goals clouded my judgement. However, as will be later realised, this approach was counterintuitive. Upon reflection and remembering the greater significance of my research, I slowed down and carefully considered what methodology would be best suited for my research, as opposed to what may have been easier to get to the finish line. As a result, when writing the proposal based on my newfound topic, I referred to a series of data collection techniques across several locations. This included completing an ethnography in mosques across Birmingham, Leicester, and London alongside disseminating questionnaires nationally. The reason I wanted to apply an ethnographic methodology was to immerse myself in the natural environment, which, in this instance, was mosques and surrounding communities. In doing so, I believed this would allow me to observe the safety risks and be able to converse with mosque staff and worshippers. It was important to apply an immersive methodology, as there was a lack of academic scholarship focusing on mosque safety, which applied an ethnographic methodology. Reflecting on this, the decision to conduct ethnographic research exposed me to the realities which are the cornerstones of my research. A picture began to form, a picture that was far greater than just my own career aspirations.

Returning to when I was still contemplating my research topic, I wanted to connect with academics across Britain who specialise in Islamophobia. I thought this would be an ideal time to solidify connections since I have the early conceptualisations of a PhD study. Upon emailing a prominent figure who specialises in Islamophobia, he initially welcomed a conversation about my PhD and suggested I put my idea on paper (resembling a proposal). At this point, I was confident to reach out to prominent academics who specialise in Islamophobia, as the last time I did, I received constructive feedback. At this point, I was happy to have found my potential topic area, which could lead me to complete the PhD. The feedback I received from this academic included: 'Maybe you should consider a different path – the PhD is probably not for you' and 'your study is unlikely to amount to anything'.

This was a gut punch. My entire sense of self, what I was capable of, and my carefully laid out plans for the future disintegrated before my eyes. This was an academic who I had grown familiar with throughout my studies, and to receive such feedback, to put it bluntly, broke my heart. The document I sent to this person was highlighted with tracked comments with similar jibes, each more painful than the last. These comments from one individual knocked me back to a point where I considered not pursuing academia, and I felt like a fraud. Like how the snake oil salesman of the Old West was lambasted and chased out of town, I felt like I wanted to run away and bury my head in the sand. These initial feelings of sadness soon transformed into anger. I was disgusted with the words used by this senior academic as this left me in a state of confusion. I did not know which path was meant for me. Although I did not say it out loud, I began to look into alternative career paths. As a master's student, I often spoke to lecturers in their offices and the university coffee pod. One day at university, two lecturers, one of them being Adam Lynes, were having an open discussion regarding their journal articles receiving harsh criticism from peer reviewers. These comments from what was discussed sounded harsh, and I could not help but think about the comments that I had received. Their reactions took me back, they seemed to so easily brush these comments off and quickly think of a strategy to address the feedback pragmatically. I asked my lecturers if the comments they received bothered them. Their response, spoken from experience, included: 'You are always going to get people who will try to put your ideas down. It is part of the job.'

This advice, which was not aimed at my situation, but at theirs, provided a spark of motivation. At this point, I had successfully located the gap in the literature which I was confident could provide real-world impact. I decided to reply, addressing the comments I had received. I gave my thanks for his time and said that I would consider certain factors but that I do believe the PhD is the right path for me and that I have confidence in my research topic; he did not respond. At this point, I had spoken to several influential academics, and they were all so supportive. It is important to emphasise there are considerate people out there and this experience should not dissuade budding students from reaching out to academics. After overcoming criticism, I became more motivated than ever to pursue this study. In terms of the impact of this criticism, this has had substantial benefits. Throughout the PhD journey, I realised that I would need to constantly defend, justify, and rationalise my study and this provided my first experience, which occurred before I officially commenced.

Finalising the topic after PhD enrolment

In September 2020, I submitted my PhD proposal to Birmingham City University and was delighted that three senior academics were interested in supervising this project. I attended an online interview in October 2021 and received approval the same day. The panel was impressed by my passion and in-depth answers, especially regarding how I would navigate ethical issues, namely the COVID-19 pandemic. I officially commenced the PhD in February 2021. When I officially started the PhD, although I had a robust idea of what my questions and strategies were, there were still factors which needed addressing to ensure it was focused and, importantly, feasible.

To re-iterate, at this time, my PhD topic involved completing an ethnography of mosques across several cities in Britain alongside disseminating surveys online. Looking back, it is clear that this idea was unrealistic and messy. Through critical conversations with supervisors and academic peers, I was able to come to the realisation that my focus was too broad. I was under the impression that because my thesis would be a lengthy submission, this had to correlate with a large scale of the study. Through this process, I realised the focus of the PhD should be precise. I then shifted my focus towards understanding the experiences of Birmingham's Muslim communities. During my review of existing literature, it was found that Muslim communities in Birmingham were particularly vulnerable and treated as 'suspect communities' (McCann, 2018). For example, funded by terrorism and allied funds, CCTV cameras, including covert types, were implemented seemingly overnight in a Muslim-majority ward, which highlights how Muslim communities are viewed and treated as suspects. Furthermore, after an anonymous letter was sent to the Home Office regarding hard-line Islamists plotting to take over a Birmingham school, which lacked any concrete evidence, law enforcement agencies and media outlets treated Muslim communities as a threat (Awan, 2018). As a result of placing my attention toward Birmingham's Muslim communities, I was able to explore the history, context, and impact of Islamophobia and risks to mosque safety with a critical approach, which would not have been achievable if I included additional locations and methods. As a result of refining my scope, I was able to build bridges and rapport with a demographic with whom I share a spiritual connection. With this established connection, I was able to understand the detailed, complex, sensitive experiences of a vulnerable demographic, which involved spending extended time in the field; time which would have been limited if I had kept the original topic.

Although, admittedly, the process in which I undertook to locate a topic and refine this into a practical research question took longer than I expected. This, however, was a time of great personal, as well as academic growth. As outlined throughout this chapter, I learned much about myself and what initially drove me to undertake a PhD. It was not until I began to question my motivations that I began to make progress in identifying and conceptualising my research topic. I truly believe that this journey of self-discovery, while painful at times, was necessary in order to see the true value and impact of what a PhD can hold beyond my own ambitions. These lessons will hopefully serve me well and keep me grounded as I continue to pursue my PhD and career as an academic.

Conclusion

The aim of my chapter was to document my journey about conceptualising a PhD topic in the hopes this would provide comfort, support, and insight into what is involved and what should be taken into consideration. The path between wanting to undertake a PhD and actually starting one is anything but straightforward; it is instead marked by twists, turns, and dead ends. To undertake a PhD involves overcoming trials and tribulations. Within this chapter, I have documented the process in which I spent approximately

18 months conceptualising a PhD topic while I was in the final stages of my undergraduate degree, undertaking my master's degree and during the initial stages of my PhD journey. During this process, there were times I questioned myself: 'Will I ever find a topic?' I was being pressured by a self-imposed countdown clock to conceptualise a topic. There may be an incentive to conceptualise a question due to a deadline; regardless, it is important to go through the stages of choosing a topic of genuine interest and engaging with the literature, and when forming a question, you need to have a practical impact at the forefront.

Although the process of conceptualising the PhD topic was extensive and difficult, at times it made me think that perhaps the PhD is not for me. However, I would not change my journey at all. In other words, yes, I would do it all over again. The journey of starting off with the broad topic of Islamophobia, which I then refined to focusing on mosques, which then connected to applying an immersive methodology, all stemmed from undertaking this complex, exhaustive process. The process of completing the PhD, although it included some difficulties, was relatively smooth as I was fully aware of my aims and I believed in the study as I undertook the organic process of conceptualising the PhD topic. It is hoped that readers of this chapter gain a deeper understanding of the process involved in conceptualising a topic during this part of their journey; there are challenges along the way and at times this can be disheartening, but when you push forward, these experiences strengthen your resiliency, which will serve you well.

Summary of reflections

As I reflect upon the process of conceptualising a PhD topic, as an established academic who now holds a PhD, I am grateful to have undertaken the rigorous, often disheartening process. This journey allowed me to identify an area of scholarship in which I have developed a sense of purpose. I advise those of you who are considering undertaking a PhD and who want to conceptualise and refine your topic, to allow yourself to understand that this process is often organic in nature. It is a process of trial and error, and it is okay not to get it right the first time, or the second, or even the third! Be sure to seek advice from your peers and most importantly, believe in yourself.

4

New horizons: moving countries to start the PhD

Eliska Suchomel Duskova
University of Cambridge

Eliska's PhD research focuses on the experiences of Czech children with incarcerated parents, with an emphasis on how children of prisoners are informed about parental incarceration.

Introduction

This chapter provides an account of the relocation process to pursue higher education studies in another country, with a specific focus on my move from Czechia to the United Kingdom. It illustrates my fluid journey towards adjustment, in line with Oberg's (1954) theory of 'culture shock'. In addition, the chapter reflects on my experience of moving from one higher education institution to another, describing the process of getting used to different institutional settings and the benefits of being part of an international cohort of researchers. Finally, my chapter provides an account of maintaining research ties with one's home country and argues for the possibility of the symbiotic co-existence of multiple spatial identities.

Moving from one country to another country – Czechia to the United Kingdom

Completing my secondary education at the Austrian Grammar School in Prague, I was exposed to an omnipresent culture glamorising studying abroad, and thus making the most of my obtained language skills. Having obtained both Austrian and Czech A-Levels, it would have been expected of me to study either in Austria or Czechia. Many alumni of my Austrian Grammar School did, but I chose to move to the United Kingdom instead. The simple reason for this was that neither Austria nor Czechia could 'criminology' be studied at an undergraduate level. This decision presented me with many challenges; challenges which I believe I share with many international students who decide to relocate to pursue their studies.

Emotional costs of leaving the family home and the financial costs of relocation

The preparation for moving abroad was, in itself, an uneasy task – bringing about both emotional and financial costs. At the beginning of my first relocation journey, I only experienced positive emotions about my choice to move out of my parent's house and start living with my – then-partner – on our own. For my parents, it generated rather mixed emotions. For my mother, in particular, the idea of my relocation to pursue studies in a different country resulted in a crisis of her identity, something common for parents dealing with their children growing up and moving out (Baumeister et al, 1985). For years, she kept insisting that I come back one day. As years went by, her worry about my permanent physical absence from the family home (and my home country) transformed into fearing the possibility of, one day, having her grandchildren abroad, resulting in missing their important milestones.

The financial costs associated with relocating to Birmingham included completing IELTS tests required by the university to demonstrate my language abilities. More importantly, it was necessary to pay a large deposit to rent an apartment in a foreign country – it was hardly possible to find a guarantor as me and my partner both faced the reality of not knowing anyone in Birmingham prior to our relocation there. These costs may represent one of the many obstacles international students face. Moving from a post-communist country in Central Europe to a Western European country also meant facing higher living costs, which ultimately led to having much lower living standards (see, for example, Brown and Holloway, 2008; Gu et al, 2010; Newsome and Cooper, 2016).

Navigating in a 'foreign' city and experiencing culture shock

Even though preparing for moving to a new country was an exciting occasion, everything changed after I arrived in the UK. Getting used to living away from one's family home for the first time can be challenging, but living away from one's family home for the first time in a 'foreign country' brings about additional stress. Most notably, one has simply no one to ask for help. My partner and I had to find ways to navigate not only a new city, but also a complex, nationally specific bureaucracy, very different from what we have been used to. Going to a Job Centre to secure a National Insurance Number and applying for a pre-settled status were some of the many things we had to do and simply knew nothing about. As it turned out, the university became the only place where we could ask for help, and in many instances, it was a place we could rely on for help when needed.

Moving to Birmingham to study our preferred degrees meant learning to navigate in a completely new environment – knowing very little about local safety. International students are exposed to an increased vulnerability through their lack of social bonds and limited knowledge of local 'rules'. Our first apartment was almost in the city centre, in Ladywood. While the accommodation itself was nice and modern, in an area where mostly young professionals resided, just across the street was a socially deprived area. This meant that over the years, we experienced not only seeing people being arrested but also shootings in broad daylight – an experience which can hardly be erased from one's mind. Shootings and arrests were something we were not used to witnessing in Prague. It is known that exposure to violence in a community can have adverse effects on young people (see, for example, Scarpa, 2003; Holt, Buckley, and Whelan, 2008; Moffitt, 2013). I experienced emotional problems in the wake of witnessing a shooting in the neighbourhood, and I consequently refused to leave the apartment for days after the shooting.

The initial phase of adjusting to living in a new country meant experiencing culture shock: the anxiety resulting from losing all familiar signs and having limited socialising options (Oberg, 1954). Being used to the European mainland café culture (see Battle, 2012) supportive of independent businesses, the ultra-capitalist chain culture seemed unrelatable. There was an omnipresent 'excess' of everything, an excess we had to get used to – in both a positive and negative sense. On the one hand, there was this broad spectrum of what is possible to buy (for example, I particularly enjoyed the 24/7 gyms and the range of fitness products available). On the other hand, there was so much waste (for example, many restaurants do not allow the taking of leftovers home). The demographic differences between Czechia and the UK meant that I could not spend as much time in the countryside as I was used to. Whereas in Czechia, many families have cottages, where they spend weekends and holidays together, this is less common in the UK. In Czechia, during the communist years, the conditional and restrained nature of travelling abroad led to people purchasing homes in the countryside instead (Rosenbaum, 2015).

A significant part of experiencing culture shock was missing home in the first 6–12 months post-relocation (Barbieri et al, 2019). Boss (2016: 281) writes that her father, a Swiss immigrant in the USA, always had a postcard of Switzerland in his leather wallet as a symbol, reminding him of his family and home country. Similarly, and quite comically, I was assigning a great value to everything I received and had even slightly reminded me of my home country – packages sent by my parents from Czechia and Czech products, which could be bought in Eastern-European grocery shops. Grief and feelings of losing one's cultural identity without knowing how to navigate such feelings can be challenging. In 2018, I remember going home for Christmas during my first year of living abroad and looking forward to it, very much holding to the idea that my home is still Czechia, and the

UK is only a place where I am focusing on my studies. I was not able to think dialectically about living and studying abroad as a Czech citizen, thus effectively prolonging my adjustment process.

Apart from adjusting to local safety 'rules', different patterns of consumption, and the lack of familial support, I also had to learn to understand the different approaches to higher education in the UK. Unlike in Czechia, universities in the UK are much more supportive of individual talents and place an emphasis on creativity – instead of tests with exact results, essays and group presentations are preferred forms of assessment. This meant I had to learn how to write an essay, something I had never done in Czechia. Even though the university provided some guidance, my first essay was not particularly successful, and I remember feeling sad and defeated when I received my first feedback. It was the day after my birthday, and I was on my way from Dublin to Liverpool when I received the news of getting a 2:2 from my first essay. Some feedback was centred around my grammar (for example, my occasional use of American English), and much of the feedback focused on my essay's 'problematic' structure. Both were undoubtedly influenced by my identity as a 'foreigner' not being used to writing traditional, English-style essays. Little did I know that this unsuccessful first essay was precisely what I needed to adjust and learn, despite adjustment being an 'ongoing' and fluid process (see, for example, Newsome and Cooper, 2016).

Overcoming challenges and discovering meaning in living abroad

After receiving unexpectedly negative essay feedback, I decided to focus all my attention on academic achievement – similar to the successfully adjusting international students in a study by Newsome and Cooper (2016: 211). I was determined to improve my academic writing, and thus, I decided to contact the university's Centre for Academic Success to discuss the feedback I received. I was immensely grateful for the academic writing support I got, and every time I wrote an essay, I booked an appointment with the same tutor to talk about the structure of my work and academic writing style. She was always very helpful and kind, offering valuable advice without judgement – making me feel like I was not alone on my academic journey.

Second, I talked to a British classmate and shared my first essay experience with him. He assured me it is normal to struggle with one's first essay, even for native speakers, and we started discussing criminology topics together. I highly value our friendship to this day, and I am grateful for our conversations in both professional and personal dimensions. I eventually started attending a 'Reading Club' he and our other classmates organised. It was a student support group focusing on helping first-year criminology students better understand their reading lists. This student support group significantly helped me improve my critical thinking and academic writing skills, ultimately leading to better grades, and most importantly, it gave me a sense of belonging. I finally started feeling settled, discovering meaning in focusing on what would later be my career. Third, I met a lecturer who inspired me – and continues to inspire me today – through her student-oriented teaching style, selfless dedication to casualty recording research, and, most importantly, her kindness. I felt like I could talk to her beyond the scope of the modules she was teaching, for example we could discuss her book together and share experiences of living in the UK as 'foreigners'.

All of this meant that while I was still having friends and family in Czechia, I started building new support networks in the UK, which ultimately allowed me to begin thinking dialectically about my life abroad. I started being comfortable with the idea of having two homes, in the UK and Czechia, rather than feeling that my home was in Prague. I befriended some of my classmates and found a coffee shop that reminded me of those in Prague. The coffee shop was of profound importance to me as it allowed me to create a weekly ritual reminding me of my other home and letting me create a new routine in the UK, far from the initial 'survival mode' I was living in.

It is important to note that my hometown, Prague, is not the same place after five years of living abroad, and neither am I the same person I was when I moved to Birmingham. People and places change over time. Sometimes, this can feel like belonging to both countries and yet not really to any of them – being a foreigner in both places – pointing towards the idea of the insider/outsider paradigm and experiencing reverse culture shock (Gaw, 2000) in a place I once considered to be my hometown. As suggested earlier in this chapter, adjustment is an ongoing and fluid process, and perhaps home is a place where dreams come true.

Moving from one higher education institution to another

As soon as I began to feel settled in Birmingham and graduated with a first-class degree – something I never even dreamed about achieving when I first moved to the UK – I faced the hard decision of moving again to pursue my MPhil degree and then a PhD. My then undergraduate dissertation supervisor talked to me over our 'goodbye' coffee about the importance of change in life and persuaded me that I should not apply to the same university to continue my studies, thus being supportive of my decision to follow a dream of studying at the University of Cambridge. This section will provide an account of relocating from one part of the UK to another due to leaving a higher education institution I was satisfied to be at to pursue my studies further.

The route to Cambridge

Beginning my PhD studies at the Cambridge Institute of Criminology was an important transition in my academic and personal life. This period was more than an intellectually demanding challenge; it demanded a significant emotional investment and required a level of commitment that undoubtedly exceeded all my previous educational experiences. From the very beginning, I was aware of the high expectations of the PhD programme I chose. The beginning of my PhD can be described as stepping into an unknown territory. The level of academic discourse characterised by the increased depth of research skills required and the requirement of originality in my work were initially overwhelming. I found myself in an environment surrounded by intellectually exceptional scholars with impressive careers and diverse backgrounds. This environment initially made me question my own abilities and triggered a sense of imposter syndrome. As time went by, I reframed these challenges as opportunities for my own professional growth.

The relationship with my PhD supervisor has been crucial in shaping my experience at Cambridge. Her expertise and guidance have been extremely valuable, but her student-centred approach was of the utmost importance. The student-supervisor dynamic she created allowed me intellectual freedom while ensuring that I stayed focused and progressed well with my PhD. Our regular supervision meetings were not only academically indispensable, but they also provided the emotional support I particularly needed during my fieldwork in Czechia. Planning fieldwork in Czechia for my PhD was a complex task as I had to manage relationships with gatekeepers and stakeholders well in advance of conducting my fieldwork. This was particularly challenging because of the geographic distance. Additionally, I had to maintain my ethical approach to research at all times, requiring me to apply for the Ethics Committee's approval soon after I embarked on my PhD journey. Despite the challenges, the fieldwork aspect of my PhD journey proved to be immensely rewarding, as it reconnected me with my home country and allowed me to substantively contribute to academic discussions at Czech conferences, as well as strengthened my relationships with some of the Czech NGO directors helping prisoners' families.

During my PhD, I have become increasingly appreciative of the distinctive scholarly nature at Cambridge. I am particularly grateful for the strong emphasis on critical thought, originality, and the collaborative nature of my research centre's meetings, which helped me overcome the many initial challenges. The friendships I made with other Cambridge students facing similar obstacles gave me a sense of belonging to '*something bigger*'. And it was the community support at Cambridge, both within and beyond the academic, that played a significant role in my integration into the Cambridge environment; the support of friends and academics made Cambridge a better place.

Getting used to different institutional settings

Relocating to Cambridge meant facing yet another lifestyle change. Significant financial costs were associated with moving from the West Midlands to the East of England. Accommodation costs are much higher in Cambridge than they were in Birmingham. The only affordable accommodation was the one offered by the college. Such an accommodation was the cheapest option, but still more expensive than the private apartment I rented in Birmingham. Unlike the light apartment with big windows that felt like home and was located in a residential area, I had to adjust to a darker, tiny student flat with safety signs everywhere, which had to be vacated after each academic year. The increased financial costs of such a relocation became much more apparent when I learned that students at Cambridge are not allowed to work for the duration of their degrees as the degrees are too demanding. Exceptions are made for part-time jobs, for example college jobs on the college site or supervising students. Such a situation arguably leaves many students dependent on their families, partners, and/or funding bodies' financial help.

College life did not only mean living in college accommodation but also learning to navigate a completely new environment, with various previously unknown rules and traditions, barely understandable to outsiders. I had to buy a gown for formal dinners and graduations, learn the Cambridge jargon, and, most importantly, become a part of my college's postgraduate students' community. Unlike at my previous university, I did not mostly know people studying for the same degree. Still, I became part of the broader university community through socialising with people from different fields due to being part of the same college or society. I met one of my dearest friends at a dinner at the Cambridge University United Nations Association, of which we are both members. We both attended the dinner despite her affiliation to the Department of Psychology and my affiliation to the Department of Criminology, being members of different colleges. I did not lack a sense of belonging thanks to my college's friendly and supportive environment for students and their partners, who are welcomed even if they are not at Cambridge. It was only bittersweet when after completing my MPhil degree, some of my Cambridge friends, who started the Cambridge journey with me, moved on while I stayed to pursue a PhD.

Becoming a Cambridge student did not only mean being part of a friendly and inclusive community of inspiring international researchers but also having to get used to a significantly higher workload than I was used to at my previous university. At first, I struggled with my readings. I felt like

I was always behind my classmates and later PhD colleagues, many of whom came from Ivy League universities, studied at Oxford, or were professionally successful in their respective countries and areas of expertise. Learning about both the relevance and prevalence of 'imposter syndrome' at Cambridge was helpful in respecting that everyone's educational journey is different, and Cambridge is a place where students are allowed to make mistakes and learn from them. One wise professor quoted John A. Shedd at the introductory MPhil lecture: 'A ship is safe in harbour, but that is not what ships are for'.

Being surrounded by international scholars and building new professional as well as personal support networks

One of the key benefits of the MPhil degree at Cambridge was being surrounded by international scholars, who were often very successful in their areas of interest, and their presence offered useful insights regarding global perspectives on crime and criminal justice. I learned a lot from them; they truly made me feel like I was part of the criminology cohort. After all, we were in the same boat – foreigners passionate about studying criminology. We were navigating the unpredictable waters of essay writing at Cambridge together. Unlike at my previous university, essay guidance was minimal, leaving students with hard-to-answer one-line questions. My international classmates inspired me through their hard work, dedication, and endless courage to study for a degree in a new environment, many coming from outside the EU, having faced much more contrasting lifestyle changes than I ever have experienced. They were supportive, kind, and generous, and it was emotional to see many of them graduate and continue on their exciting career paths, making decisions that change the world for the better.

A supportive criminology cohort with international scholars paired with being taught (and now supervised) by leading experts in criminology meant that Cambridge opened a new world of social opportunities for me and enriched me in the most valuable way possible by enabling me to form meaningful connections. I am constantly inspired by the omnipresent openness to critical discussion. Simultaneously, I feel grateful for my college's approach to students, offering Study Skills Sessions aimed at improving students' academic writing skills. During the seemingly countless hours of Study Skills Sessions at my college, I was allowed to talk about my ideas in a safe and supportive environment. I benefited and still benefit from my tutor's background in philosophy. His outstanding teaching skills and immense passion for his subject assure me that I made the right decision by stepping out of my comfort zone and moving to study at the University of Cambridge.

Relocating to Cambridge meant suddenly having two homes within the UK. I never stopped coming back to Birmingham to see friends and acquaintances, and sometimes, I miss the 'old times', despite knowing that staying and not deciding to study at Cambridge would not bring me happiness. Nonetheless, I am always happy to be back in Birmingham, and I would be open to the possibility of moving back in a professional capacity after finishing my PhD.

Maintaining research ties with Czechia

Throughout my entire higher education journey, I have always focused my research on the Czech context, and the reasons for this went far beyond the 'gap in research' argument I used to justify my decision. It provided a meaningful connection to a place I once called 'my home'. It was the safety and comfort of dealing with the 'known', both the spatial and cultural familiarity, I sought or perhaps feared to lose if I did not write about my home country. This section will provide an account of keeping in touch with home through research.

A Polish lecturer supervised my undergraduate dissertation, with whom I could share much of my cultural understanding. We had a very different working pattern, and I learned a lot through being under his supervision. Most notably, I learned that waiting for a supervisor's feedback can be a good thing – allowing one to reflect and detach a bit from one's research and rest – my supervisor always worked towards deadlines. In contrast, I wanted to have everything submitted in advance. My undergraduate dissertation was titled: 'A comparative study of institutional responses to sexual harassment at Birmingham City University and Charles University', and it was more than just a bridge between my life in the UK and my life in Czechia; it was my therapy and a symbolic way of coming to terms with my own experiences of sexual harassment in Czechia. I am grateful to my supervisor at Birmingham City University for allowing me to heal through academic writing and leave this painful chapter in life behind me. Owing much to his support, my undergraduate dissertation writing has been an enjoyable and reflective process during which I never felt alone or misunderstood.

Relocating to Cambridge to pursue a nine-month MPhil degree in criminology meant choosing a new dissertation topic. I was strongly advised against doing empirical research collecting my own data because there was too little time to do so, given that I did not choose to study the twelve-month MPhil degree in Criminological Research instead. I knew that I could do it simply because I felt like I needed to be, in one way or another, connected to my participants to write a dissertation; I needed to be personally attached to the topic I was writing about. It always has to be personal for me, so I begged to be allowed to collect my own data back in Czechia. I was warned that no one could help me if I failed to collect my data, and I was determined to prove that I could do it – in nine months' time.

Thanks to my supervisor's student-centred pedagogical style, allowing much freedom to students' ideas and pace of work, I could focus on researching the experiences of Czech children with incarcerated parents who live in institutional care. My MPhil dissertation was a precursor to my larger-scale PhD study focusing on the experiences of Czech children who live in institutional and non-institutional settings.

Collecting data in Czechia for both my MPhil and my PhD meant having to remotely manage relationships with gatekeepers and stakeholders in Czechia before travelling to do the actual fieldwork. At times, I was treated like an 'outsider' during initial meetings with NGOs as they wanted to make sure that I knew enough about my prospective participants and their experiences prior to conducting my research. Once I gained their trust, they showed me support I could hardly ever have imagined getting. They went over and above what they promised, always helping me find a way to do my research as comfortably as possible – for example offering their premises to conduct the interviews (even though this was not needed) and treating me like one of them while doing my ethnographic observation.

Navigating fieldwork in Czechia could be difficult in terms of having to travel extensively and securing enough funding for that purpose. I would like to express my gratitude to the Institute of Criminology for giving me the funding I needed and to my participants, gatekeepers and stakeholders, who made the fieldwork rewarding despite being emotionally challenging. I felt supported by the prison staff members in Czechia, my family, and the many Czech NGOs and government organisations who were willing to help me with the realisation of my fieldwork. Simultaneously, I could always count on my supervisor's support, who kindly checked on me during the data collection process. Our fortnightly Zoom calls helped me reflect on the data collection process, and I was allowed to share the emotional burden of fieldwork with her, which I am utterly grateful for. In both instances of finishing my fieldwork in Czechia, regardless of whether this was for my MPhil degree or my PhD, I felt like I could feel at home both in Czechia and the UK. The unconditional support of others in both places made me feel like I was a part of both countries. Since my MPhil research and subsequent graduation, I have been in touch with a small Czech NGO helping prisoners and their families. At first, I was a social worker and then a researcher, in both roles, offering consultancy on various issues centred around the NGO's activities. Most recently, as part of my NGO work, I delivered a speech at an award evening, where winners of a creative writing competition for Czech prisoners were announced, and I talked about Arts in Prisons in the UK. Working for a Czech NGO can be seen as a way of seeking belonging while staying connected to my own roots and giving back to my home country. Still, the example of delivering a speech about the UK context of Arts in Prisons illustrates that it is possible to have more than one spatial identity. These multiple spatial identities can co-exist symbiotically.

Conclusion

This chapter has provided an account of moving locations to pursue higher education. First, it has illustrated that change can be challenging but rewarding. Moving from one country to another and/or moving from one higher education institution to another can have emotional, financial, and social opportunity costs. Simultaneously, these costs can be turned into many benefits, for example building new professional and personal support networks and always having somewhere to go when things get difficult. Second, it showed that stepping outside one's comfort zone can make us grow, and the loss of a spatial identity because of relocation is, like most losses, rarely absolute. Therefore, it is important to focus on the meaningfulness of life despite facing difficulties. Moreover, facing difficulties and finding ways to overcome obstacles can lead to and significantly help with adjustment. Adjustment can be seen as an inherently fluid and ongoing process. Third, and most important, building multiple support networks to stay connected to more than one place is at the core of managing the process of 'relocating'. And, perhaps, home is a place where dreams come true. These dreams are made true thanks to others who have been with me on this journey. I am grateful for the support of my family, friends, colleagues, supervisors, tutors, and research gatekeepers. It is a blessing to be alive at the same time as all these people who continue to inspire me *endlessly*.

Summary of reflections

Reflecting on my educational journey, and the transition to studying a PhD at Cambridge in particular, it has been a journey of personal and professional growth through challenge and adaptation. Experiencing relocation and adjustment to different academic institutions was demanding but enriching. While these relocations and adjustments came at significant emotional and financial costs, these costs were outweighed by the personal and academic growth that resulted from stepping outside my comfort zone. My PhD journey has been a transformative experience requiring me to confront not only my personal insecurities, such as imposter syndrome, but also demanded a level of discipline and creativity that I had not previously encountered. My account shows that the support systems, consisting of my supervisor and my personal support networks, were pivotal in helping me navigate this demanding yet inspirational academic landscape. These relationships helped me build the emotional resilience needed to persevere through the PhD alongside providing academic guidance. My journey proves that growth often comes from discomfort, and the process of adapting to new environments is arguably a fluid and ongoing one. Having to construct multiple homes – geographically and metaphorically – has changed me as a person.

5

From home to the unknown: applying for postgraduate study in the UK from the global south

Manikandan Soundararajan
Staffordshire University

Manikandan's PhD research topic is closely connected with international issues, specifically exploring the lived experiences of undocumented migrants in the West Midlands region.

Introduction

This chapter is all about my reflections and personal experiences while pursuing postgraduate study or a PhD in the UK. Currently, I am pursuing my PhD in criminology at Staffordshire University, a full-funded course offered by the University. My decision to embark on this academic path is driven by a quest for a more enriching research environment, one that transcends the limitations I have faced in my home country. There is a lot of debate on the Indian education system from both positive and negative sides. However, in my experience, criminology and criminal justice often lack emphasis on critical thinking and practical research skills, which compelled me to seek opportunities abroad. I was drawn towards the UK and its higher education system because of its research environment, innovation, critical thinking, and its long history of excellent education. It was not just about getting a degree but about joining a worldwide community of research scholars. In this chapter, I will reflect on my motivation, the challenges encountered, and the insights gained throughout the process of applying for postgraduate study in the UK from an Indian perspective.

Indian education and my experience

During my time in school, I never considered pursuing a PhD, and at that time, I did not even know what a PhD was. My experience with the Indian education system has been consistently challenging because I do not fit the 'ideal' student profile they arguably want. The Indian education system primarily assesses students' knowledge based on memorising capacity through written examination rather than emphasising critical thinking, analysis, and skill development (Sivasubramanian, Sridharan, and Saravanan, 2013). I struggled in many exams and tests due to difficulties memorising information for them, which led some of my schoolteachers to perceive me as an academically weak or below-average student. Memory-based education limits students' critical thinking abilities, creativity, and innovation (Hoque, 2018). This has proven to be a challenge for many international students who enrol in higher education in developed countries such as the UK, US, Canada, and so on, and particularly for Indian students who are accustomed to memory-based education systems (Hayes and Introna, 2005). As a result, they often face difficulties in writing assignments and have an increased risk of submitting plagiarised work (Pallela and Talari, 2016).

Higher education in India has developed significantly, but there is still a need for further research production and quality development. Premier institutions such as the Indian Institute of Science, Jawaharlal Nehru University, and the Indian Institutes of Technology uphold the quality of education and research (Singh, 2011; Altbach, 2014). However, not everyone has access to study in these institutions due to various deciding factors, including funding, guidance, entrance tests, and recommendations (Sivasubramanian, Sridharan, and Saravanan, 2013).

When I started my master's in criminology in 2014, I did not know anything about conducting research, and I was unaware of the potential research opportunities in postgraduate study. I chose to study criminology because I was fascinated by the subject, as it offers valuable insights into crime and criminal behaviour, which are crucial for policing jobs. I aspired to become a police officer, believing studying criminology would provide a pathway to a policing career. During my course, I was introduced to research methods and criminological research. However, the focus was mostly theoretical and did not include practical guidance on conducting research in the real world (Altbach and Mathews, 2015). In the UK, many undergraduate programmes are research-led courses, and universities often encourage students, including undergraduates, to conduct research in their area of interest (Healey, 2005). However, in India, even master's students struggle to conduct research and write plagiarism-free dissertations (Altbach, 2014). From my perspective, the primary reason for plagiarism is that Indian students were never taught to write without plagiarism and faculty members' lack of emphasis on research quality. Many Indian universities lack effective systems to detect plagiarism and do not have an ethics committee to uphold academic integrity. It is crucial to recognise the urgent need for pedagogical reforms with a greater emphasis on improving the quality of research (Altbach and Mathews, 2015). These reforms are necessary to align our educational system with international standards and prepare students for global challenges (Altbach and Mathews, 2015).

My decision to pursue a PhD abroad

The shortcomings I experienced in the Indian education system, particularly in my field of interest, motivated me to seek academic opportunities abroad. After completing my master's degree and gaining some insight into research methods, I realised there is potential for growth and development in a more conducive academic environment. The decision to pursue a PhD abroad was not just about acquiring a prestigious degree; it was about immersing myself in a research-intensive culture that fosters critical thinking, innovation, and the practical application of theoretical knowledge. As mentioned, my decision to study criminology was driven by my fascination with the subject and my aspiration to become a police officer. However, my interactions with some police officers during my course led me not to join the police career. Instead, a senior police officer advised me to pursue a research career and contribute to society through research. This marked the moment when I began contemplating pursuing a PhD abroad and initiated my search for potential avenues to achieve this goal.

My decision to apply for a PhD in developed countries such as the UK, the US, and Europe was driven by multiple push and pull factors (Mazzarol and Soutar, 2002). India's academic and research environment is not that favourable for PhD students, primarily due to a high dependency on supervisors. This relationship often goes beyond academic guidance and mentoring, placing students in positions where they are expected to undertake personal tasks and non-research-related tasks for their supervisors (Sivasubramanian, Sridharan, and Saravanan, 2013). Such expectations extend beyond the bounds of academic mentorship, blurring into personal service without payment. During my master's studies, I witnessed numerous events where PhD students were assigned a wide range of tasks, including those related to their supervisors' personal projects, and frequently these involved unpaid responsibilities. This depressing situation with PhD students in India deeply affected me and significantly influenced my decision not to pursue a PhD in India. Moreover, it is concerning to note that PhD students sometimes work more than 12 hours per day on tasks unrelated to their doctoral research, leading to a lack of work-life balance (Ganesha and Aithal, 2022). However, this situation is not limited to the criminology department alone but applies to many social science and humanities departments across Indian universities. However, there are exceptions, and I have observed a few professors who treat their PhD students with respect and dignity.

Moreover, PhD candidates in India experience low pay and excessive workloads. They typically receive University Grants Commission (UGC) fellowships or University fellowships but are often reliant on their supervisors for approval and disbursement. Failure to obtain supervisor approval can result in the withholding of a fellowship by the department. Consequently, PhD students find themselves unduly dependent on their supervisors, creating an academic environment resembling contemporary servitude. This was one of the primary motivations for seeking a PhD programme outside of India.

Furthermore, the reputation of a PhD degree obtained from India is not highly regarded. Many international researchers and experts believe that Indian PhDs lack quality and do not meet research standards. It is quite prevalent in India that numerous PhD projects do not meet established research standards, with many universities failing to adhere to ethical guidelines for research, plagiarism and data integrity issues, and producing substandard research reports (Sahay, 2015). While some students and supervisors strive for high-quality research and maintain research standards, the overall reputation of Indian PhDs often hinders recognition. This factor also contributes to my decision to pursue a doctoral degree abroad. I recognise challenges within Western education and research, such as the higher cost of education and an overreliance on the process rather than outcomes in research. However, it is undeniable that the quality of education and research in India lags significantly behind (Altbach, 2014; Sahay, 2015; Altbach and Mathews, 2020). This is disappointing, as historically, India was known for its indigenous educational system, research, and innovation. My decision was further reinforced when I struggled to publish a paper from my dissertation. After completing my master's degree, I realised that my dissertation did not meet the required standards due to the absence of an ethics committee at my university and the lack of quality needed for publication. Eventually, I withdrew my intention to publish my dissertation due to this setback. This is when I realised that to establish my research career, I must seek opportunities to acquire knowledge and engage in high-quality research.

Criminology in India is underdeveloped (Thakre and Jaishankar, 2018) and only receives limited government funding for research. Moreover, criminology is not widely recognised as valuable for the functioning of the government or police department in India, which can be attributed to several factors. Unlike in the West, criminology and sociology have significant importance in society and are valued by scholars who often collaborate with government policymakers (Blomberg, 2019; Thakre and Jaishankar, 2018). I have never seen such things in India, and these differences influenced me to seek opportunities in Western countries. As a criminology student, I have always been intrigued by the criminological theories developed by Western scholars, such as Edwin Sutherland's Differential Association Theory and Evidence-Based Approaches. This also influenced me to pursue my criminology studies at a university in the West.

My motivation to pursue a PhD degree abroad is firmly based on my desire to be part of a research group that is more supportive, ethical, and progressive. Have you ever been drawn towards something that feels like it holds the key to unlocking your career potential? For me, the academic environment in Western countries presented such an opportunity for my academic and personal development. This decision represents not just the pursuit of higher education but also a step towards making substantial contributions to the field of criminology from a global south perspective.

Choosing the UK over other countries

One of the primary factors influencing my decision to pursue doctoral research in the UK was the connections and interactions I had with academics from the UK. During my MPhil programme, I had the opportunity to meet scholars from different parts of the world who were visiting India for various purposes, such as research projects, academic visits, and conferences. I encountered challenges in networking with many academics and scholars, as they were less approachable. However, I was fortunate to find some good people, particularly from the UK and they were exceptionally helpful and easy to approach. This experience motivated me to seek their support and guidance for reviewing my research proposal for funding opportunities or when applying for a PhD in the UK.

Regarding financial support, countries such as the US, Australia, and European countries such as Germany, Italy, France, Poland, and the Netherlands tend to prioritise domestic students for scholarships and fellowships. In contrast, the UK offers separate funding opportunities for international students and support for domestic students. I have observed cases of Indian students receiving fellowships and grants in the UK and had conversations with some of these individuals when I was applying for my own fellowship. However, it is uncommon for the US, Australia, and European countries such as Germany, Italy, France, Poland, and the Netherlands to offer fellowships to international students except in exceptional circumstances.

I have previously applied for PhD programmes at universities in different countries, such as the UK, the US, Germany, Italy, the Netherlands, Australia, Japan, and New Zealand. Among these nations, I found the UK application process for PhD courses for international students comparatively straightforward compared to other countries. In the UK, a master's degree with good grades, a research proposal, and an International English Language Testing System (IELTS) score are sufficient for a PhD application, along with additional written elements such as a motivation or personal statement. In contrast, in countries such as the US, Australia, Germany, France, and New Zealand, applicants must submit officially certified transcripts directly to the university in sealed envelopes by a certifying officer. Additionally, the students must take the Graduate Record Examination, attend multiple rounds of interviews, and, in some cases, demonstrate proficiency in the local language even when the course is conducted in English.

Additionally, I reached out to numerous university professors and noticed that UK professors were more responsive. Many of them even offered feedback on my research proposal, which helped me to understand the flaws in my research proposal, and eventually, this process boosted my confidence. In contrast, professors from other countries were less responsive and not as helpful for enhancing my application. This motivated me to focus primarily on applying to more UK universities and contacting professors from UK universities. Furthermore, the colonisation of India by the British Empire has had a significant impact on its language and culture which has influenced me to apply for the UK universities. My education in the English medium has played a pivotal role in my decision to apply to universities in English-speaking countries. Additionally, many students from India are inclined towards studying at UK universities due to various factors like colonial connection, the existence of huge Indian communities in the UK, and former students' experience and fascination with London, which I also shared, influenced my choice (Hercog and Laar, 2016).

As a criminology student, I regularly follow international news and developments, enabling me to gain insights into hate crimes and racism in developed nations. Through various sources, including news articles, social media, and conversations with peers, I concluded that while hate crimes exist in the UK, their severity is less pronounced compared to the US, Australia, or other European countries (Myers and Lantz, 2020). This observation also significantly influenced my decision to pursue a PhD programme in the UK.

Challenges encountered during the application process

I began to apply for PhD programmes in 2016, after completing my master's degree in criminology. I secured admission to a PhD with a full scholarship at Staffordshire University in September 2020 after an extensive four-year application process to over 50 universities worldwide. My first application was to Victoria University of Wellington in New Zealand. As expected, I received a prompt rejection within a week; however, it was disappointing. Throughout this journey, I lacked adequate support, guidance, and mentorship (Bhagat et al, 2022). I still remember that for my first PhD application, I had to make multiple requests to the head of the department of my alma mater and physically visit his office to obtain the reference letter. In India, the PhD application process is often similar to the undergraduate programme and very rarely involves the rigorous approach adopted by developed PhD applications, which involves writing research proposals, motivation letters, and acquiring reference letters. Due to this reason, getting a reference or recommendation was a difficult task for me.

Have you ever experienced a setback that left you feeling lost and uncertain about your future? Following my rejection from Victoria University of

Wellington, I sought guidance from professors at my alma mater with hopes of receiving support. However, I had a disheartening experience as they responded by humiliating and mocking me. One professor went so far as to express doubt about my abilities and skill set, suggesting that obtaining a self-funded PhD would be exceedingly challenging for me. This experience made me question whether I lacked the necessary skills and abilities. It was a moment of profound disappointment that demotivated me greatly, but it also made clear to me that this journey ahead would be very tough. Despite these challenges, I was fortunate to connect with a professor from the political science department. Although I was unfamiliar with him, he generously offered his assistance and furnished me with a reference letter for my upcoming applications.

Throughout my application process, I encountered limited assistance and guidance. Writing application documents such as motivation letters, personal statements, research proposals, CVs, and other materials was undertaken independently by me. I relied on my own judgement to compose each section and sought out online examples for reference. However, I received some support and guidance from an immediate senior who reviewed my application and provided valuable feedback, which helped me to revise and strengthen my PhD applications.

After facing several more rejections, I felt deeply disheartened and discouraged. It became apparent to me that there were significant shortcomings in my application and qualifications. Subsequently, I took the initiative to reach out to the universities and professors who had turned down my applications, seeking their insights and feedback. This process helped me to understand that my research experience was insufficient and that I lacked the ability to conduct research independently. To overcome this, I actively started to look for research positions and possibilities to publish. Some advisors also recommended pursuing a second master's degree in criminology abroad to overcome these issues. However, financial constraints prevented me from pursuing this option due to my hailing from a lower-middle-class family without substantial financial support. The financial constraints significantly affected my academic aspirations, and I started to have self-doubt about myself and my future.

After carefully considering and contemplating my career path, I decided to pursue an MPhil degree in India rather than a second master's abroad. When I spoke to my elder brother and family about this, they expressed some disappointment in my choice to pursue another degree instead of providing financial support to the family, particularly during a period of extreme financial crisis for the family. Despite their concerns, I remained resolute in pursuing an MPhil degree and began contemplating where to undertake it. Finding suitable institutions for studying MPhil courses in criminology proved challenging due to the limited academic offerings in this field in India. I was very careful about choosing a supervisor for my MPhil research and choosing an institution that would support my academic research goals. As mentioned, criminology in India constitutes only a small group of academics, and only a few universities offer criminology courses. Due to this, I was unable to find as many options as I had hoped for to pursue my MPhil degree. Furthermore, many universities have discontinued MPhil courses in criminology and many other subject areas due to a lack of student numbers and interest in MPhil degrees. Ultimately, upon learning about Rashtriya Raksha University, which specialises in education and research related to internal security and policing, I found it a good option for pursuing my MPhil. Fortunately, I was assigned an exceptional supervisor during my MPhil programme, who shared my objectives and offered valuable support in achieving them right from the beginning of our collaboration. His encouragement and support were a great source of inspiration for me, which increased my confidence and belief in my ability to accomplish my goals.

During my MPhil programme, I encountered significant financial difficulties as my family was undergoing a severe crisis and could not support me. As a result, I had to borrow money from friends to cover tuition and engage in part-time work to sustain myself. Balancing work with the rigorous, research-focused coursework was challenging, but I remained committed to my academic goals and focused on my research project despite these obstacles. Choosing an original and impactful research topic for my MPhil thesis was crucial. I was a bit ambitious about my research project, and I chose to pursue research on the plight of Rohingya refugees who were forced from Myanmar to Bangladesh. Despite initial resistance due to prevailing prejudice against Muslims in India and institutional alignment with right-leaning ideologies, both my supervisor and the institution's head supported my decision to explore the plight of Rohingya refugees. When I presented my proposal and mentioned my plan to travel to Bangladesh for ethnographic research to study the lives of Rohingya refugees, it surprised many people, including my supervisor.

Even my supervisor suggested conducting similar research on Rohingya refugees in India who arrived before 2017. However, I was not completely convinced, as the persecution of Rohingyas escalated after 2017, leading to the exodus of approximately 750,000 individuals from Myanmar. I take pride in having undertaken research on Rohingya refugees during that period, which was an under-researched area, and it brings me great satisfaction to know that I could advocate for these marginalised individuals. I am proud that I could give a voice to these marginalised individuals by publishing my research in the *British Journal of Criminology* in 2023 and as a book chapter in Routledge's *Handbook of South Asian Criminology* in 2019. I never thought I could publish in Routledge's book and the *British Journal of Criminology*, both known for their exceptional work. This reminds me of one thing – even when people discourage you, believe in your abilities and hard work.

I successfully completed my MPhil degree with high distinction and gained valuable research experience through part-time work as a research assistant, as well as two publications by that time. I thought getting an extra degree and fulfilling other criteria would be enough to get PhD admission with funding abroad. Despite meeting the additional requirements, I faced unexpected challenges and rejections that disheartened me. While I was determined not to give up on my dream, I also struggled with pressure and feelings of depression. Meanwhile, many of my classmates from the master's programme had already begun their PhD studies in India or were close to completing their data collection process. During social interactions at conferences in India, peers often asked questions and made remarks, 'When are you going to the UK?' or 'Going to the UK or US?' These comments deeply affected me because I was struggling to achieve my goals and feeling depressed due to rejections. On the other hand, close friends and my MPhil supervisor suggested that pursuing a PhD was simply a gateway to academia and advised me not to take the rejections too personally. Although they were very positive and supportive, they advised me to accept this reality and suggested considering a PhD in India. The realisation of this reality, alongside these conversations, had convinced me to reconsider pursuing a PhD abroad; however, the next question was, 'If not abroad, then where to do a PhD in India?'.

I was fortunate to marry a woman who is equally ambitious about her career and life. In 2019, I was about to give up on my dream and decided to pursue a PhD in India. She reignited the passion that I had lost. She suggested: 'I've already spent three years improving my qualifications and research skills; why not give it one last try before considering other options?' She also advised me to focus on my goal rather than be influenced by others' opinions. I agreed with her and started applying to more universities. Despite receiving further rejections, it was encouraging to note that I was shortlisted for multiple opportunities. I was shortlisted by two universities – one in the UK and another in the Netherlands – although ultimately, they did not select me after the interview process concluded. This inspired and motivated me as it showed progress towards reaching my goal. This achievement meant a lot to me, as no university had considered me for over two years.

Following this progress, while facing rejections during interviews, there were moments of disappointment combined with encouragement. Following a rejected interview outcome, I received constructive feedback from a professor who expressed genuine interest in my research idea. He explained why I had not been selected and helped revise my research proposal. In addition, he also indicated a willingness to facilitate admission into their PhD programme. However, the downside was that this opportunity was a PhD without funding, which meant I had to organise external or self-funding. Yet, I was fully committed to pursuing a self-funded PhD, as this was the first time I had received any opportunity to pursue my doctoral research. Subsequently, I had a few online meetings with the professor and started to work on the proposal.

During this time, a professor from a UK university whom I had met at a conference in India advised me to apply to highly ranked universities if I am self-funding my PhD. He convinced me that it would be worth investing in a top university. Following his advice, I reached out to professors at well-ranked universities to discuss my research proposal and seek their support for my application. However, I received only a few responses from these professors. Meanwhile, I also applied for several funded PhD programmes to keep my options open, including fully and partially funded ones. One such programme was at Staffordshire University, where I am currently pursuing my PhD.

In 2019, I was happy with being accepted into two PhD programmes out of five applications. This boosted my confidence, even though the offers did not include funding. Previously, I faced rejections when applying for funded PhD programmes and doubted my research profile. However, this experience helped me recognise that rejection does not necessarily reflect on the candidate but can be influenced by factors such as strong competition, research experience, publications, research focus, interview performance, and more. After discussing with mentors and family regarding joining one of the PhD programmes, one of my mentors from the UK warned me about the high international fees and living costs in the UK (Rajan and Wadhawan, 2014; King and Sondhi, 2017). Despite his caution, I remained focused on pursuing this opportunity without fully considering the financial implications at that time. I began calculating the costs and contacted several banks to secure a loan for my education. Unfortunately, I soon discovered that obtaining a loan would be challenging as the banks required collateral, such as property or land, which I did not possess. I attempted to secure the necessary funds by seeking support from my friends and family. I also considered selling some of my wife's gold jewellery to finance my doctoral studies. Despite these efforts, I could only raise approximately £10k, leaving me short by £15k for expenses, including tuition fees, visa costs, airfare, and initial living expenses totalling around £25k. Once again, I was at a dead end with nowhere to go. This was a deeply depressing and hopeless moment for me.

New horizons

After a few months, I was shortlisted for PhD programme interviews at two universities. One was at Staffordshire University, and the other was from a Russell Group University, which was unexpected. However, I lacked confidence this time due to uncertain feelings about my career and fear of further rejection. Additionally, the shortlisted PhD programmes required me to work on pre-planned projects based on UK research topics. I feared another rejection since these topics were unfamiliar and I had never experienced British culture, community, or the criminal justice system. Both universities interviewed me. The interview with Russell Group University went much better than the Staffordshire University interview, as the latter's research project was not in my area of interest, and I was unaware of many developments in British policing. I had high hopes for a positive outcome from Russell Group University. However, after a month, I was informed that the decision was between myself and another candidate. Ultimately, they chose the other candidate over me due to their extensive experience in that research area. This was the biggest disappointment of my life, as I missed a fully funded PhD opportunity at Russell Group University by just one step. Furthermore, after this rejection, I did not have much hope from Staffordshire University because I felt that my interview performance was not good enough and I lacked experience and knowledge about British policing, which was the focus of their research project.

Finally, it was a big surprise when they selected me for the PhD programme and requested further documents for the next process. They chose me and another candidate, even though they had initially planned to offer only one PhD position. They informed me that my application stood out as the strongest but recognised that I wouldn't be a good fit for the policing research project. As a result, they proposed a research project aligned with my MPhil research on undocumented migrants due to my interest in refugees and migration. Due to the time zone difference, I received my decision late in the evening. It was an incredibly happy night as thoughts of my future PhD and life in the UK kept me awake.

Through perseverance and determination, I overcame numerous challenges to secure a place in a PhD programme at Staffordshire University despite facing initial rejections and financial hurdles. The journey has taught me the valuable lesson that setbacks and disappointments are part of pursuing higher education. Each rejection and setback have only made me more resilient and determined to succeed. Being chosen for the PhD programme at Staffordshire University, with a research project aligned with my interests, validated my hard work and commitment to my research interests. It was a dream come true to be given the opportunity to explore deeper into a subject that is not only academically stimulating but also holds personal significance for me. I have already finished three years of my PhD and am moving towards finishing my PhD research.

Summary of reflections

My decision to pursue a PhD in the UK was a crucial moment in my life. The journey, filled with many ups and downs, helped me learn valuable lessons. Getting accepted on to a fully funded PhD programme requires strong perseverance. Despite having self-doubt about my abilities, I was committed to my goals. Following a structured approach and working on the feedback from my rejected applications helped me to overcome these obstacles. Building a strong network with like-minded individuals and experts who can provide valuable feedback, mentorship and opportunities is important. However, it is essential to maintain these relationships with realistic expectations, as overreliance on them can lead to disappointment and affect the relationship itself. A positive attitude is essential for any competitive funding application. It is important to maintain an optimistic mindset – this will help you in achieving your goals!

Editors' reflections: Part I

Imagine the PhD as a literal journey across a vast landscape filled with mountains to climb, swamps to wade through, forests to explore, and seas to cross. Along the way, we would need to pause to catch our breath, assess our supplies, and plan the next phase of our adventure. This is our first rest stop on this journey, where we will take a moment to reflect on the key themes and challenges we have encountered.

Chapter 1, by Sarah Jones, provides valuable insights for those contemplating a PhD. Her narrative begins with a profound personal tragedy that shifted her life away from academia and led to years of grappling with grief and self-doubt. Sarah's return to education was driven by a desire to rebuild her life, and her story highlights the transformative power of learning and personal growth. Through the support of mentors and loved ones, she started to understand how to navigate imposter syndrome, which allowed her to recognise her potential. Sarah's journey illustrates that pursuing a PhD is deeply intertwined with personal challenges and identity. Her reflections emphasise the significance of self-belief, support systems, and the courage to reshape personal narratives, providing reassurance and a sense of support for anyone at the crossroads of deciding whether to embark on a PhD journey.

Chapter 2, by Alexander Black, offers a raw account of the competitive struggle to secure PhD funding. Alex's narrative sheds light on the personal and professional hurdles encountered in academia, including the fierce competition, the need for originality in research proposals, and the psychological toll of imposter syndrome. His experience as a Visiting Lecturer, compounded by ageism and homophobia, adds complexity to his journey. Alex's chapter serves as both a guide and a cautionary tale, urging doctoral candidates to cultivate resilience, self-reflection, and authenticity amid the increasingly competitive landscape.

Chapter 3, by Mikahil Azad, explores the challenges of conceptualising a PhD topic. Mikahil's journey began with a broad interest in criminology but evolved as they faced difficulties narrowing down a research focus. Despite setbacks and criticism, they learned the importance of perseverance, dedication, and a clear research question driven by a genuine desire to make a real-world impact. This chapter underscores the evolving nature of research development, and the resilience required to navigate academia.

Chapter 4, by Eliska Suchomel Duskova, provides a personal account of the challenges faced as an international student transitioning from Prague to the UK. She discusses the emotional and financial costs of relocation, the culture shock in Birmingham, and the complexities of adapting to a new academic environment. Eliska's transition from undergraduate studies to a

PhD at Cambridge highlights the significance of building support networks to combat isolation and imposter syndrome. Her experiences emphasise the transformative impact of studying abroad, where overcoming adversity leads to substantial personal and academic growth.

Finally, Chapter 5, by Manikandan Soundararajan, tells a story of perseverance and hope in the pursuit of a PhD in criminology in the UK. Manikandan's motivation stemmed from a desire for a research environment that fostered critical thinking and practical skills, which they found lacking in the Indian education system. Their journey, marked by academic culture challenges and numerous rejections, shaped their resolve. Manikandan's narrative provides intimate insights into their motivations, struggles, and ultimate triumphs, offering inspiration for others in their pursuit of their own academic dreams.

These chapters present a rich tapestry of themes crucial for those considering or navigating a PhD. From the interplay between personal adversity and academic ambition to the value of support networks and battling imposter syndrome, each chapter provides valuable insights and words of encouragement for you, the reader, as you embark on or continue your PhD journey.

Now, as we pack our metaphorical bags for the next leg of this journey, let us consider what lies ahead. Chapters 6 through 9 delve into how life outside the PhD can profoundly influence one's academic journey while offering solace and practical guidance for overcoming significant challenges. Chapter 6, by Rio Waldock, shares their experience of coping with the profound loss of a father during their early PhD years and the decision to shift from full-time to part-time study. In Chapter 7, Charlotte Rigby discusses balancing the demands of being both a lecturer and a PhD student, emphasising the importance of work-life balance and a strong support network. Chapter 8, by Suzanne Baggs, continues this theme by highlighting the sacrifices made for doctoral pursuits and the need to acknowledge personal limits. Finally, Chapter 9, by Abigail Shaw, addresses mental health and neurodiversity in the PhD experience, tracing their personal journey through institutional and cultural barriers. These chapters offer valuable insights and support as you navigate the complexities of integrating academic and personal life.

PART II

6

Navigating the depths of grief: a journey through grief while pursuing a PhD

Rio Waldock
Birmingham City University

Rio's PhD research explores the impact and psychological harms of Imprisonment for Public Protection (IPP) sentencing on both prisoners and their family members.

Introduction

Grief doesn't know the concept of time and is a weird process. Some days, you act like it doesn't exist, and then there are days where you feel everything, like a tonne of bricks lying over your chest. Losing a loved one is an experience for which nothing in life truly prepares you and is sadly a reality that eventually touches everyone. The most difficult truth about grief is that it never truly disappears. Whether triggered by a special milestone, birthday, anniversary, or a song that evokes memories, something will always remind you of them and intensify feelings of grief. Anyone who has lost a loved one knows that grief is not a linear process, and there can be many different stages. For me, it has been an emotional rollercoaster characterised by its unpredictability; however, it is becoming easier to navigate with time and self-care. In this chapter, I will share some of my personal experiences and discuss what I have found helpful for coping with bereavement. I will begin by recounting key moments from my life journey and then delve into how I have managed the complexities of grief while pursuing a PhD. This chapter touches on some very sensitive topics and experiences.

From GCSE failure to PhD pursuit

If someone had told me 20 years ago that I would end up attending university and doing a PhD, I would have laughed in their face and thought they were off their head. None of my family had been to university, and it was certainly never on my agenda. As a child, I hated education and could not wait to leave school and earn some money. Academically, I did not do well and failed most of my GCSEs, so in 1999, when I left school at 16, I went straight into the factories working as a picker and packer. I tried a few college courses over the following years, but they never lasted more than a few months as I became bored quickly. Nothing seemed to be stimulating my brain and making me want to learn. Honestly, I just wanted a job to make money and go out partying on the weekend with my friends. That all changed at age 19 when I found out I was pregnant with my daughter, and I suddenly had to grow up and get my life in some order. Even though working two jobs and being a young single parent was a struggle, it catalysed my personal growth and aspirations. I knew to get a better job, I would need to get some education behind me, so in 2014, I decided to try another course at college. I didn't know what I wanted to do career-wise. Still, I knew I was passionate about justice and fairness, so I started an Access Course in Social Sciences that covered criminology, sociology, social policy, and psychology. I was surprised that I really enjoyed the Access Course and looked forward to going to college to educate myself. Never in my life had I enjoyed education, yet here I was, wanting to learn as much as I could. The only part of the course I hated was maths, but because I had failed my GCSE, it was a requirement that I had to re-sit the exam. I don't know what it is about me and maths, but I just cannot grasp it, and my brain goes into a meltdown even just thinking about it!

Anyway, as I knew I would, I went on to fail the exam and the subsequent four attempts. However, I did well with everything else, which afforded me enough UCAS points to get into university. In 2016, I started a BA Hons in sociology and criminology at Birmingham City University. I enjoyed it so much that I decided to complete an MA in criminology. My dad always said that the biggest law breakers tend to be lawmakers, and this became clearer to me the more I studied criminology. With an unwavering passion for fairness and upon uncovering profound injustices within the criminal justice system, it felt only natural to take the next step in my academic journey and apply for a PhD. I decided to focus my research on the impacts of the now-abolished Imprisonment for Public Protection (IPP) sentence, which I believe to be a miscarriage of justice. As I delved deeper into the inhumane IPP sentence regime and its psychological impacts on those subjected to it, my frustration and anger intensified, so I knew this was an area I would be passionate about and focused on. Initially, I applied for a PhD scholarship, but my proposal was turned down, so I went down the student finance route again to self-fund. I tried not to think about how much money I owed student finance already as I sent off my application. Feeling proud of myself, the first people I called were my mum and dad to tell them I had applied. I don't think anyone would have imagined that when I started my Access Course, it would lead to me applying for a PhD, but here I was. As I lapped my family's praises, I felt a real sense of achievement and pride. Looking back, there were challenging moments throughout the journey, requiring a lot of discipline and dedication. Balancing a full-time degree alongside two jobs and being a parent is demanding, yet the thought of giving up had never entered my mind because I enjoyed what I was learning and how it was taught. I had a year before I was due to start the PhD (all being well, and if my proposal was accepted!), and life was going well, but I had no idea how much things were about to change.

Identity crisis

On 26 May 2022, at 1:21 am, I was woken up by two police officers knocking on my door. At first, I thought maybe there had been some trouble on my estate, and they were perhaps doing door-to-door enquiries. As I walked down the stairs to let them in, it suddenly dawned on me that they would not be doing door-to-door enquiries in the early hours of the morning. Opening the door, I noticed their faces looked sad, and they had their helmets under their arms. Instantly, my legs started shaking as I knew they were about to deliver devastating news. I have seen moments like this happen on TV, but you never think it will happen to you. They told me they had come to inform me that my dad had passed away, and it was not suspicious circumstances, but they could not give me any further information at that point. It seemed to take a while to process what they had said as I thought I was in some nightmare, but the scream that left my body as I slumped to the floor in shock soon brought me back to reality. As they helped me off the floor, I was shaking and felt sick. They asked me if they could do anything to help, and I said, 'Yeah, tell me this isn't fucking true'. They both just put their heads down and apologised again for my loss. I felt sorry for the police officers standing in front of me. They were no older than 25, and I remember thinking, what a shit thing to have to do as part of your job, wake people up to tell them their loved one is dead. I don't know why that came into my thoughts when I had just been given the worst news of my life, but I think I was just trying to distract my brain from processing the fact that my dad was dead. After hearing my screams, my daughter came running down the stairs to see what was going on, and it suddenly dawned on me that now I was going to have to tell her that her grandad was dead. As I delivered the devastating blow to her, I watched her heart break, and I felt mine break even more. My dad had helped me bring her up and had always been the most significant male figure in our lives. As I rocked my daughter while she sobbed uncontrollably in my arms, I knew I had to try and be strong. I kept thinking that my dad would hate to see us upset, and I needed to somehow find the strength to get through this. But how could I possibly be strong? I had just been told that I had lost my dad, my hero, my protector, the man who taught me everything I know.

So many thoughts were flying through my head. What did they mean my dad was dead, he wasn't ill, and he is only 63? How has he died? Why has he died? Surely, they had the wrong address, and this was an awful mistake. Maybe this isn't happening, and I will wake up soon and realise it's a horrible nightmare. Unfortunately, it wasn't, and in the following months, it is hard to describe the emotional turmoil that took over me. Processing that my dad was gone for good was a difficult adaption, and it triggered an identity crisis. I felt empty, sad, frightened, angry, confused, confused, you name it, I felt it, but more than anything, I felt exhausted. My brain was tired from all the thinking, and my heart was broken from all the pain. I did not want to be around people; all I wanted to do was sleep. I couldn't seem to grasp how the world was just continuing as normal, and my dad was dead.

Father's Day was a few weeks later, and there were reminders of this everywhere I went, and that felt painful. I walked into one shop, saw the Father's Day cards display and walked straight back out, tears streaming down my face. Flicking through social media and seeing friends and family posting their dads on Father's Day, I felt emotional and somewhat envious. I wanted to be out with my dad, having a meal and posting pictures, but instead, I was planning his funeral and still unsure of his cause of death. Two months after losing my dad, it was my graduation, and it was supposed to be one of the best days of my life, but there was a profound feeling of emptiness and sadness. I just remember seeing other graduates with their dads and feeling upset and wanting to get out of there as quickly as possible. I also felt guilty for feeling so sad as I looked at my 80-year-old nan, who had caught the train up with my mum to watch me graduate. I wanted to try and be happy that day, so I could make some nice memories with the family I still have, but nothing could shift the empty feeling and the heartache. I couldn't wait to get home, go to bed and be on my own.

Turning pain into power

A month after graduating I received an unconditional offer to start my PhD, and the first person I wanted to tell was my dad, so I called his number, clearly without thinking. For a few seconds, I had forgotten he was dead, and as it hit me, he was gone; it felt like someone had taken the wind out of me. How could I forget he was dead? And how could I possibly consider doing a PhD with my dad no longer here? As the pain ruptured through my body, I let the tears flow and curled up on the floor in a foetal position, shaking back and forth and making some weird noises. I say weird because I have never heard the noises come out of my mouth before. I just figured it must be some kind of trauma release of all the emotions I had been bottling up. I knew I had to release everything I had been suppressing, so I just lay there until the noises stopped. It was exhausting but very needed.

After what seemed like forever, I got off the floor and sat on the sofa, and although I felt drained, I was overcome with a sense of peace and calmness. I started to self-reflect on my childhood, which made me realise how much influence my dad had in shaping my beliefs and values. I had never thought about it before he died, but I suddenly remembered how people had always said to me 'You are just like your dad', and I used to just roll my eyes and laugh. Now, I was sitting down, reflecting, and it suddenly felt like a massive compliment. My dad was a go-getter who worked hard and was never afraid to use his voice to stand up for others. He was passionate about that, and he had drummed into me from my childhood to always stand up for what was right, even if you must stand alone.

Reflecting on one of my and my dad's last conversations, we talked about what I wanted to base my PhD research around and he said he was unbelievably proud. Believing my dad was still watching over me gave me a reason to want to continue. It motivated me to want to turn my pain into power and achieve what I had told him I would. My focus now would be to continue his legacy of helping and standing up for others, and in that moment, I felt a real determination to succeed. That was the first time since he had passed away that I had felt any form of strength, and I smiled to myself as I held the acceptance letter in the air and said, 'I'm going to do it for you, Dad … I'm going to do it for you!' To dedicate my PhD to my dad, I knew it would serve as a powerful motivation to see me through.

Roots and reflections

Born in 1983 into a working-class family, I was aware of social inequality from a young age. With the implementation of economic policies by Margaret Thatcher's government that predominantly impacted working-class communities disproportionately (Tomlinson, 2021), my dad had a strong hatred towards the Tory government. So much so that he decided to get into politics to argue their decisions and to be a voice for the working class (as he used to say). First, he started as a Labour councillor, and then he became the mayor of the town where I grew up. As a child, I remember going around all the estates, posting vote Labour leaflets through doors, and I recall walking uptown with my friends and seeing him cut the ribbon to a new charity shop that had just opened. I was so embarrassed as he called me over to have my picture taken with him for the local paper. I never fully appreciated or thought about the effort and dedication he put into trying to stand up for others, sadly, until he passed away. I found a letter he must have written to himself after a few beers, which said …

> A journey throughout my life in my own words … I did not know my destination in life until I realised people needed help and support.

I realised that I was given a gift to supply that and set off upsetting people who tried to hurt my own sort. They frightened me at first, but after a while, I knew that they were just bullies, so I gave them some of their own back. Their big words and education made me feel small at first, but I then smelled their fear of my passion. They quickly understood that they would get my opinion or listen to it until they did. My voice was my own people's thoughts being relayed through my mouth! At the end of the day, I was, and always will be a true representative of my people. If I die tomorrow, I will always be the voice of my own if they want it!

Reading this brought tears to my eyes. I could never imagine my dad being frightened as he had never displayed such an image to me. He always seemed so confident, and if he had something to say, he would say it, regardless of whether he was the only person saying it. Suddenly, I was overcome with strong feelings of pride and respect for him as I thought of all he had achieved throughout his life, considering his hard, challenging childhood. Raised in the North of England during the era of deindustrialisation (Forster, Petrie, and Crowther, 2018), my dad faced economic hardships throughout his childhood and experienced periods within the care system. With limited formal education, having been expelled from school at 14, he decided to join the Merchant Navy so he could (in his words) travel the world for free. My dad left the Navy when he married my mum and had me and my siblings and went into factory work. As a socialist, my dad harboured a deep disdain for capitalism and its inherent issues and inequalities and motivated by this belief, he pursued a career as a trade unionist and dedicated himself to championing the rights of workers. Despite facing significant challenges early in life, my dad persevered and strived to better himself, driven by a desire to advocate and stand up for others. Only after his death did I recognise the myriad traits, beliefs, and values he instilled in me. He had such a profound impact on my life. He shaped my identity, and this fuels my determination to carry forward his legacy, particularly in advocating for the rights and well-being of others.

The intersection of grief and education

A few months after my dad's passing, I walked into my first PhD lecture and recall feeling overwhelmed as I observed the happy faces of the other students. Everything felt so raw, yet here I was embarking on a full-time PhD while juggling two jobs, just so I could keep my mind occupied to try and limit the over-thinking about my dad. As time passed, everything started to take its toll on me mentally and physically, and I knew something had to give, so I decided to change my studies to part-time hours, and I cut down on picking up extra hours at work. Realising I couldn't continue suppressing my grief, I decided to allow myself the space and time to process the emotions. The initial stages of grief were exhausting as my brain was doing a lot of thinking, and there was so much to process. Finding out my dad's cause of death was SADAM (sudden adult death alcohol misuse) hit hard, and it was emotionally devastating and challenging. After my nan passed away in 2016, he started drinking more than usual to deal with the pain. However, he wasn't drinking every day, so I wasn't too concerned at that point. When the pandemic hit, and he had to stay at home, I started to notice he was drinking more, but when I would try to talk to him about it, he would brush it off and say he was fine and there was nothing to worry about. I couldn't see him as he lived over a hundred miles away, and he was no longer married to my mum, so I had to take his word for it.

I remember feeling relieved when he had to go back to work as I knew he would be in a routine and this would hopefully cut down the alcohol intake, but unfortunately it didn't. A report published by Public Health England found that there was a 20 per cent rise in alcohol-specific deaths in 2020 compared with 2019 due to changes in alcohol use during the first part of the pandemic (Davis, 2021). Two studies analysing the potential long-term impacts of the trends of heavier drinking in England during the pandemic have estimated that up to 25,000 more people than usual will die over the next 20 years due to developing heavier drinking habits through the COVID-19 lockdowns (Campbell, 2022). I am aware my dad experienced a lot of traumas from his childhood, and I think alcohol misuse would be his escapism. Research around alcohol dependency suggests that it can be used as escapism for coping with unpleasant emotions and notes a link between experiencing childhood trauma and alcohol misuse (Jouhki and Oksanen, 2022; Burton and Dryer, 2023). Discovering my dad's death was alcohol-related stirred up a lot of guilt for me. Sometimes, when my dad called me in the evening, I would ignore his calls as I presumed he was going to be drunk, and I was not in the mood for him to be singing songs on the phone to me. As I looked at all the missed video calls on WhatsApp, I hated myself for not answering. Could I have helped him? Could I have done more to get him support with all his trauma? Why did I not think to get him help? I was beating myself up, and I knew I had to stop. Fortunately, I spoke to him just before he died, and we ended the call saying 'I love you' as we always did. Knowing they were our last words to each other did bring me some comfort, but I still had deep feelings of regret and guilt, which I could not seem to shift. Turning the pain into power at this point seemed like a real task as my energy was low. I was slacking when it came to working on my PhD, and I had lost all motivation for it. My first deadline was the day after my dad's first anniversary, and as the date drew near, I started to panic as I could not seem to get the work done.

Every day, I would set myself study goals, but after an hour of sitting at the computer and writing a few sentences, my brain would decide to give up, and I would end up cleaning my house instead. Roughly a week before the deadline, I had a bit of a meltdown and decided that now was not the time for me to be doing a PhD. I felt emotional writing out the email to my supervisors explaining my decision, but before sending it, I called Sarah Jones, who was also on the course, and we had become close. When I told her my decision, she was adamant I could not quit and spent over an hour convincing me why I should not give up. The conversation was just what I needed, and I came off the phone feeling empowered and determined and went on to complete my work and meet the deadline. To those of you who uplift others and make them feel better about themselves, I cannot thank you enough! Fortunately for me, I am surrounded by amazing people, and their support has been instrumental in helping me navigate this journey. Passing the first year was a huge relief, but it was clear I needed to put more effort into my studies and, to do that, I had to start taking care of myself. The first year after losing my dad, I had stopped going to the gym, was eating loads of crap, and working, on average, 50 hours a week while also trying to do a PhD. Looking back, it was no wonder I was burning out and failing to put effort into my studies. I knew going forward, prioritising self-care was paramount and made a promise to myself that this would be my focus.

Love transcends death

Grief, for me, has been a rollercoaster of unpredictable emotions where some days are marked by strength and determination, and others find me feeling low and withdrawn. However, I've noticed that the latter occurs much less frequently since I have started to prioritise self-care. Lately, when I start to feel my energy dipping, I will engage in activities that will help lift my mood. Walking regularly in nature is always my top go-to, as I find it provides an opportunity for mindfulness and reflection. When studying, I always try and take a walking break, as I find it can be useful for conquering things like writer's block or imposter syndrome. To motivate me and reinforce positive messages in my mind, I have started listening to positive affirmations and uplifting podcasts. This has been a useful tool to help me overcome self-doubt and negative thoughts. Additionally, changing my diet to healthier options and getting back into regularly exercising at the gym has done wonders. Never underestimate the power of exercise. I have never once worked out and regretted it, but I do know when I don't work out, I regret it, and my mental health takes a dip! Exercise serves as a good stress outlet and always leaves me feeling determined that I will get through whatever that day decides to throw at me.

Having counselling was cathartic as it helped me explore complex emotions and be able to address the feelings of guilt I had been harbouring. Another source of solace for me is the belief that I receive signs from my dad, which provides me with the reassurance that he is still watching over me. While I appreciate not everyone shares this belief, being a believer has been immensely comforting throughout this journey and the signs always seem to arrive at moments when I need them the most. My dad passed on the belief to me, as he used to believe that when he found white feathers, they were a sign from my nan to let him know that she was still around protecting us. The day he died, I kept repeating out loud for him to give me signs he was still with me and was requesting he send me white feathers. A few days later, I had to go and clear out his shed, and when I was walking out, the biggest white feather I have ever seen fell at my feet, and instantly, I was overcome with a warm fuzzy feeling and a sudden sense of ease. Now, it isn't every white feather I see that I think is a sign from my dad because, as you know, they are everywhere. It is just certain ones, like those I find in random places, such as on my car seat, in my bathroom cabinet, or in my laptop bag. While out on walks, a few have also fallen from the sky and landed at my feet or in my hair when talking or thinking about him. It might sound a bit weird, but I have kept all the feathers I think my dad has sent me and have them all in a glass jar next to his ashes. Other signs I receive will be things like hearing my dad's favourite song as I walk into a shop or when he visits me in my dreams. I like to believe they carry messages that he is still watching me, and this way of thinking provides me with a sense of comfort. Love transcends death, and despite my dad's physical absence, his presence continues to influence and support me every day, and the thought of this keeps me pushing through. While his absence leaves a huge hole in my heart, I am driven to continue to turn this pain into power and complete my PhD, and to do this, staying on top of self-care will continue to be my top priority.

One thing I can say about the journey so far is that time is a healer (as cliché as it may sound), and you will eventually find ways to adapt to their loss. I've learnt to be kind to myself and now I find it easier to shift negative thoughts to positive ones (thanks to listening to positive affirmations daily). There has not been a day since my dad passed away that I have not thought about him, talked about him, or talked to him, but as the days go by, the pain is becoming easier to manage. I now consciously try to recall all the cherished memories and think about the invaluable life skills and values he instilled in me rather than start guilt-tripping myself over whether I could have done more to help him. I will forever be thankful for the traits my dad passed on to me, like being passionate about standing up for justice and fairness, and it is my heartfelt commitment to honour his memory by persevering on my doctorate journey.

Summary of reflections

When thinking about summarising my chapter to enable me to concisely offer support to those of you who may be searching for guidance within your PhD journey or within your journey of grief, my eyes fill with tears. Tears of joy, that encapsulate the pride that I feel in myself for pursuing something that was once unthinkable. But also tears of sadness that represent the sorrow of loss and thoughts of a future without my dad. I know I am not alone in this sentiment, and one of the central reasons for me sharing my story and writing this chapter is to let you know you are not alone either. Here is where I will tell you, the reader, that if you relate to any part of my story, we will be ok. Self-doubt, especially in times of despair, is unavoidable, but understanding the importance of self-care in its many forms will help carry us through. Throughout your PhD, try to reflect on why you decided to embark on this journey in the first place, as I have done within this chapter and will continue to do so throughout my studies. This can help us turn our pain into power.

7

Double duty: undertaking PhD research while being a full-time lecturer

Charlotte Rigby
Staffordshire University

As a cultural sociologist and social historian, Charlotte's PhD research is centred around policewomen's experiences throughout the 1970s, the 1980s and 1990s.

Introduction

As the earlier chapters of this book have captured so far, all PhD experiences are unique. In my case, the recent cost-of-living crisis meant that I needed to secure full-time employment earlier than initially planned. In this chapter, I will reflect upon my experiences as a first-generation student navigating the barriers of Higher Education while working full time. I draw upon time management, creating a sustainable work-life balance, the importance of a strong support network and navigating imposter syndrome. I also offer insight into lessons learned for anybody who may find themselves in a similar situation.

At the time of writing this chapter, I have been working as a full-time lecturer for just over 12 months. After finishing my master's degree in Sociology and Social Justice at Staffordshire University in August 2020, I was awarded a partial scholarship. This meant that, in exchange for teaching and marking support, my tuition fees were paid for by the University.

Where my story begins

When I was offered a partial scholarship, I jumped at the opportunity. Although I had fallen in love with academia early on, I was uncertain about whether I would be able to pursue a career within it because of my 'untraditional' background. For the entirety of my schooling, I received Free School Meals (henceforth referred to as FSM). In England, FSM eligibility is determined by household income (DWP, 2013), and pupils who receive

FSM before age 15 are considered 'disadvantaged' (DfE, 2023). The latest statistics show that only 29 per cent of pupils who receive FSM go on to study at university by the age of 19 (DfE, 2023). While access to Higher Education is certainly better than it was 30 years ago (Montacute and Cullinane, 2023), many FSM students who make it to university are the first in their families to go. I am one of those 'first gen' students, and proudly so – but, owing to my socio-economic background, financial constraints meant that self-funding a PhD would never be feasible. The scholarship was and continues to be, my only way into a world that was otherwise closed to working-class academics.

Although the partial scholarship made my entry into academia possible, funding only covered my tuition fees. As such, I have always worked in some capacity throughout my doctoral studies. I worked as a research assistant on various projects and, alongside my 'free' scholarship hours, worked as an hourly paid lecturer at my PhD institution. However, as any doctoral student knows too well, hourly paid contracts do not provide financial security. While the partial scholarship alleviated some of the monetary pressures, I ultimately made the decision to search for full-time employment due to financial constraints. The recent cost-of-living crisis – or 'cozzie livs', as it is satirically known as in Britain (Touma, 2023) – meant that, for a lot of postgraduate researchers, taking on paid employment alongside their studies was essential. A recent study found that 97 per cent of PhD students have, to differing extents, felt the pressure of the cost-of-living crisis on their studies (Munro, 2023). Support for PhD students has also been somewhat lacklustre, with many receiving little to no support from their respective institutions (Munro, 2023). I was certainly not exempt from this, which ultimately led to me beginning my job hunt 12 months early. It was not an easy decision; I was fully committed to my PhD and wanted to give it the time it deserved, but I also felt the financial pressures associated with postgraduate study. Had it not been for securing full-time employment early on, I am not entirely confident that I would have been able to continue with the PhD at all.

The opposite of yes: boundaries, time management, and prioritising your workload

As a keen, enthusiastic, and perhaps naïve first year, I attended every webinar I could find in a frantic attempt to learn more about being a PhD researcher. It was important to me as a first gen student that I understood what, exactly, a doctorate involved. I was firmly under the impression that postgraduate study was not for the likes of me, and I desperately wanted to uncover the unwritten rules of academia. I now understand this was my attempt at building my cultural capital (Bourdieu, 1986) and establishing an academic identity of my own (Bourdieu, 1999).

For the purpose of this chapter, I flicked through my diary from the 2020/21 academic year. In total, I attended 15 webinars in the space of two months, all of which varied in length and price. Some were hosted by universities, while others were hosted by private companies. Topics ranged from writing journals and book reviews to the importance of edutainment and TEF. I attended subject-specific talks and listened to academics reflect on their teaching experiences during the COVID-19 pandemic. Impressively, I learnt how to pronounce words I had only ever read on paper – who knew there were so many ways to incorrectly pronounce the word 'pedagogy'? Even now, I have a notebook near my desk containing pages upon pages of detailed notes, quoting the speakers verbatim as they shared academia's hidden secrets with an audience of optimistic early career researchers.

And while I was grateful to hear from these speakers, none of these talks stressed the importance of the word 'no'.

When I started working full time, the opposite of 'yes' was something of a mystery. I knew the word existed, of course, but I was unable to say it. 'No' was a dirty word. And it felt wrong to decline opportunities because, well, why would I? I recognised how lucky I was to secure a full-time lectureship before the end of my PhD, and I wanted to give it my all to prove my worth in a notoriously competitive industry.

The reality of working full time alongside your PhD, however, is that you have to say 'no'. And this was a lesson I learnt the hard way. There have been moments over the last 12 months where I felt that I would never be able to get my thesis fully drafted because I had taken on too much. Saying yes to conferences miles away from my desk, taking on new and exciting writing projects, and catching up on marking while keeping a close eye on my emails past 5 pm meant that my thesis frequently fell to the bottom of my 'To Do' list. There were times when I felt that working 9–5 in academia and then 5–11 pm on the PhD was not enough, and I needed to seek out new projects to put my name to. And while this seemed manageable initially, it quickly led to burnout. When I had my first week of annual leave in August 2023, I spent a great deal of it eating copious amounts of chocolate and feeling like I had made a terrible mistake entering full-time employment while finishing my PhD.

So, to echo the advice of my long-suffering supervisor, it is important to set boundaries early on so that you can manage your workload accordingly without sacrificing valuable PhD time. One of the biggest advantages of working in academia while undertaking a PhD is that you are responsible for managing your own time. In practice, this means that if you can shuffle things about and plan ahead, you can carve out time for your PhD.

As a general rule, I allocated a couple of hours per week – usually on a Monday or Tuesday morning – to work on my thesis. I made a point of turning my emails off during this period to avoid distractions. Around my students' assessment periods, I hosted writing retreats. While students worked on their assessments, I focused on a small portion of work, and we were able to hold one another accountable. I also ensured that I allocated periods of relaxation, too. While writing on trains might work for some people, I decided early on that my commute to and from work would be reserved for intense people-watching – or ethnography, as we social scientists call it – and listening to music. Doing this has encouraged me to be kinder to myself, and to prioritise my doctoral studies above monitoring emails every hour. Of course, that is not to say that it is easy – the guilt is *always* there – but it is important to remember that just because you now have fewer hours to work on the thesis, you are still entitled to a little bit of downtime! Carving out dedicated time can often lead to bursts of productivity, and it is ultimately quality over quantity.

Letting go of perfection: navigating fieldwork, expectations, and realities

When I made the jump from part-time to full-time work, I was fortunate that the bulk of my research had already been completed. My interviews had been transcribed, the majority of my archival research had been collected, and my thematic analysis had been finalised. The remainder of my PhD was, at least provisionally, just a case of writing up my thesis.

But as anyone who has been through the writing-up period knows all too well, it is rarely ever a linear process. In my case, I still had some fieldwork to complete. My data collection, which took place between December 2021 and June 2022, had been severely impacted by the various COVID-19 lockdowns and restrictions. Due to this, I had not been able to visit as many archive centres as I would have liked and had initially planned to reschedule my visit during my write-up year. In addition to this, the nature of my thesis – a collection of narratives from 35 retired policewomen – meant that there always was, and continues to be, a reason to locate the 'perfect' archive source to supplement a participant's narrative.

Gathering data while working full time, however, is tricky. First and foremost, archive centres generally operate during work hours, so it becomes a logistical nightmare to try to schedule an appointment. Second, it is difficult to predict exactly how long you plan to stay in the archives because you are not guaranteed to find the source you require straight away. And when you work full time, time is already limited. This meant I had two options: make the most of the data I already had, or risk falling behind on my other responsibilities. This, for me, was difficult. From the start of my PhD journey, I made a promise to myself that I would tell my participants' stories in the most genuine and heartfelt way possible. Archival research was a huge part of this, as I wanted to substantiate their claims with photographic evidence. Working full time, however, required me to reconsider my priorities somewhat. I accepted, albeit reluctantly, that carrying out another round of fieldwork was impractical and unrealistic. Instead, I organised one final visit to the archives on a weekend and agreed to move on if I could not find what I was looking for.

Reflecting on these experiences, I recognise that I was in pursuit of perfection. The perpetual feeling of needing 'one more archive visit' or 'one more interview' persisted and never truly went away. There is always a feeling of wanting to do just that little bit more to ensure things are perfect. However, as a colleague once told me, the only 'perfect' PhD is a finished PhD. In 2013, Times Higher Education reported that only 72.9 per cent of full-time PhD students finish their PhDs within seven years (Jump, 2013). Universities do, of course, have different completion rates, and I think lots of us set ourselves the goal to finish within four years. Irrespective of the timeframe, though, it is important to remember that the end goal is to finish and pass the viva rather than perfection. That is not to say that you should submit something you and your supervisor are unhappy with; rather, you can only do your best in the timeframe that you have.

Before I submitted my PhD in August 2024, I used the last of my annual leave to fully dedicate some time to working on my thesis. Letting 'go' of the thesis was hard. There were paragraphs I wanted to rewrite, sources I wanted to revisit, and sentence structure I wanted to revise. In an unexpected series of events, my 'favourite' data chapter about policewomen's role in the Miners' Strike suddenly became my worst enemy. I was, in no uncertain terms, frustrated. This feeling was then exacerbated because I had taken on full-time employment and, as discussed earlier in this chapter, had been unable to dedicate the time my thesis deserved. However, after speaking to my friends and colleagues, I now recognise that this feeling is fairly normal. There will always be things we wish we could have done differently.

Work, eat, PhD, repeat: work-life balance, friendships, and the importance of a strong support network

As a working-class PhD researcher entering the world of academia for the first time, my main priority has always been to survive. Nothing too ambitious, or at least so I thought. In hindsight, I now recognise that survival in academia is multifaceted and, contrary to popular belief, may not be as straightforward as it initially seems. Alongside learning how to say 'no' to opportunities and letting go of perfection, I also needed to learn how to navigate the toxic occupational culture within academia.

Much like canteen culture in the police force, academia has its own iteration of occupational culture that normalises an unsustainable work-life balance. This, to an extent, is to be expected; the demanding and complicated nature of academia requires effort, as well as time (Kinman and Jones, 2008; Santos and Cabral-Cardoso, 2008). Unfortunately, it is common for academics to work six days a week, 16 hours a day, and still feel dissatisfied with their productivity and output (Forrester, 2023). Subsequent studies around the realities of academic workloads have uncovered the ways in which the promotion of an unhealthy work-life balance can impact lecturers' personal lives, such as missing important family events, experiencing stress, and feeling undervalued (Griffin, 2022; UCU, 2022). And while research often demonstrates the devastating effects of a toxic culture with academia, it seldom acknowledges the experiences of scholars undertaking PhD research simultaneously.

Early on in my academic journey, I was advised that a PhD should be treated as a full-time job. It was repeated to me over and over – in webinars and conferences, on social media platforms and online forums – that the minimum amount of time a 'good' PhD student should dedicate to their thesis was 40 hours per week. There was never a good enough reason to have a day off – especially not festivities such as Christmas and New Year – and if you were not particularly fond of such intensity, doctoral studies were not for you. Then, of course, I heard academics use the term 'publish or perish'. Alongside dedicating every hour of our existence to our research, we were then expected to publish regularly or risk fading into the abyss. As I noted earlier on in this chapter, I have always worked alongside my PhD to some capacity. By the time I started working full time, I had already grappled with the work-life balance dichotomy – and the burnout that follows. Nothing, however, could have prepared me for the intensity of occupational culture while working full time.

In my experience, the lines between 'work' and 'non-work' eroded to the point that it felt like I was always working in some capacity (Kinman and Jones, 2008). As a lecturer, I was (and still am) contracted to work 37.5 hours per week – Monday to Friday, 9–5. I led modules on our undergraduate and postgraduate programmes, marked hundreds of papers during assessment periods, provided ongoing dissertation support, and line-managed a small team of Associate Lecturers. As soon as it reached 5 pm, my shift as a full-time PhD researcher began. In the evenings when I felt particularly productive, I worked from 5 pm until 11 pm. I kept up to date with scholarly publications, responded to my supervisor's feedback, and drafted conference abstracts. And since COVID-19, I have predominantly worked from home, resulting in my 'home' life becoming synonymous with work life. Simply put, there were times when my life was quite literally 'work, eat, PhD, repeat'.

When I have spoken about this with my PhD friends who, like me, also work full time, they also agreed that the lines had become blurred. Any attempt to move away from this mentality instilled an overwhelming and inexplicable feeling of guilt, and because of this fear of switching off, I experienced an overwhelming sense of reluctance to create any distinction between 'work' and 'non-work' (Kinman and Jones, 2008). And yet, despite knowing that this is fundamentally unhealthy, academia and academic culture normalise this to an unnerving degree.

The best way to avoid internalising harmful occupational practices, such as an unsustainable work-life balance, is to surround yourself with a strong support network early on. I am fortunate enough to have never worked for an institution that has encouraged its academic staff to work beyond their contracted hours. We are regularly reminded of the importance of having a life outside of academia. And, as Dumitrescu (2020) rightly notes, heroism is not part of the academic job description. Ergo, nobody will thank you for the hours you put in past 5 pm. Earlier this year, I made a conscious decision to distance myself from specific pockets of academia to avoid worsening the guilt I felt for not being able to live and breathe my PhD while working full time. And while I still experience feelings of guilt to some extent, I am in a stronger position to be able to rationalise what, exactly, this means for me.

Of course, that is not to say that all aspects of academic culture are negative and problematic. Instead, I became more selective about the areas of academia I associated myself with. Among my PhD friends, we were transparent with one another, and regularly discussed the hardships associated with working full time in academia while writing up. Having this level of transparency meant that I personally had a more realistic understanding of where I was at. We set ourselves weekly writing goals and check in with one another after an agreed number of days to see what progress has been made. A strong support network also held me accountable, too. If, for whatever reason, my PhD fell to the bottom of my priorities, I knew that somebody in my circle would be prepared to have a candid discussion with me about this. My friends and family outside of academia were particularly good at holding me to account, too. Investing my time and energy into this type of support network contributed to a much more positive experience while working full time and provided me with a much more grounded view of what I am realistically capable of in a working week.

The elephant in the room: imposter syndrome, mentorship, and self-belief

In 12 months, I conquered various aspects of academia. My understanding of what a sustainable work-life balance looked like improved significantly, and I felt adequately prepared to meet my thesis hand-in date. That said, there are still things I struggled with while working full time. The biggest challenge of all, and something I am still working towards, was managing imposter syndrome.

Imposter syndrome in Higher Education is not a new concept. Almost 50 years ago, American psychologists Clance and Imes (1978: 241) defined imposter syndrome as an 'internal experience of intellectual phoniness'. Imposter syndrome was recognised as being the main cause of anxiety, frustration, and, crucially, a lack of self-confidence among PhD students (Clance and Imes, 1978). Such feelings led to a fear of failure and an inability to accept praise and created a deliberating sense of self (Matthews and Clance, 1985).

As a first gen student, I experienced imposter syndrome throughout the entirety of my academic career. When I was an undergraduate student and proudly posted on social media that I had achieved a first, I was told that, had I gone to a Russell Group, I would have never achieved such grades. When I was awarded a scholarship, I was reprimanded by postgraduate researchers at other universities for having it 'given to me on a plate' while simultaneously 'not being good enough'. At conferences, I have had my Black Country accent mocked. In the first year of my PhD, I was told that, while I may be considered good enough *now*, I would never secure a permanent academic post because I was not, nor would I ever be, good enough. And when I was offered my first full-time post, the most common response was '*you?*'.

Acutely aware of my lack of habitus (Raey, 2021), I spent the first few years of my PhD worrying about the possibility that I would never secure full-time employment in academia. Indeed, when I was offered my first full-time academic job, one would be forgiven for assuming that the overwhelming feeling of not being good enough would, at the very least, be alleviated to some degree. The reality was staunchly different. For the first few weeks of my new job, I was crippled by my fears of being 'found out' that I was not good enough to work in academia. Every mistake I made, such as an email that went unread for longer than an hour or a forgotten exclamation mark in a Teams message, I would scrutinise myself for hours upon hours. In hindsight, I now recognise that I was holding myself to a set of impossible standards because I was a first gen academic navigating a largely unfamiliar world (Holden, Wright, and Sims, 2021). This feeling was aggravated further when I started turning down writing opportunities and conference spaces because, as discussed earlier on in this chapter, I simply did not have the time to commit to them. Truthfully, I felt like I had failed as an academic.

I still struggle with this feeling today. I look back on the plans I had for my PhD, some of which were scaled back because of my work commitments, and feel disappointed with myself. Momentarily, I will agree with the comments I heard in my first year of postgraduate study; perhaps academia was never truly for me. Indeed, as my submission date got closer, I counted down the days on the whiteboard next to my desk. When I got to 30 days until hand-in, the overwhelming feeling of guilt was inescapable. I was stuck in a cycle of self-doubt, regretted my choices, and felt as though I would never finish on time. I often joke that I had to schedule in cries between work and PhD time, but that was sometimes the reality. In hindsight, a lot can be achieved in 30 days – but at the time, it certainly did *not* feel that way and I was convinced I had bitten off more than I could chew. This feeling was worsened by my background. As a working-class researcher, I had made a lot of sacrifices, both financially and socially, in order to pursue doctoral studies. While my friends outside of academia had bought houses and cars, I had bought books and stationery. And now, here I was, unable to finish my PhD. Of course, this was not true; I submitted the PhD thesis on time, with approximately an hour and eight minutes to spare. Despite this, though, it was a feeling that I struggled to shake and only worsened as I got closer to handing in my PhD to the Graduate School.

Regrettably, there is no magical 'cure' to imposter syndrome. There is, however, a way to make it less crippling. In my experience, having a mentor – or a role model – can make a world of difference (Van Bueren, 2021). My PhD supervisor, a fellow working-class academic, offered me a great deal of support. We met regularly, sometimes weekly, and chatted. She knows from first-hand experience how challenging that first academic post can be – and, after working in academia for over ten years, she is able to offer me some much-needed guidance. When I felt guilty for being unable to dedicate 40 hours per week to my PhD, she was the first to remind me about how much I was doing and how difficult it can be working full time. She was always empathetic towards the sacrifices I have made and continue to make while balancing employment and my write-up year. When I felt exhausted, and the thought of working on my PhD made me nauseous, I remember her advice: 'Just spend an hour or so working on your references'. This technique helped me to work on my PhD in smaller, more manageable chunks.

I now try to channel this energy into my job, too. As a working-class academic, I have pursued employment at two universities, both of which attract a high number of first gen students. And, like me, a lot of my students balance full-time work alongside their studies and experience the wrath of imposter syndrome. I am open and honest about this with my students which, in turn, helps to establish a trustworthy relationship. They know that, if they are experiencing any difficulties, they can approach me, and I will have empathy with their situation because of our shared experiences. We have conversations about time management, and how to make the most of an evening after work. When they tell me that university is 'too hard' or 'not for the likes of them', we unpack these feelings in more depth. A lot of the time, students just need to see for themselves that there are various ways to navigate academia. The conventional route is not the only way, and working alongside their studies does not detract from their dedication. More importantly, it provides me with the opportunity to instil the next generation of working-class academics with the confidence to pursue postgraduate research, despite financial constraints and feelings of self-doubt. On a personal level, this makes my hardships feel worthwhile. And while I still experience bouts of imposter syndrome, I recognise ways that I can use my experiences to help others.

Summary of reflections

My chapter has provided you with a small insight into some of the challenges associated with working full time while doing a PhD. A central theme within this chapter is the importance of saying 'no' and maintaining healthy boundaries. Here, I reflect upon why I initially said 'yes' to everything, and how I eventually came to the realisation that this was not sustainable. I also reflect upon letting 'go' of perfection. As PhD researchers, it is common for us to have high expectations. However, when working full time, it is important to be realistic about what can be achieved in a short period of time. I also explore the difficulties of maintaining a healthy work-life balance, and the challenges associated with this when every waking hour is spent working in some capacity. Finally, I reflect upon my personal experience of imposter syndrome, and the 'guilt' that arose from working full time caused me intense feelings of self-doubt. Simply put, reading for a PhD has been the hardest thing I have ever done in my academic career. Nonetheless, it can be manageable – and, dare I say it, rewarding, when you can finally see the finishing line.

8

Balancing act: balancing family life with the PhD

Suzanne Baggs
University of Plymouth

Suzanne's PhD research focuses on women and the impact of online gambling. The theoretical framework adopted is that of the emerging Deviant Leisure perspective. Suzanne also looks at the marketing techniques used by the gambling industry, particularly TV advertising, and how they are directed specifically towards women.

Introduction

When I was in my mid-30s, and my twin boys were five years old, I started studying for a master's in criminology with a vague intention to move on to a PhD afterwards. I was new to the social sciences (my previous qualifications were in Philosophy and Law), but I found the sheer breadth of the discipline fascinating, with my optional modules including policing, white-collar crime, and leisure, consumerism and harm. This last module introduced me to the idea of gambling as a criminological topic, as two of my lecturers had recently written an article on the harms of lifestyle gambling as a male leisure activity. The article was excellent, but I felt that it wasn't reflective of my own personal experience as an occasional female gambler. On further investigation, it seemed that women's gambling was generally under-researched, and that was an opportunity that aligned with my own interests; so, the following year I started my PhD in criminology, focusing on the gambling industry and its impact on female gamblers. I studied part time, and for the duration of my studies (over six years), I was a lone parent, having divorced a few years previously. My ex-husband lived in a different area of the country, so childcare was my responsibility on weekdays, weekends and most of the school holidays, apart from the odd few days or weeks here and there (never planned in advance) when I would find myself completely alone in the house and suddenly free to work on my thesis. At times like these, I imagined that this sense of freedom must be what child-free PhD students experience all the time. That's not to say that any PhD student has it easy – we all face the very real demands of being a responsible adult – but if you're embarking on your PhD as a parent there are definitely some significant challenges that our child-free colleagues do not experience.

I have separated this chapter into two distinct sections which I have called 'university life' and 'family life'. It will come as no surprise to anyone that the distinctions between family and university in real life are not so easily compartmentalised, and this will be reflected in several messy overlaps (for instance, is 'time management' a university or family issue?). However, as you'll hopefully learn as you follow in the footsteps of the many PhD parents who have gone before you, the intention and semblance of organisation is sometimes all you'll be able to manage and is often enough. The final point of housekeeping, before we begin, is to apologise in advance if I ever come across as patronising. That is obviously not my aim, and I don't doubt your ability to work out all of what I'm going to say on your own. It's just that sometimes it's helpful when someone takes us aside at the beginning of an adventure and imparts some of their learned wisdom. Even when we find we already know some of that advice, hearing it from someone else can have an affirming effect. That is what I hope to offer to you.

Going back to my story, the first and most important piece of advice I'll give is to have your 'why' figured out. Not long after I started my PhD, I was given the advice to write down why I was doing it. Honestly, this felt unnecessary to me. After all the effort I'd put into my application, research proposal, interview, and presentation, it seemed clear to me that I was serious about doing it; I felt super motivated to get started and complete it in a time faster than anyone was expecting. How naive I was. Setbacks, obstructions, and the demands of life quickly stacked up, and my motivation to continue was tested more times than I care to remember. Knowing why I was doing it was vital to face these challenges, and I would advise anyone starting this long and arduous journey to seriously consider your 'why' too. What will keep you going when the going gets tough?

University life

I am going to start with university life as this encompasses some of the biggest decisions you'll have to make about this whole process. Some of the things discussed here are relevant to all PhD students regardless of your parental status, but being a parent adds a different dimension which heavily influences the decisions you make and the freedom (or not) you have over those decisions.

One of the most important decisions to make at the beginning is whether to do your PhD full time or part time. Based solely on my own personal experience, admittedly, I'm not sure I know anyone who did their PhD full time who was a parent too, or at least no one who completed in the original time frame they'd intended. Some applied for extensions; others switched from full time to part time during the programme. These are obviously valid options and may have come about because of a change in circumstances, but to lessen the stress of changing plans, it is best to be brutally honest with yourself from the outset. Many new or prospective students seem to focus on how many years they want to complete it in (where full time is usually three years and part time is six years) but I think it's much more important to consider how many hours a week you can realistically devote to the programme and use that as an indicator of whether you can do it full or part time. For instance, a recent study on UK PhD students found that the average full-time student works on their PhD for 47 hours a week, but in actuality, many work up to 60 hours (Cornell, 2020a). This varies between disciplines, but in any field, full time really does mean full time. The same study also states that the average age for a full-time PhD student is between 24 and 25; meanwhile the average part-time student age ranges between 32 and 33 (Cornell, 2020a). Given that the average age for women in the UK to have their first child is currently 30.9 and men is 33.7 (ONS, 2023) it seems likely to me that many who begin a part-time PhD in their 30s are parents or considering becoming parents in their near future.

Choosing to study part time is sensible if you currently have a family life and a job (that you intend to keep), and a social life – these things probably already take up most of the week, so there's no way you can add a full-time PhD into that without giving something up. Even studying part time, you may have to be prepared to give up or drastically reduce other demands on your time. Certain things (like parenting) are simply non-negotiable as they carry numerous demands. Work often, also. Other pursuits like clubs, hobbies, or interests may need to take a back seat, at least temporarily. That's not to say you can't have any interests outside of the PhD (please don't give up everything you love – it's no good for anyone), but you need to factor everything that matters to you into that initial decision to go full or part time.

The next thing to consider is whether you plan to teach alongside your PhD, and this will likely be tied into your funding arrangements and career aspirations. It is generally accepted that either the stipend you could get from a research council or the government's doctorate loan does not provide a living wage (Cornell, 2020a). Factor in that living off a loan or stipend will mean that you may not be entitled to the same childcare funding that traditional employees get – if your children are of pre-school age this may be a significant amount of money that you cannot claim. For many reasons, then, students take on roles as associate lecturers or graduate teaching assistants (different universities use different terms), which can be anything from assisting in seminars right up to creating and leading modules, depending on your experience and the needs of your university. Personally, I started my PhD as a Doctoral Teaching Assistant (DTA), which combined a 0.6 FTE teaching contract and a part-time funded PhD. For me, this was ideal, as I was already in my late 30s and had a successful career behind me, which, for a number of reasons, I could no longer pursue, so I saw this as a route into a new career in academia. Your long-term career aims are important to consider here. If you want a career in academia, then doing some teaching is vital to gain the experience necessary for a future lecturer position. The money may feel like a necessity too, even if you have funding (it hardly needs saying to factor in that there are quite a few months during a typical year when there will be no teaching, and therefore no money).

Alternatively, you might consider taking on some projects as a research assistant. Of course, you don't have to teach or research alongside your PhD, and particularly if an academic career is not your long-term goal, you may be happier earning money from a completely unrelated job, or one related to your PhD subject. When you spend a great deal of your time grappling with intellectual academic thinking, then a job that is more practical or allows you to tap into different skills and experiences can be rewarding. For me, starting from the beginning as a DTA felt at first like I was disregarding some of the skills I'd acquired in my previous careers. I had once been a project manager for the implementation of large-scale IT systems into international organisations, responsible for managing people and budgets and creating staff training programmes. After that I was a self-employed copywriter, having complete autonomy over my own work, marketing, and client management. Being a DTA was like being a trainee again – no management responsibility, leading seminars that other people had written, and being seen as one of the least experienced members of the team. This could have been demoralising, but I treated it as a learning experience, and after four years, I was able to secure a full lecturer position before finishing my PhD, an achievement that would have been much harder without my previous experience and/or the amount of teaching I had done as a DTA.

I believe that most students feel that teaching is a necessity, but unless your PhD funding comes with a teaching requirement (as mine did) it is your choice how much teaching you do. It is not unknown for universities to take advantage of students' willingness to impress, as their financial incentive to hire DTAs and Associate Lecturers often aligns with PhD students' desire to earn money. The thing to consider is what fits in with your studies *and* your family. What can you do that won't take over so much that you end up not doing any PhD work? This sounds dramatic, but over my years in academia, I've seen more than one fellow student succumb to a teaching load that left them completely unable to make any progress on their PhD for weeks or even months at a time (and if I'm honest, at times, that student was me). Remember your priorities. If the PhD is the first step in an academic career, then don't sabotage that by working so much that you never complete the PhD. Of course, almost all PhD students have to grapple with the work/PhD balance, but as a parent, you must balance your family too. For me as a single parent, for instance, weekend and evening work outside of the home was out of the question. And, at least in the early days, I was sometimes paying almost as much in after-school childcare as I was earning. Only you can know your own situation, considering working hours, childcare arrangements, family support, distance between home, school, and campus, and so on. But whatever your personal situation, it can't be an afterthought. I was lucky enough under my contract to be able to get timetable constraints that meant I didn't have to teach the 4 pm to 6 pm slot, but even finishing at 4 pm and rushing back to my children's school saw me paying for quite a few hours a week after-school club, not to mention the breakfast club that I sometimes had to use when I was teaching a 9 am class. Navigating some of these issues will be picked up again in the 'family life' section (one of those messy overlaps I mentioned at the beginning), but for now, just add it to the list of things to consider before you start.

While all this planning is necessary, the topic inevitably leads rather logically to the issue of interruptions, extenuating circumstances and unexpected 'life stuff'. During a standard three to six (or more) year PhD, and as an adult in your 20s, 30s, 40s or beyond, you're likely to encounter some significant changes in your life. Without being too specific or pessimistic, this could include more children, house moves, relationship breakups and/or start-ups, and family emergencies, of all descriptions. I somehow managed to avoid many of these, beginning and ending my journey as a single parent to two children and living in the same house. But I did get hit, along with everyone else, by a global pandemic, which had both positive and negative effects in terms of many of the plans outlined. For instance, teaching online at home meant I didn't have the expense of childcare to worry about, but teaching online at home with two bored kids roaming around definitely brought its own challenges, not to mention the difficulty of teaching certain criminological subjects in language suitable for a (covertly listening) nine-year-old audience. My takeaway from this time was that while my financial stresses eased temporarily, the additional family and workload stresses stunted my PhD progress for a while.

Whatever your personal challenges, if your PhD is adversely affected then you must seriously consider applying for interruptions or extensions at the earliest possibility. At the risk of sounding cliche, a PhD is a marathon not a sprint, and the effects of pushing through a long-term difficult family situation has the potential to derail not only your PhD but your family too. Well-being and good mental health – that means you, your children, and your partner (if applicable) – are necessary in order to complete a PhD. If something is threatening any of those things, then consider how to make the PhD more manageable in the short term. All universities will have policies and procedures around interrupting your programme for weeks or months or to give you extensions on various milestones or deadlines. Explore these, preferably before it becomes an issue so that you know what your options are. At the end of the day a PhD is a PhD, regardless of how long it takes. I've heard stories of people who have taken much longer than six years to complete, but it doesn't make their final achievement any less significant than those who knock it out in less than three years. It's the same qualification in the end – what matters is getting there in one piece.

The final thing I would say is important, in terms of university life, is the relationship with your supervisor/s. Are they parents too? I'm not saying that a supervisor who isn't a parent cannot guide you through the specific difficulties that go with being a PhD parent, but I do think that the all-consuming nature of parenting is one of those things that non-parents often do not understand. You want your supervisor to challenge you and not to let 'being a parent' be your excuse for missing deadlines or not making as much progress as you should, but the reality is that sometimes parenting does affect our progress, and a supervisor who understands how that really feels from their own experience is valuable. Again, I was lucky here. My two main supervisors were of a similar age to me with kids also of a similar age so it was easy to discuss some of my ongoing challenges with them. Ultimately though, your supervisor should take time to understand your personal situation, so it is something you should be willing and proactive in explaining to them.

Family life

As I write this chapter, I am personally grappling with the very real challenge of not having a 'room of my own' in which to write. Throughout my PhD, I had this luxury, but I've recently sacrificed it in the name of trying to be a good parent. When I started my PhD my children were only six years old, and they and I were happy for them to share a room, especially as (often the case in a three-bedroom house) the third bedroom is very small, which made it a perfect office space for me. However, as my kids grew and I approached my completion date, I started to feel a bit guilty for taking up that space. So, after I had submitted my thesis and all the arguments and negotiations about who would have the small room were complete, I moved my desk and other office things into the living room. It has meant a change in the logistics of my working time and their TV/Xbox/sitting on the sofa time, and those adjustments are still a work in progress. I found that marking out some space for yourself is important, whether it's a home office, a desk in the corner of the living room, or even just a section of the kitchen table. I think it's fair to say that it is *possible* to get work done in any scenario (especially with a good pair of noise-cancelling headphones) but I do miss being able to go upstairs and close the door on my own private working space. Still, what better environment in which to write this section about the realities of how a PhD affects your home life (and vice versa) than the soothing sounds of computerised gunshots, TikTok videos, and the many, many phone pings that teenagers get.

Let's start with adult relationships, particularly as they relate to parenting. It's almost impossible to discuss parenting without discussing gender roles and expectations. Obviously, every relationship is different, and some are more traditional than others with regard to who does the cooking, cleaning, and caring duties, but certain trends persist. There have been various studies on how domestic duties are shared in modern families, and despite significant strides forward in gender equality over the past 50 years or so, they all seem to agree that women take on the bulk of domestic work and caregiving (Dinh, Strazdins and Welsh, 2017) and this includes the mental load, such as budgeting, planning childcare, and booking medical appointments, and so on. This unequal division of domestic labour leads to a situation in academia whereby 'There is a perception that doctoral student mothers are less committed to their work, progress more slowly, drop out at greater rates, and perform less well than academic fathers and childless women' (Mirick and Wladkowski, 2018: 256). There are numerous exceptions and probably plenty of mothers who do not feel they suffer this stigma, so whatever your gender or domestic role, it is worth noting that academia, particularly the doctoral stage, can be challenging for all parents. An interesting study which used personal reflections by two doctoral students during the pandemic lockdown found that even though there were significant differences in their experiences as female and male parents, they both concluded that 'As PhD parents, we cannot escape the ticking of time and looming deadlines; we constantly feel this pressure, even at the best of times' (Abdellatif and Gatto, 2020: 731). The most important thing is to have honest conversations and set realistic boundaries with your partner *early on* about the division of domestic labour and who takes responsibility for what. A PhD may mean a lot of flexibility compared to a partner who works 9–5, but don't mistake flexibility for free time (for example, 'Since you're home today would you mind popping to the shops, hanging up the washing, and giving the downstairs bathroom a quick clean?') or resentment can quickly set in.

I didn't have to have these conversations when I started my PhD, and like me, you may be lucky enough to be a single parent. As I mentioned earlier, my kids saw very little of their father during the years I was working on my PhD, so all the cooking, cleaning, and caring duties fell to me. My experience of being a lone PhD parent affected many things, not least of all my ability to keep up with the networking/social side of academia. Conferences anywhere other than my own university were logistically difficult as I didn't have any overnight childcare options. COVID-19 had a positive effect in this regard as more events moved online and I have been able to 'attend' many events that I would never have been able to before. However, while online events can be great, the natural networking that I was able to do at the few conferences I was able to attend could not be replicated online. If a career in academia is your aim, do discuss with your family your need to attend events and conferences that may be some distance away.

Whatever your parenting situation, my two best pieces of advice would be to accept help and ringfence your PhD time. Firstly, accept help – from everyone. From whoever offers it whenever it is offered. Whether it's car sharing the school drop off, alternating pick up days with friends, or letting the kids go around to a friend or family member's house when you need a bit of writing time. I'm not advocating taking advantage of anyone's kindness, but many parents are reluctant to accept help, even when it is offered, so try to get out of that habit (and offer to help others whenever you can so that you really are giving back). The other part of this is to be prepared to work on your PhD as and when the opportunity arises – even at short notice! Second, while those opportune moments need to be seized, the other piece of advice is to ringfence or schedule the time you know you have. That doesn't mean you have to somehow find huge swathes of time, just to make the most of the time you have. To say I wrote my PhD in small time/word blocks would be accurate. I did sometimes have an epic writing session and knock out a few thousand words in a day, but this was the exception rather than the rule; some days, I would completely focus for 30 minutes, and then, that was it. Dinner needed to be cooked, kids needed to be taken to clubs, and the washing up couldn't be avoided any longer; but that 30 minutes and 250 words was more than I had at the beginning of that day. It was forward momentum, even if only a bit – progress is progress, however much you write or read.

My personal approach (which I followed, admittedly, a bit on and off) was to do an hour's work at 5 am every day. This won't be for everyone, I know, but it worked wonders for me and I'm not sure I'd ever have completed it if I hadn't given myself this early morning gift of productivity. On a good day (and not all were this perfect) I would get out of bed just before 5 am, go downstairs and make a coffee, then sit at my desk and start writing, continuing until about 6 am when I would need to start getting myself and the kids up and ready for school. On a weekend or holiday, I would keep to this schedule but might manage a couple of hours before the rest of the house starts to stir. Vitally, during this hour I never checked emails or did any marking, lecture writing, seminar prep, or anything else related to my day job. Sometimes if I needed to get my thoughts in order, I would do a 10-minute meditation to get myself focused, but I found the best way to focus was to always finish any PhD session by deciding what I wanted to work on next. That way, when I sat down at my desk, I didn't have to waste time working out what to read or which chapter to write – I would already know. Other PhD parents I spoke to found that this early morning approach really didn't work for them as they couldn't physically wake up earlier than their kids, and if you're a parent of toddlers or very young children you might find that too. Working in the evening might be your thing if you're more of a night owl. Personally, I very rarely work in the evenings because my brain seems to have a 7 pm off switch, but the important thing is to find what works for you, get into a habit of scheduling that time in, and then use it wisely. In fact, scheduling time and making the most of the time you schedule are probably the most important aspects of time management for PhD parents. Scheduling everything isn't always the most exciting way to live but it's vital when you're running a family and a PhD at the same time. It also helps you to choose what you can say yes to and what you need to say no to, without overextending yourself.

Even the best-laid plans, though, cannot predict our moods and mental state. Sometimes I would get up early in the morning, but I just couldn't write. Physically and logistically, I had the time available, but my concentration, creativity, and/or motivation were somehow missing. This can happen to anyone, and I don't assume that parents have a monopoly on writer's block or PhD procrastination, but the effects are more pronounced because, as parents, we may have less flexibility in our day, and once a session is gone without progress being made, it's gone. I found it helpful at times like these to have a few strategies up my sleeve.

First, if writer's block was a real issue I wouldn't write. I might read an article or if I couldn't even concentrate on that, I would search for more articles to add to my reading list. Or I would immerse myself in my data or send emails to potential participants. Admin tasks, transcribing, coding, or simply thinking about your findings must be done too. Even if you spend an hour thinking, perhaps making a few notes, and generally getting your thoughts in order, *that is progress*. Second, I tried to be as kind to myself as possible. If I made progress of any kind, then I recognised that. And if I genuinely didn't make any progress at all, then I accepted that not as a failure but as part of the process as well.

We are humans, not machines, and if concentration becomes an issue, then it could be the dreaded burnout rearing its ugly head. A PhD is hard work sustained over several years, and many people who start one don't finish it. Specific statistics on this claim are lacking because universities simply do not publish this data. However, Block (2023) claims that over 30 per cent of mature (over 30) part-time students do not complete their doctoral studies. He suggests that this has to do with universities' inability to adequately support the 'nontraditional doctoral student', many of whom are parents. It is a difficult route for anyone of any age, but embarking on it as a parent is especially challenging. Undoubtedly, universities could do more to support the specific needs of this demographic, but in the meantime, there are things you can do to help yourself. Learn to recognise tiredness, burnout, and other concentration deficits and deal with them. Take a rest. Journal. Meditate. Go for a run or a walk, or a swim. Meet some friends for coffee and a chat. Enjoy some family time. Embrace things that move your body or relax your mind and make them part of the process, too.

Several times during my PhD I sat down to reflect on why I was finding it difficult to get motivated. One time this led to the realisation that when I found myself scrolling social media instead of working on my thesis, I was actually craving more social connection. I had been neglecting quality time with my friends at the expense of getting on with life. Even though I saw people during the day, I was missing the very real and tangible good effects of a deep conversation with trusted friends. There were also times when I stepped up my exercise regime because I sensed that my body needed it – far from time in the gym taking me away from time on my thesis when I had nourished my body properly, I could concentrate better, felt more motivated, and crucially, got more done. These are not wishy-washy concepts. You can't expect to do something as cerebral as a PhD without preparing your mind and body for the journey and recognising that maintenance along the way is necessary too.

Final thoughts

I hope that through the combination of my experience and advice throughout this chapter, you have now created your own plan (or at least thought of the things you need to think about) and if you're already a decent way through your PhD project then I hope it's given you some strategies to help you carry on and finish. If that means taking a break or interruption of studies, then don't resist that option, but reach out to your supervisors and Doctoral College for practical support and advice.

My personal belief is that I reached the finish line through a combination of sheer determination, a lot of compromises, a great deal of support from various quarters (both personal and professional), and a clear sense of *why* I wanted to achieve this thing. I said at the beginning that the best piece of advice I could give is to figure out your 'why' and for me, that was the main thing that saved me when I was floundering during the last few months before submission. At that time, I was struggling to even write a word, and I sought out help and advice from a number of places, eventually discovering a coach online who specialised in PhDs. In one of her videos, she advised writing out my 'why' on an actual piece of paper (not just typing it in an online journal) and putting it somewhere where I could see it every day. I did that and pinned it to my noticeboard (on the wall behind my screen) and seeing it every day was one of the things that kept up my motivation when

I most needed it. Your why is a personal thing and you don't have to share it with anyone, but I don't mind sharing a couple of sentences from mine.

> I want to turn my life around – from being a penniless single mum to a qualified university lecturer – and I want to model that achievement for my kids and show them that anything is possible for them too. Now it's time to get this done so we can get our space sorted and move somewhere bigger.

We haven't moved somewhere bigger yet, but that will come in time. However, not long after I submitted my thesis I spent several days sorting, clearing, and rearranging the house (as noted about the downgrade to my writing space in the last section!). While I was deep in my PhD, I was basically incapable of doing those big tasks like sorting through the clothes, toys, and books the kids had grown out of. It wasn't that I was working all weekend every weekend (although sometimes I was), it was more that I didn't have the mental capacity to take on a big domestic project when I knew my PhD was sitting waiting to be worked on. And this is totally normal. Doing a PhD took a toll on my family because, in some ways, we were in suspension for those years as I prioritised it above things like cleaning, organising, and holidays – even when I wasn't actively working on it. There's a selfish element to that because I did the PhD largely for me (although see also my previous point about modelling achievement) but it had a huge impact on my kids, and if I'd had a partner, it would have impacted them too. There's no avoiding the fact that as a parent your PhD is not entirely your own, and therefore, you can't compare what you're doing to non-parents who embark on this same project. But at the end of it you gain a qualification that may be worth all the challenges along the way, and for me, it is one that I consider as much belonging to my kids as it does to me.

Summary of reflections

Reflecting on my chapter has allowed me to help guide you, the reader, with some of the challenges that you may currently, or will face within your PhD journey. Whether you are contemplating funding options, considering what your long-term goals are, whether you want to go full or part time, are concerned with childcare funding, or are worried about how you are going to balance work commitments alongside your studies. It is important to be realistic when thinking about these potential challenges. Regardless of your individual circumstances, remember that you are not alone, and your decisions may impact those around you. Discuss the implications with those close to you, whether that be your partner, your parents, children or friends. However, it is also important not to assume that everyone will fall into line, just because you are undertaking a PhD. This journey will impact those closest to you, as revealed within my own reflections. Just be sure to stick to boundaries and responsibilities. Regardless of your circumstances, make sure you ringfence the time that you allocate to your PhD and guard it vehemently. A thesis doesn't write itself!

9

Managing the mind and PhD'ing

Abigail Shaw
Birmingham City University

Abigail's research focuses on Black women from African and Caribbean backgrounds who have histories of offending and explores their desistance pathways. Her objective is to uncover the diversity within these communities and emphasise the importance of considering this diversity when providing support to Black, African, and Caribbean women with offending histories. It is noted that grouping these women together could present challenges in their treatment within the criminal justice system and their successful reintegration into the community

Introduction

Completing this chapter is seemingly bittersweet because, for me, reflection is never an easy road to tread. It evokes the many years of feelings I have tried to suppress to get by – anger, hatred, disappointment, grief, and mental turmoil. Yet, simultaneously, I feel a sense of honour and gratitude whenever I share my experiences because it means more than just reflecting. It provides an affinity space for me and enables my story to reach the people – especially Black women who can relate to this journey of what I like to call 'Mind Management'. More importantly, I am managing a multifaceted persona and balancing family life while ensuring I can fit in and be accepted in and outside university. I think, for context, I should start from the beginning, my childhood.

It started as a kid

Growing up was definitely a challenge for me, but a challenge I didn't recognise or understand until early adulthood. I say this because it is widely documented that within the Caribbean community, we tend to have a 'Get on with it' attitude and we are taught the mentality that 'We should remain strong when confronted with adversities' (Vance, 2019). As a matter of fact, the elders are foreign to the idea of mental health and do not understand the burden it creates in someone's life. I grew up in Handsworth, Birmingham, an inner-city area that is situated in the Northwest of Birmingham, which is also well known and ridiculed for rioting in the 1980s, serious crime, drugs, gangs, and violence (McCarthy, 2022). When you think about a young girl navigating their life around these intersections, what are the chances of success and opportunity? Let me paint a (not-so-pretty) picture! From what I have written thus far, you would expect my upbringing to be filled with anguish, dread, and regret but it was the complete opposite. I grew up in a two-parent household, an only child until the age of 11, never wanting for anything and feeling what I thought was love. However, as I reflect on my younger years, I now recognise that emotional detachment was apparent between my parents and me. It was not common in my household to show affection, say 'I love you', and greet each other with a hug, a smile, or a kiss – this was something I learned as I got older – showing affection, that is. Negative and unhappy domesticity definitely impacted my school, with the early onset of negative behavioural and academic issues. In the same way, I had a difficult time forming friendships and manifesting a positive learning experience. My relationship with teachers was challenging and that was expressed in my school reports. From as young an age as I can remember, I was labelled a 'bully' and 'disruptive' and told 'I will never amount to anything' in my senior year – I was always in isolation. Isolation was used as a form of discipline for children who had misbehaved in some way. It was used to exclude problematic children from mainstream education, as they were sent to a designated room separated from their peers. It is now recognised that the use of isolation or seclusion in school perpetuates mental health and challenging behaviour (Kljakovic, Kelly, and Richardson, 2021). I do not remember the school assessing my situation to identify whether I had experience of previous trauma or any other vulnerabilities. One thing I do remember is that it was a distressing situation and was one of the main reasons I truanted – I was always isolated. In the classroom, I found it difficult to stay idle for long periods of time and I would frequently fidget and get out of my seat. I now know that these are signs of behavioural and learning difficulties, but it was never observed or understood as that. I would be put on a school report to manage my behaviour and academic performance, but support would not go beyond that. Undoubtedly, this was another factor that led to my disinterest and disengagement from the school environment.

McLeod (2022: 6) noted: 'Whilst Black boys continue to face higher rates of exclusion overall, rates of permanent exclusions of Black girls rose by 66% in the five years prior to the coronavirus pandemic, compared to a rise of 27% for boys'.

The most common reason for both permanent and fixed-term expulsions is persistent disruptive behaviour. However, school policies prohibiting Black hairstyles, kissing teeth, and fist-bumping have also played a role. As I reflect on my early education, I find it arduous to locate a positive, memorable moment at school. Besides those that involved me being removed from a classroom for disruptive behaviour, suspension, and ultimately permanent exclusion. My secondary schooling was short-lived, but the teachers all echoed the same attestation. However, I would say this is when I had a slight inclination that I was emotionally and mentally immature due to a lack of understanding of what I was experiencing, in the sense that I was not fully aware of how and why I was feeling depressed, frustrated, and always angry. I was a very violent teenager and used violence to express my emotions because I had no other release or a positive escape. I was participating in deviant excursions such as running away, truanting, and getting involved in toxic intimate relationships, consequently exposing me to inappropriate promiscuous behaviours. I associated and developed relationships with older people, relationships my family disapproved of, but I was obstinate, and I did not comprehend the difference between, and the impact of, healthy and unhealthy relationships. It was never spoken about at home, and I vaguely remember this being a serious topic at school, but then again, I was not there long enough or had the capacity to absorb what I was being taught. My behaviour at home was disciplined using a mixture of verbal and physical punishments which was not a positive reinforcement for me. Despite my abhorrent and impudent behaviour towards adults, I do not recall a specific person(s) or service(s) identifying, acknowledging, or supporting the underlying issues that may have contributed to it. Instead, I was simply labelled as a 'potential troublemaker', 'bad', and a 'disobedient' child. Despite this, no intervention or support was given to me or my family. The people I associated with had similar experiences, and my peers also had a similar upbringing and experiences. We all had anger management issues, no respect for authority and were resistant to consequences. My complete disregard for authority eventually led me to engage in criminal activity, resulting in contact with the criminal justice system and a custodial sentence in a youth offending centre. It was a trajectory I was warned about but never understood or expected. As a child with a vulnerable mind, it was easy for me to become susceptible to radicalisation. I was easily manipulated and swayed by the opinions of others, and I often found myself compliant when participating in deviant behaviour. My emotions would guide my decision-making.

This is how my mind works

Dyslexia is a learning difficulty that mainly affects a person's ability to read and spell words accurately and fluently. People with dyslexia experience challenges with phonological awareness, verbal memory, and verbal processing speed. It is important to note that dyslexia can occur in individuals with varying levels of intellectual ability. (The British Dyslexia Association, 2019)

To me, this definition is quite generic, but what the British Dyslexia Association (2019) has done is amplified additional traits dyslexic individuals embody. It also exemplifies and recognises that some individuals with dyslexia may experience visual and auditory processing difficulties, which can adversely affect the learning process. However, some dyslexic individuals may have strengths in other areas, such as problem-solving, creative skills, and interactive skills.

I was 14 and serving a custodial sentence when I realised I was experiencing something peculiar, but as a child, you do not recognise it and cannot define it. I enjoyed reading as a child, and although it would take me weeks to read one book, it was a form of escapism. I could be engrossed in the lives of the characters and forget about my own situation – momentarily. However, asking me to read aloud in public was a terrifying task, and anxiety filled me, knowing that I would stumble over words and sentences, read too slowly, and mispronounce words. Refusal meant I was being defiant and accused of dereliction – I felt tormented. As I previously mentioned, I had difficulties with my education and regulating my emotions. Part of my custodial order required me to participate in anger management and education, but I was having difficulties engaging. I did not feel normal; I felt isolated, and I would find myself daydreaming in class or meetings. Education was difficult for me, and when it was mentioned, it was a trigger because I was a slow learner in comparison to my peers. My aggressive behaviour was also a way of communicating an unmet need or unsolved problem. I lost confidence and self-esteem, and my depressive state deteriorated to the point I did not want to be here. I had never considered or experienced self-harming or suicide before, but my mind was starting to consider this as a form of release – it made me feel worse! I was overstimulated and under-stimulated and struggled to process my environment, which led to hiding and masking out of shame and embarrassment. I did not have the ability to define what I was experiencing due to a lack of knowledge and support, and this impaired my ability to develop strategies to function.

From as far back as I can remember, I have always been an overthinker, sensitive, and I suffered from anxiety. However, this tendency would not only arise in distressing situations. I often found myself getting overwhelmed by the simplest things (and still do), and this could sometimes be detrimental to how I process and confront situations. Support in the young offender's institute was inconsistent and more like a tick-box exercise. There was no opportunity to build a rapport, and due to the circumstances, I felt compelled to share. Upon my release from young offenders, my challenging behaviour was still a bane, and my time of tribulation did not end there.

I had a strong sense of self-hatred, and I would indulge in recreational drugs, bury myself in a secluded place, and try to forget, these were my coping mechanisms – 'laugh out loud', as they say nowadays – feeling hungover never helps. I literally couldn't talk about my life and experiences as it exasperated my emotions and thought process. It became challenging and exhausting trying to suppress my authentic thoughts and feelings, causing me to lash out verbally and physically. Although I received support while in young offenders, it was limited, and time restraints meant support was short-lived and not substantial. Even though I was home, hostility remained because my dysfunctional domesticity had not been addressed. My life had not changed and did not coincide with the person I was trying to become; however, it was frustrating seeking help because, in my community, we do not express how we feel outside the home. We are told from a young age to 'keep our business in the home to ourselves' and encouraged to follow a 'sweep under the carpet' mentality. When I did eventually receive some support, it was something I did not express to anyone out of fear of being judged and isolated, and to put it bluntly, I did not want my experiences to be used for idle gossip, especially among friends and relatives. I was confronted with judgement and discouragement when seeking support from my family; I would feel like I was a burden and not good enough and this was debilitating. Seeking support from professionals was also a negative and distressing experience. Some professionals did not hide the fact that they had preconceived notions of the type of people who are prone to depression and anxiety. As stated before, I found it difficult to engage with professionals because I was subjected to microaggressions.

Combating neurodiversity

Attempting education, employment, or training in early adulthood was an unsuccessful mission because although I would enrol and initially feel enthusiastic about getting my life on track, I would not finish. Then I would find myself trying again the following year and repeating the process because I lose interest and focus on other things so easily. I think I have always been impulsive, and this has been misconstrued as rudeness, irrationality, and lacking self-discipline, especially as an adult. As a result, I have found myself in conflicting and chaotic situations, causing me to be severely reprimanded and tarnished my personal and professional relationships. This caused further isolation, and I found myself masking and being dishonest about my authentic feelings. I developed strategies to cope; I became monosyllabic unless I was around certain peer groups and, especially, within a professional setting. I would wait until I got home to let out my frustrations and again indulge in self-medicating with substance abuse and bingeing on alcohol – this wasn't good for my impulsivity. I was not certain it was mental health until I was

19, had a child, and experienced domestic violence, and the demands placed on me exceeded my ability to work around them. I thought I was trying my hardest and doing the best I could. This transition to motherhood was onerous, and to put it bluntly, I disliked being a mother. There was also an element of selfishness with having to prioritise the needs of my child over my own. Eventually I did seek professional help, and the doctor advised me I was experiencing post-natal depression. Immediately and without discussing alternative support, I was introduced to anti-depressants, but the treatment was unsuccessful, and I fell into a deeper depression. Over time it was apparent that the coping strategies I was using were ineffective, and things were spiralling out of control; my life was unorganised, and my mind was cluttered. Then the 'mum guilt' kicked in, and this heightened my depression and anxiety, I felt depleted and defeated. I could not provide the most basic level of care for my child and instead of comforting me, my parents would suffocate me with critique and expectations instead of allowing me to learn from my mistakes and positively guide and support me without passing judgement. Consequently, I made a conscious decision to contact the local authority and have my daughter placed with my maternal grandmother. As expected, these changes in my circumstances had a significant impact on my lifestyle. Following the short-term childcare plan, it was paramount that I utilised this time to work on improving my situation.

What I was unaware of at the time was that social workers play a significant role in improving the lives of families in need. However, their main priority was the well-being and safety of my child. Regarding my care and support, I had to seek this independently as it was not offered to me. Mediation was provided to some degree, but neither I nor my family was receptive to it at the time because the situation was fresh and hostile. There was a clear breakdown in communication within my immediate family, resulting from my decision to involve the local authority. Eventually, reconciliation happened organically through the management of expectations and reflection over a period of time. I utilised this time to focus on seeking professional support for my mental health and getting back into education. To ensure my transition was successful, I obtained my own rental property for the first time, which brought with it some challenges. I must say it was an exhilarating experience, even though it came with a lot of responsibilities, physical labour, and emotional strain. Moving out of my parents' house was another step towards independence. I was now in a position where I had to manage the general upkeep of a home, including managing finances, and become self-reliant. As I reflect, although I was deprived of my liberty, I do think incarceration prepared me for this moment. The experience instilled discipline, the value of time and productivity, problem-solving, and the ability to think outside the box. However, what was absent was the practical and emotional support needed to succeed in living independently. Additionally, the lack of prior preparation and knowledge made the transition stressful and overwhelming, which triggered my mental health.

It took some time to settle into my new environment, and my circumstances started to improve. In spite of this, my mental health was still negatively impacting my decisions and lifestyle. I was tired of masking my authentic feelings and made an informed decision to seek further support. The local authority provided me with information on local services that could help me overcome some of the difficulties I was experiencing. I contacted a local women's group, and they invited me for an initial assessment. We worked together to create a plan which involved coping strategies, participating in affinity spaces and engaging in one-to-one support. For the first time, I felt I was being heard, and I had a clear plan of action and then I was introduced to talking therapies. I think I was receptive to these methods for a variety of reasons, mainly because I was engaging and listening to the lived experiences of other women who were trying to navigate their own obstacles. It was also a safe space where we could come together and engage in open and honest dialogues. During this time, I was encouraged and decided to enrol to college on an Access to Biology and Psychology course and due to my previous unsuccessful attempts, I was nervous and filled with anxiety. On the other hand, I felt prepared for the transition because I was now receiving some support and a place where I could escape life's challenges.

Escapism

> Escapism
> /ɪˈskeɪpɪz(ə)m/
> *noun*
> 1. *the tendency to seek distraction and relief from unpleasant realities, especially by seeking entertainment or engaging in fantasy.*

I was a 24-year-old, mature student and the college I attended was women only. This was a positive for me because of my previous experiences, and more importantly, college was a form of escapism. It was easy for me to build relationships with the women, and as time progressed, we built a strong enough rapport that we would confide in one another. It was a congenial environment and atmosphere, and I realised these women and girls had similar experiences. My attitude towards learning was changing, and I was gaining new insights into coping strategies that did not involve participating in deviant behaviour. In fact, attending college was like another support group and I was finally enjoying my academic experience. I was surrounded by other mature students and supportive academic staff, creating a welcoming and engaging environment. However, I was still experiencing learning difficulties such as poor concentration, daydreaming, retaining information (especially for exams), forgetfulness, and difficulties processing spoken and written language. I was referred to the college's dyslexia assessor for a diagnostic assessment and it was confirmed I was dyslexic: 'Dyslexia is defined as a learning disorder that affects both children and adults. Its symptoms are different with age, and severity can also vary. Generally, people with dyslexia have difficulty breaking down words into simple sounds' (NHS, 2022).

I had never considered that I may have learning difficulties because this was never spoken about or communicated to me. It came as a shock to my family as well because they had accepted the labels that had been bestowed upon me. For me, the diagnosis was an emotional experience because I associated dyslexia with being a barrier to achievement, being marginalised, having special needs requirements, and illiteracy. I am not entirely sure why or where I learned this. Still, my guess is back then (over ten years ago), that's how learning difficulties were portrayed and illustrated – a societal misconception. Importantly, the diagnosis provided clarity, and I could now receive the educational support I had been deprived of for many years. I would say that I was lucky because if my tutor at the time did not have the knowledge and intuition to identify the signs relating to my learning difficulties, I would have been overlooked. As a matter of fact, without the support, I probably would not have exceeded my academic expectations or be contributing to this chapter. I suddenly realised that the problem was not me, it was our education system, for allowing my learning disability to go unnoticed. Now I had a 'needs assessment' report I was eligible for Disabled Student Allowance, and they provided me with financial support to pay for assistive technology and other support while I was on my course. Once support systems were in place I thrived academically, receiving merits and distinctions – much to my surprise. Interestingly, because of my struggles with mental health I wanted to pursue a psychology degree, but I did not receive the level in numeracy required to enrol. After attending university open days, I was introduced to criminology and based on my lived experiences this aligned well with my future endeavours. I had submitted a personal statement and achieved the required University and Colleges Admissions Service (UCAS) points needed to secure my university place at Birmingham City University (BCU).

Neurodiversity vs university

Starting university was a highly prestigious accomplishment for me, especially being the first in my immediate family to attend. More importantly, everything I had to contend with up until this point had prepared me for this new venture. Contrastingly, it was a daunting point in my life because although I was industrious, I was still struggling with anxiety, low self-esteem, and feeling inadequate. I thought it was a fluke and pure luck that I had managed (against all odds) to reach this level within academia. Due to my experience at college, my feeling of social anxiety decreased, and I found it quite easy to blend in and establish a strong social network. To be clear, although I did not struggle in creating new friendships, academically I was still feeling overwhelmed and overstimulated. I have always considered myself an average student and never really compared my academic achievements to those of others. I believe I was putting too much pressure on myself because my expectations were high, and I would overreact when I made a mistake. This was my initial encounter with imposter syndrome – adding to the roster of ailments I was enduring, and as previously stated, I would not dare speak of this. Also, this was something else I would need to manage and find a form of escapism to mask – another burden. For me, it was another stigma, another barrier, another thing to be demonised for – telling myself, 'It's ok you have come this far'. But how? I found myself, once again, suppressing my emotions. As a result, I would avoid occupying certain spaces and be selective about the engagements I attended to avoid public speaking or any situation that would draw attention to me. This was extremely frustrating, and at times it caused me to become discourteous, and experience mood swings. Stepping out of my comfort zone, adjusting, and adapting to new environments takes a lot of adjusting for me. Suppressing my emotions to fit in, I would mentally shut down and find myself in a mental and internal crisis because I was evaluating my entire self-worth. I struggle with executive functioning (Rodden, 2021); what this means is I have difficulty prioritising, organising, planning, starting, and completing tasks which also impacts every aspect of my life.

Caring for the mind and PhD'ing

I continued to engage with professional services externally as it was having a positive impact on my personal life. The academic support I received was tailored towards supporting academic-related issues and provided me with tools to help. I consider myself to have a blended learning style and, depending on the setting, this determines how I learn and retain information. However, what was crucial for me was taking the initiative to seek help managing my emotions, which impacted my mental health, especially when confronted with the demands and pressures of university life. The thought of being left behind and unable to complete the tasks required to gain my degree haunted me daily. I decided to reach out to the mental health and well-being support services provided by BCU to gain a fresh perspective and receive guidance.

While studying for my undergraduate and master's degrees, I found the lectures and seminars were not tailored to meet my specific needs. As a result, I had to create my own structure and approach to learning. However,

I must give credit to the teaching staff who did their best to help me despite their limited knowledge of learning disabilities. I felt that the counsellor assigned to me lacked cultural awareness, the advice was generic, and there was no follow-up. However, I am in no way blaming the counsellor or the university, and I am conscious of the fact that there could be a variety of reasons why this was the case. Occasionally, when divulging my challenges, I have been met with incredulity and feeling the need to belabour my traumatic experiences, this became and continues to be a tormenting issue. Previously, my experiences have been defined as 'unlucky', suggesting that I had just drawn a short straw. As I reflect, I realise that I probably was not receptive; I lacked trust and struggled to divulge my experiences to new people, this felt a laborious and exhausting task. Seeking professional support in the community was scarce, and mental health services were stretched. As a result, I was continuously met with long waiting lists. Luckily for me, I had established a positive social network through university and the women's group; thus, I always had someone I could depend on in times of need. I also received support from the university, this was also helpful, and I was grateful. After years of constantly avoiding situations that made me feel vulnerable and presenting myself as perfectly fine, unbothered, and smiling, I now present myself as honest and transparent and use my vulnerability as a strength and a lesson.

Without doubt, over the years, I have adopted negative beliefs about myself, but I continue to find strategies that enable me to adopt a positive mental attitude. For several years, I have been navigating biases and stereotypes to access opportunities, but I also understand that I come from a less fortunate and opportunistic background. I learned to plough through the shame and embarrassment I was feeling, even when my motivation was at its lowest. Occasionally, I would feel uncomfortable doing so; I would think people were misconstruing my cry for help as 'crying wolf'. Well, let's just say the façade gets tiring and leads to a state of deep depression. I must admit that I have been learning as I progress, using the effective strategies I have developed over the years. I have realised that taking small steps and functioning adequately is enough to get by, even through the suffering of mental chaos. With my recent diagnosis of Attention-deficit hyperactivity disorder (ADHD), I am now accepting that mental health has become a massive part of my identity and acknowledge that I am a Black woman with dyslexia and ADHD – and that's okay. In fact, this diagnosis has enabled me to understand some of the challenges I have been experiencing over the years, in particular my inability to regulate information in a typical way and my regular burnout intervals. I also understand my neurodivergent brain deviates from the dominant societal standard of neurotypical, and I am becoming comfortable with this. Recently being diagnosed with ADHD combined type, a mixture of inattentive and hyperactive symptoms, has not caused a hinderance. Instead, it has provided me again with clarity. Although I find myself leaving therapy feeling fatigued, I understand that this is part of the healing process. I finally understand how to manage my feelings and returning to a balanced state has empowered me to not be discouraged from divulging and expressing myself.

Conclusion: Navigating the academic space

Regarding my academic performance and managing my PhD, I have become comfortable with sharing my experiences of managing mental health, academia, and lone parenting. It's a struggle trying to manage a household and mental health and provide quality time to my child and her education. However, through the support of professionals, my supervisors, colleagues, and friends, I have incorporated learned coping strategies and developed through them, as well as been proactive in finding strategies of my own. It is important to note that my support network has expanded since starting my PhD. I now participate in online support groups tailored and organised by people from a similar background. These affinity spaces are less judgemental, encompass an increased sense of empathy, and are also a safe space to share. I find online support networks work best for me because I meet women from different backgrounds with similar and different experiences, and we discuss a variety of topics, from mental health to DIY techniques. Also, family intervention has been supportive and assisted in helping me understand the impact of my behaviour and, more importantly, how it made others feel. My past and current situations have taught me that I do not need to feel guilty or ashamed. Compartmentalising coping mechanisms allow me to function, and as a lateral thinker, I have a unique thinking and learning style, and I am becoming proud of this. 'Black and Black British women are more likely to experience increased mental health problems (29%) compared to White British women (21%) and non-British White women (16%). Also, Black people are more 4 times more likely to be detained under the Mental Health Act' (Mind, 2021).

For me, this suggests that support needs to be holistic, and professionals need to exercise active listening and empathy and, importantly, provide support tailored to the individual's needs and without judgement. Therapy and support groups should be a safe space, one that steers away from cultural implications and myths. It's not an easy road, and I can only speak for myself and provide a reflection of my own experience, and I hope I have accomplished that here. Sometimes, a lifestyle change can be challenging but necessary. This means incorporating meditation, new eating habits, living healthily and getting regular exercise, which are methods I have used to overcome the challenges. Overall, with the right support, access to resources, and constructive coping mechanisms it is possible to maintain a healthy mind while completing a PhD.

Summary of reflections

Within my chapter, I highlight the significance of transparency and openness when addressing mental health challenges. I also acknowledge the prevalent tendency to suppress emotions, especially among individuals contending with long-term mental health issues or within communities that do not prioritise mental well-being. I want to stress the possibility of overcoming these challenges that you may face through tailored support and coping strategies. Within my chapter, I also advocate for creating a supportive environment and fostering open communication with peers to mitigate feelings of isolation. I offer you guidance for acknowledging, addressing, and managing mental well-being throughout the doctoral process. I believe that engaging with internal and external support services both before, during, and after the doctoral journey is essential. While encountering inevitable stress during the pursuit of a doctoral degree, I have learned that the integration of diverse coping strategies is favoured to cultivate a positive and resilient mindset. Additionally, the paramount role of thought in shaping one's reality and the significance of cultivating a positive mindset as the catalyst for change and improved outcomes are crucial when navigating the PhD journey.

Editors' reflections: Part II

As we move forward on this grand expedition of the PhD journey, we find ourselves approaching the next pitstop – a crucial waypoint on our path. Picture this rest area not just as a chance to regroup but as an opportunity to delve deeper into the evolving terrain we have traversed. At this juncture, we will reflect on the rich landscape of experiences and insights from our recent chapters. It is a moment to pause and examine how the diverse elements of our journey interconnect, revealing patterns and pathways that might not have been visible at first glance. Just as a traveller examines their map and adjusts their route based on new discoveries, we, too, will assess the key themes that have shaped our expedition so far.

In Chapter 6, Rio Waldock took us on a deeply personal journey through the intertwined challenges of grief and academia. She began by recounting her initial struggles with education, reflecting on how her unexpected academic path – from failing GCSEs to pursuing a PhD – was shaped by her evolving sense of purpose and passion for justice. Rio shared the devastating loss of her father, an event that triggered an identity crisis and emotional turmoil. She described how grief affected her, manifesting in feelings of exhaustion, anger, and sadness. Despite these challenges, Rio emphasised how she gradually transformed her pain into a source of strength and motivation. By dedicating her PhD journey to her late father, she found renewed determination to continue his legacy of standing up for others. Ultimately, this chapter explored the profound impact of grief on one's identity and aspirations, something which transcends beyond the confines of academia and underscores the importance of self-care in navigating such a complex emotional landscape.

Chapter 7, by Charlotte Rigby, offers a candid reflection on the challenges of pursuing PhD research while working full-time as a lecturer, particularly as a first-generation student from a disadvantaged background. She shares her experiences of navigating time management, maintaining a work-life balance, and coping with imposter syndrome. Charlotte emphasises the importance of setting boundaries and prioritising tasks to avoid burnout, advocating for self-compassion and realistic expectations. She also highlights the value of a strong support network and mentorship in overcoming the pressures of academia. Ultimately, Charlotte's narrative serves as a guide for others in similar circumstances, encouraging resilience and self-belief.

In Chapter 8, Suzanne Baggs provides a sincere exploration of the challenges of balancing family life with the demands of a PhD, offering practical advice and personal insights that may assist in guiding you through this complex journey. Suzanne stresses the importance of clearly defining your motivation before starting a PhD, as this will sustain you through challenges and potential setbacks. She discusses critical decisions, such as whether to study full-time or part-time and the implications of teaching or working alongside your research. Suzanne shares her experiences as a single parent, highlighting the need for careful time management, accepting help, and setting realistic boundaries. She also stresses the importance of maintaining your well-being and flexibility and provides important advice if you ever find personal circumstances impacting your progress. The chapter underscores that while balancing a PhD and family life is challenging, it is manageable with strategic planning, support, and resilience.

In Chapter 9, we were guided through the deeply personal journey of Abigail Shaw as she navigated her complex educational and emotional landscape, shaped by her childhood in Birmingham's inner city and her struggles with undiagnosed dyslexia. The chapter explores themes of resilience, the challenges of growing up in a household where mental health was dismissed, and the impact of an unsupportive educational system that led to her disengagement, criminal behaviour, and eventual incarceration. Abigail reflects on how these experiences fuelled her determination to pursue education despite battling anxiety, low self-esteem, and the all-too-common theme of imposter syndrome. Her story illustrates the importance of self-advocacy, the power of support networks, and the need for accessible mental health resources for those navigating similar challenges. Abigail's story is a testament to the strength required to manage and subsequently succeed against overwhelming odds.

The recent chapters highlight the emotional and practical challenges that often accompany the pursuit of a PhD, such as grief, balancing personal and academic life, managing time, and overcoming self-doubt. A recurring theme is the importance of resilience – whether in transforming personal pain into motivation, navigating the pressures of academia, or balancing family responsibilities with research demands. Self-care and self-compassion are emphasised as essential tools in managing these challenges, alongside the value of setting boundaries and seeking support. The narratives underscore that while the PhD journey is demanding, it is also a path of personal growth and empowerment. By recognising and addressing the complex interplay of emotions, responsibilities, and aspirations, we hope that you can navigate your own PhD journey with greater resilience, purpose, and clarity.

As we pack up our supplies and extinguish the fire at this rest stop, we prepare ourselves for the next leg of our PhD journey – one marked by the hidden challenges and barriers that may lie ahead. Chapters 10 through 13, written by Lisa Edge, Kyla Bavin, Kavya Padmanabhan, and Liam Miles, serve as vital guides through the often-overlooked obstacles of doctoral study, shedding light on the institutional, methodological, and ethical hurdles that many may not anticipate when they first set out on this path. These chapters reveal the potentially treacherous waters of higher education, where students may have to navigate the need for trauma-informed supervision, the exploitative nature of some PhD scholarships, and the ethical dilemmas that arise in research. Each account emphasises how these barriers can shape, challenge, and sometimes threaten to derail the journey. Yet, within these stories lies a common thread of resilience and adaptability. As we press forward into this unknown terrain, these insights provide us with the knowledge to overcome the obstacles ahead, reminding us that, despite the challenges, there is a way through.

PART III

10

Safety in cultures of precarity: complex trauma and the value of 'trauma-informed' PhD supervision

Lisa Edge
Birmingham City University

Lisa's PhD explores the impact of trauma on the lives of criminal justice-involved women who have used violence. Lisa is designing and applying a trauma-informed methodology to capture the experiences and biopsychosocial processes which provide context for understanding women who have used violence, the worlds they live in, the motivation behind their use of violence, and the interventions required to improve the quality of their lives.

Introduction

In the neoliberal university, which heavily markets itself on values of equality, diversity, and inclusion (EDI), mental health awareness campaigns are regularly flaunted throughout higher education (HE) institutions. Being seen to challenge mental health stigma with messages like 'it's okay not to be okay' is a popular business strategy. However, accepting poor mental health as 'just the way it is' prevents critical enquiry into the multiple, often socio-economic factors which generate and maintain suffering and inequality among some of the most disadvantaged sections of society. The chronic destitution endured by many with complex trauma is not 'okay', and within the backdrop of a culture which insists 'mental health matters', there appears to be little genuine enthusiasm within UK universities to acknowledge and actively tackle the structural part they play in sustaining this adversity.

This chapter, written in the third person, is a critical and personal reflection on the systemic and cultural barriers faced by a PhD student with complex trauma, in particular reference to the importance of building trust and safety in supervisory relationships. After a brief introduction to the concept of complex trauma, the chapter will describe some obstacles faced when attempting to integrate into a post-graduate research (PGR) culture committed to the values of the current political economy. The chapter will then discuss the commercialisation and subsequent misrepresentation of the term 'trauma-informed' (TI) before concluding with how a TI model of supervision can assist in mitigating some of the additional challenges encountered by PhD students with complex trauma histories.

Complex trauma

Complex trauma, also known as complex post-traumatic stress disorder (c-PTSD), describes exposure to repeated or prolonged traumatic experiences which are interpersonal in nature and typically begin in childhood (Lawson, Davis, and Brandon, 2013). Examples include experiencing or witnessing domestic violence and abuse or suffering parental emotional neglect or abandonment. Trauma which originated in early childhood is also called developmental trauma because of the devastating neurobiological impact it has on an infant's developing brain and nervous system (Van der Kolk, 2005). In addition to the indicators of post-traumatic stress disorder (PTSD), which are reexperiencing the trauma, avoiding traumatic reminders, and prolonged states of hypervigilance, complex trauma is characterised by significant nervous system dysregulation, an enduring negative self-concept and frequent interpersonal difficulties due to a chronic mistrust of others (Brewer-Smyth, 2022). The impact complex trauma has on psychosocial functioning can be immense, with sufferers frequently tormented with life-long mental health issues (including addiction and substance abuse), poor physical health, and impaired social functioning (Dye, 2018). In addition, significant socio-economic disadvantage is both a cause and a consequence of complex trauma, creating intergenerational cycles of childhood adversity, victimisation, and socio-economic deprivation (Johnson, 2019).

Threat within a neoliberal university

The debilitating effects described before explain why it is so common for traumatised children and young people to find the standard approach to education difficult to navigate. Those few who succeed in reaching HE and PGR as adults can find the conditions here even more challenging. Prior to the 1990s, HE was predominantly a public service free at the point of entry. However, the rise of the current political economy saw practices and policies reconstructed around market logics. There was a shift in ideology away from the fundamental pursuit of knowledge for the greater good and towards goals of individual success and long-term financial gains (Raymen, 2022). The commodification of HE requires universities to aggressively compete against one another to attract more students, research funding, and the highest ranks in research performance, with the sole aim of generating increased revenue. Academics are also expected to follow the capitalist tenant of competitive individualism (Hall and Winlow, 2015) or rigorous, narcissistic competition with their closest peers to achieve status and success, thus earning their place in the institution's hierarchical power structure. Competitive individualism is unashamedly displayed through the academic custom of securing your name to as many publications as possible, the acute need of which often seems to surpass any genuine passion for the work being produced. The cultural pressure on PhD students to enter the game and start publishing begins immediately, and while high-stress, adversarial working conditions ultimately harm the mental health of the majority, a culture of precarity, competitive individualism, and justified inequality can be particularly challenging for those with complex trauma because these conditions will emulate the traumatic experiences of their past. Put simply, the neoliberal capitalist ideology which underpins contemporary HE effortlessly generates a neurobiological state of threat. PhD students with complex trauma must find ways of working within a system and among people who can feel intensely threatened and unsafe.

Remote working and interpersonal hypervigilance

Complex trauma makes trusting others a significant challenge, and for PhD students, the threat of further mistreatment and exploitation in an academic environment can feel pervasive. Interpersonal hypervigilance refers to the excessive scanning of social interactions for signs of threat. This behaviour is an evolutionary, neurobiological adaption to interpersonal harm designed to detect danger quickly to increase the chances of survival. However, analysing social interactions in such excruciating detail, and with an attention bias to threat, enhances the likelihood of inaccurate interpretations. For example, if we enter a conference event looking for signs that we are unwanted, the red flags received from one preoccupied attendee who failed to return your greeting will take precedence over the receiving of a warm welcome from the rest of the room. Interpersonal hypervigilance can suggest great animosity, mistreatment, or neglect from people and in circumstances where no harm is intended. In addition, repeated or prolonged traumatic experiences, especially in early childhood, can make regulating emotions as an adult considerably challenging. The difficulty arises due to a narrowing of what Dr Dan Siegal calls the 'window of tolerance' (Siegal, 1999). The window of tolerance describes our nervous system's zone of optimal arousal, a place of psychological safety and calm. Only here can we effectively regulate our thoughts, emotions, and behaviours. However, experiencing trauma can cause this zone to reduce significantly in size, meaning even minor stressors can push someone outside of their window of tolerance, activating sizeable nervous system responses which may appear unnecessarily dramatic or out of proportion to the casual observer. Needing to leave a conference because one attendee ignored you may seem irrational to most academics, but for those with complex trauma histories, interpersonal hypervigilance coupled with a narrow window of tolerance can mean even brief interpersonal exchanges or lack of them, have the potential to provoke intense feelings of confusion, fear, anger, mistrust, and shame. This can especially be the case with email correspondence. While it is a quick, cheap, and easy method of communication for sectors like academia, it fails to provide the primal environmental cues necessary for safe social engagement. The depersonalised, direct tone of emails risks communicating an expression of disapproval or irritation to a student who has reached out for help.

The work of neuroscientist Dr Stephen Porges explains how a heavy reliance on email communication can force someone with complex trauma outside of their window of tolerance. Polyvagal Theory demonstrates the significance of another's body language, facial expressions, and tone of voice in helping us evaluate our own levels of safety (Porges, 2001). It's the connection between two nervous systems transmitting and receiving social cues of environmental safety, or coregulation, which supports our capacity to remain inside our window of tolerance. In other words, warm, receptive, face-to-face communication can be immensely reassuring, especially for those with complex trauma, and delivered consistently over time, can build relational trust, making interpersonal exchanges far less likely to activate overwhelming feelings of threat. However, the mass rollout of remote working post-pandemic has become a significant barrier to this authentic social connection. The barrage of formal emails, online webinars, and virtual meetings makes it even more difficult for some to regulate their nervous systems, unsure of how to accurately interpret social exchanges or the safety level of working relationships. While it could be argued that virtual meetings still provide some social cues in the form of facial expressions, neuroscientists have reported reduced neural activity in facial processing during online interpersonal connections (Zhao et al, 2023). Ultimately, there is no substitute for in-person, face-to-face social interaction and for some, this is an essential part of forming and maintaining safe relationships. Therefore, achieving the most effective and productive PhD supervision often involves making that extra effort to gather everyone around the same table to form an authentically connected social unit. The reliance and normalisation of remote working in academia post-pandemic prevents open, honest social connection, and for those with histories of trauma, it can negatively impact both the supervisory relationship and the student's ability to successfully integrate into the wider PGR community.

Student support services and mental health and well-being services also rely heavily on email communication and remote working. Emails may be automated, impersonal and lack the opportunity to authentically interact with another human being. Services specifically designed to support vulnerable students with their mental health are, therefore, providing conditions which can greatly exacerbate some of their difficulties. Moreover, these post-pandemic asocial practices are now so ingrained into a rigid institutional culture that any challenge to them is easily ignored or rebuffed. For those with complex trauma, having their needs invalidated and disregarded in this way can be re-traumatising, further damaging their self-esteem, their trust in relationships and their confidence in the institution.

On a macro level, remote working, available to the laptop class only, strengthens neoliberal capitalist values of egotism by discouraging social solidarity and compassion for the less privileged sections of society. Academics now frequently work from home because it suits their own individual needs. However, the death of on-campus working increases structural inequality by depriving some of the most socially and emotionally vulnerable students of ways to improve their mental health and achieve their full academic potential. It's those with histories of trauma and adversity who lack external support systems, internal coping strategies, and effective interpersonal skills who are further impaired and marginalised by this practice. In other words, PhD students at high risk of feelings of depression, loneliness, and isolation due to their disadvantaged home circumstances are travelling to campus in search of fellowship, connection, and purpose, only to find a soulless, empty space where a bustling and vibrant PGR community once sat.

Staying out of the spotlight

A tendency to want to stay small, keep quiet and blend into the background for protection does not align well with the belief that to succeed, PhD students must 'take up space' and compete for academic status. Even before any data has been collected, students are encouraged to present posters of their research at conferences to impress prestigious academics with their proposals. But, advocating for yourself, your work, and your ideas, however passionate you are about them, is incredibly challenging when your nervous system tells you it is unsafe. Additionally, chronic low self-esteem and a pervading negative self-concept will quickly convince you that what you have to say is not worth voicing anyway. While 'imposter syndrome' is a phenomenon experienced by many PhD students when assessing their own work, for those with complex trauma, the self-limiting belief of not being good enough is one firmly anchored in all aspects of their lives. It is the hypervigilance and attention bias to signs of criticism, failure, or rejection that maintains this belief. Because of past traumatic experiences, criticism, failure, or rejection can activate a significant nervous system response. Even gently delivered constructive criticism has the potential to generate overwhelming feelings of anxiety, anger, or shame. Perfectionist working is one strategy a PhD student may employ to try and avoid criticism and the intense emotional reactions which can follow. Unfortunately, the pathway to perfection is often equally filled with feelings of anxiety, anger, or shame, which the student is aiming to avoid.

With a firmly established negative self-concept, focus on perfection, and hypervigilance to criticism and rejection, a PhD student with complex trauma may find being the centre of attention in social situations distressing especially when giving presentations. This is because they expect to be judged and criticised by others as harshly as they've learnt to judge and criticise themselves. Social psychologists coined the term 'the spotlight effect' (Gilovich, Medvec, and Savitsky, 2000) to describe the extent to which we overestimate how much others notice about our appearance and behaviour. Through the spotlight effect, vulnerable students can become painfully aware of what they perceive to be their own catastrophic social flaws and shortcomings, even when they are unapparent to those around them. Public speaking under these conditions of intense self-scrutiny can force a student far outside their window of tolerance, which will not only be incredibly stressful for them but being in a neurobiological state of threat will cause significant cognitive impairment, negatively affecting their academic performance. Throwing a traumatised student in at the deep end with a narrowed window of tolerance is simply setting them up to fail.

Campus culture equates success with those students who can extrovertly compete to grab the limelight, with little to no understanding of how to champion and support budding academics who are neurobiologically unable to shine in this way. In 2018, an undergraduate student who suffered with severe social anxiety took her own life shortly before she was due to give an oral presentation of her work. The University of Bristol was successfully sued under the Equality Act for failing to provide the student with reasonable adjustments (Morris, 2022). HE's focus on outcomes over experience and market relationships over social relationships and social welfare leaves talented students who do not fit the neoliberal mould isolated and catastrophically failed by a hardened and inflexible academic system.

Trauma-informed or trauma-misappropriated?

The origins of the TI movement can be traced back to literature by Harris and Fallout (2001), which highlighted how frequently service systems failed to meet the needs of trauma survivors. By applying the advanced neurobiological insights of contemporary trauma theory to service design, the authors recognised effective service relied heavily on providing an emotionally unthreatening environment to prevent inadvertently activating trauma responses. To do this, service systems needed to be better educated on the impact of trauma and integrate this knowledge into their practices. In addition to increased service effectiveness for trauma survivors, Harris and Fallout believed that following a TI approach would mitigate the risk of an organisation inadvertently causing survivors any further harm.

Building on this work and through their own research, the United States government agency SAMHSA (the Substance Abuse and Mental Health Services Administration) established six key principles for a TI service approach: 1. Safety, 2. Trustworthiness and transparency, 3. Peer support, 4. Collaboration and mutuality, 5. Empowerment, voice, and choice, and 6. Cultural, historical, and gender issues (SAMHSA, 2014). SAMHSA's TI framework has become enormously influential worldwide over the past decade, with research suggesting a beneficial impact when applied to populations exhibiting high levels of trauma, for example, women in contact with the criminal justice system and the homeless (Stergiopoulos et al, 2015; King, 2017). The popularity of TI practice is also gaining ground within primary and secondary education as schools begin to understand the vital role psychological safety plays in the effectual learning, emotional development, and relational growth of all their students. While critics of TI education frequently argue there is a lack of evidence-based research into this approach, a systematic review of the impact of TI education programs revealed this approach could improve academic and academic-related outcomes in students who have experienced childhood adversity, and, therefore, potentially provide a means of escape from the cycle of generational trauma and its associated socio-economic disadvantage (Roseby and Gascoigne, 2021).

There is no doubt more research is needed in this area. Still, the popular critique of the TI movement so frequently reflects a misrepresentation or misunderstanding of its core aims and principles. As is so often the case in advanced capitalist culture, the initial buzz surrounding this topic has become commercialised and distorted to the point that it has lost all meaning. SAMHSA's key principles have become notably absent in the work of many professionals who claim to be TI. The commandeering and dilution of the concept for financial gain is a travesty for trauma survivors as they become exposed to the risk of further exploitation and harm from those in pursuit of profit. It is, therefore, essential the conversation is returned to the academic literature informed by SAMHSA's original construct and its neurobiologically informed principles. In 2022, the UK government published much-needed guidance for a working definition of TI practice, which *does* reflect SAMHSA's original concept (Department of Health and Social Care, 2022). It's hoped that this guidance will help steer organisations back towards the key aim of supporting and protecting some of the most vulnerable sections of society.

Despite the current indisputable trend towards TI system approaches, HE in the UK has been immune from any legitimate influence. Being on the frontiers of knowledge production, it may be expected for universities to eagerly embrace a more inclusive neurobiologically informed approach to productive learning. But they are not. This is made even more remarkable considering their forward-facing enthusiasm for EDI policies. Unfortunately, conversations surrounding the impact of trauma and adversity within HE is being dominated by those already possessing high socio-economic status, those already flourishing within the system. Because of this, the psychosocial harms and complex generational traumas, which are the byproducts of unequal distributions of wealth and resources, are easily dismissed and devalued. Instead of traditional class politics, it is identity politics which has had the most influence on HE's understanding of trauma. Rather than challenging a system which risks completely excluding sections of society from academia altogether, the concept of trauma has become a tool for securing additional advantages for those already in positions of privilege and influence. For example, a demand for emotionally safe environments is being used to shame and cancel views and beliefs which run counter to popular opinion, preventing diversity of thought and healthy academic debate. There is also a confounding of common emotional reactions with clinical trauma responses as students request 'trigger warnings' on material, which may generate unpleasant feelings. While a key aim of SAMHSA's TI framework is to draw attention to the wide prevalence of trauma in society, including the impact of historical and cultural trauma, these performative, often misguided gestures do little, if anything, to actively recognise and respond to the complex generational trauma suffered by those from lower socio-economic status. Instead, these practices risk sustaining their adversity and exclusion from HE and PGR by diverting conversations away from the underlying mechanisms which drive structural inequality and its associated traumatic harms. SAMHSA's work originated from the goal of supporting some of the most vulnerable, disadvantaged, and traumatised sections of society, those who have been exposed to multiple forms of violence, oppression, and exploitation. So, how have we got to a point in discussions of trauma where the experiences and needs of these people are overlooked?

This is partly due to the broad range of meanings associated with the word 'trauma'. SAMHSA defines trauma as 'an event, series of events, or set of circumstances that is experienced by an individual as physically or emotionally harmful or life-threatening and that has lasting adverse effects on the individual's functioning and mental, physical, social, emotional, or spiritual well-being' (SAMHSA, 2014: 11). What's missing from this description is any reference to the differing levels of impact and adversity suffered due to the specific form of trauma experienced. The notable lack of lived-experience advocacy for complex and developmental trauma in HE and PGR is testament to the substantial psychosocial and socio-economic barriers these individuals face with regards to participation. Consequently, the general understanding of the ways in which trauma affects HE and PGR students excludes the experiences of those who have been repeatedly failed by people and systems and those who have suffered an ongoing traumatic existence. For example, students with care experience who have been conditioned to believe their needs are less important than the needs of others, or those who trusted and believed mental health services would help ease their emotional suffering, only to be re-traumatised by its insensitive neoliberal practices. Because of their past experiences, students like these face huge internal barriers to speaking up and making their voices heard as a direct result of the relentless trauma they have suffered at the hands of society. In addition, lived experience testaments of the structural violence and traumatic social harms generated by neoliberal political economy are an uncomfortable topic for organisations who are committed to its values, as well as for those individuals who prosper enormously from it. As the principles of the TI framework are designed to counter experiences of oppression and exploitation, they are in direct opposition to the neoliberal values underpinning contemporary HE. SAMHSA's guidelines for a TI approach target organisational-level cultural transformation, but the likelihood of any meaningful change here from within HE in the current political climate feels unlikely. However, that is not to say that academics cannot begin to challenge this culture by integrating TI values into their work and in their interactions with each other and their students.

Trauma-informed PhD supervision

There is a common misconception that a TI approach is a therapeutic intervention, and supervisors may be concerned that they are expected to be trauma therapists. This is certainly not the case, and no one is advocating for the clinically untrained to assume the role of a therapist – the risk of substantial harm for all involved here is obvious. A system approach which directly addresses an individual's trauma in this way is a 'trauma-specific' model, whereas a TI framework works only with knowledge of the impact of trauma and adversity. Rather than asking the question 'What's wrong with you?' it's often said that a TI approach should be asking instead, 'What's happened to you?' however, a more appropriate question could perhaps be 'How have your experiences affected you?'. Supervisors do not need to know any details about what has happened to a student to be TI; they just need to understand SAMHSA's key principles and begin to integrate them into their model of supervision.

The first principle, and the one which runs through the heart of a TI framework, is 'safety'. Since the trauma associated with complex trauma is relational, safety within the supervisory relationship is paramount. A lack of this feeling of safety may automatically activate behaviours in the student, which, because of their past experiences, they believe will prevent or minimise the risk of coming to harm. It is important for supervisors to understand that these protective behaviours are not limited to the avoidance of physical harm. For students with complex trauma histories, avoidance of the psychological harms which result from being manipulated, exploited, deceived, invalidated, and humiliated are likely to be more prevalent. For example, a student may avoid supervisory meetings or ignore requests for updates if they feel they will be judged negatively. Conversely, a student may communicate regularly that their research is going well despite feeling desperately overwhelmed and needing guidance. Both these methods could be a student's attempts to hide their vulnerability and protect themselves in a situation which feels psychologically threatening. While the two scenarios described could be applicable to many PhD students, for those with complex trauma, it's the persistent negative self-concept, interpersonal hypervigilance, and substantial nervous system dysregulation which amplifies this feeling of threat. It may seem irrational to some supervisors that contact with them could produce such intense feelings of fear, but in a TI model, it's vital to understand that the fear generated is a conditioned, protective, physiological response, a neurobiological consequence of repeated or sustained interpersonal harm. The student's fear is, therefore, perfectly rational and understandable when given context through a lens of trauma.

Because the trauma associated with complex trauma is so often a consequence of repeated abuses of power, the power imbalance of a supervisor-student relationship is likely to intensify the student's feelings of threat. In other words, there will be a heightened emotional sensitivity to those they perceive to hold authority over them. The TI principle of 'collaboration and mutuality' can assist in minimising this power differential, supporting the development of emotional equality and mutual respect within the supervisory relationship. Sharing decision-making with the student rather than giving instructions can also facilitate the principle of 'empowerment, voice, and choice'. 'Empowerment, voice, and choice' can provide a relationship where students with complex trauma can make choices which support their individual needs, facilitating the sense of control and autonomy which they have been historically denied. For example, giving the student an option of conducting meetings in a private room or a public space enables them to choose a location which feels safest for them. A supervisory relationship where a student feels controlled, silenced, or their needs ignored will activate protective trauma responses such as avoidance or aggression. This guidance is not meant to imply that supervisors should bend over backwards or transcend their own limits to accommodate the student. It is here where 'collaboration and mutuality' becomes vitally important. Safe relationships and safe environments do not serve the voice and needs of just one person or one section of society. 'Safety' means establishing a space where students and staff feel able to voice differing needs and opinions without fear of judgement or reprisal, a place where all feel heard, understood, and are compassionately committed to working towards solutions to shared goals.

Honest and effective communication of the wide-ranging impact of trauma, including that which involves 'cultural, historical, and gender issues', can only occur within spaces which can safely tolerate discomfort.

The TI principle of 'trust and transparency' is key to developing safe and effective supervisory relationships, and as a student with a complex trauma history will struggle immensely with trusting others, establishing this trust is likely to take some time. Another common misconception in understanding more relational ways of working in systems like education is that it translates as an absence of boundaries. However, the complete opposite is true. A lack of mutually understood and consistently employed boundaries can provoke confusion, uncertainty, and increased interpersonal hypervigilance for those with complex trauma. Instead, the key to building trust in relationships is by being clear, transparent, and realistic about individual limits and by then applying them consistently over time. Having secure supervisory relationships built on trust not only makes it easier for struggling students to ask for help, but they can also serve as a buffer against the brutality of neoliberal PGR culture, especially with the elevated level of impact it can have on those with complex trauma. In a competitive environment teeming with reviews, critique, and rejection, applying the values of 'trust and transparency' can assist these students in tolerating the intense shame which often surfaces in response to feelings of criticism and rejection. Understanding a student's increased sensitivity to shame may make supervisors reluctant to give honest feedback for fear of damaging already fragile self-esteem. However, it's only through transparent communication, compassionate co-regulatory support, and the building of trust within the relationship that the student has the best chance of effectively processing these difficult emotions.

Finally, the principle of 'peer support' could be facilitated by signposting PhD students towards supportive TI PGR communities created by academics with histories of complex trauma and childhood adversity. Sharing similar experiences and belonging to a collective voice is a powerful weapon against feelings of shame, isolation, and self-blame, as well as serving as a vehicle for social change. However, these communities do not exist, and enthusiasm for their creation, outside of those few directly affected within academia, is nominal. It is incredibly isolating to be a PhD student with complex trauma, and the failure of institutions to recognise and respond to the unique psychosocial challenges faced, questions the authenticity of an HE culture committed to the values of EDI.

Conclusion

Lived experience of the psychosocial and socio-economic barriers students with complex trauma must overcome to reach a PGR level of study should be of great academic value to the social sciences. However, the pathway to applying this insight to benefit society through academia is hindered by an HE commitment to the adversarial ideology of the current political economy. System cultures which firmly integrate exploitative and individualistic values emulate the relational conditions of past traumatic experiences, activating a neurobiological state of threat incompatible with effective cognitive functioning. A TI framework is designed to assist those with trauma histories by creating environmental conditions which reduce these physiological feelings of threat. However, SAMHSA's key principles are in direct opposition to the neoliberal values which underpin contemporary HE – precariousness over safety and competitive individualism over peer support, mutuality, and collaboration. In addition, the misappropriation and erosion of TI language at the hands of those in pursuit of increased personal status or wealth is an additional hurdle to any authentic integration of its principles. While compassionate systemic and organisational change often feels insurmountable for those of us who desperately seek it, the key principles of a TI framework can be adapted for use on a micro level. By applying a TI approach to supervision, a PhD student's supervisory team are in a unique position to assist by establishing a small pocket of safety within an environment which can often feel inhospitable.

Summary of reflections

Safety in Cultures of Precarity highlights how a fiercely competitive and hierarchical neoliberal culture within universities can produce a neurobiological state of threat. As well as causing a considerable amount of mental distress, a nervous system stuck in survival mode becomes incapable of effective cognitive functioning. Consequently, students whose nervous systems have adapted to be more reactive, for example, because they have a history of trauma and adversity, continue to suffer considerable disadvantage as post-graduate researchers. Relational trauma, in particular, can create difficulties in the student-supervisor relationship and successful integration into the wider research community. Although in direct opposition to the values of a neoliberal university, the integration of authentic trauma-informed principles into supervisory relationships could be one method of addressing barriers to participation faced by post-graduate researchers with extensive trauma histories. This chapter underpins the importance of finding the courage to challenge established practices within post-graduate research if they are damaging to you. Despite contemporary proclamations of equality, diversity, and inclusion, institutions and systems are resolute in their resistance to change, especially in accommodating those traditionally excluded from educational opportunities. If you find yourself struggling to comfortably fit into post-graduate research culture, rather than blame yourself, maybe it's time for you to consider the possibility that you are just as capable, that your contribution is just as valuable, and that it's not *you* that's the problem.

11

Working for nothing: the exploitation of postgraduate students

Kyla Bavin
Birmingham City University

Content warning: this chapter discusses sensitive topics.

Kyla's research explores the relationship between contemporary identity politics using ethnographic methodology using found poetry to disseminate her findings.

Introduction: A cold wet day in January

The Early Career Academic Serf @ EarlySerf: I contemplated suicide to escape my workload. A workload that I'm not paid for. Nothing is worth that. I have been trying to live a life where I'm not so poverty stricken, I don't eat and walk miles to get to work. Bloody academia, I'm going to make this better. (26 January 2020)

The person who tweeted this was a hollowed-out shell, circles that formed under their eyes were as dark as the clouds that had formed in their mind. They had just stood shivering on a cold train station gulping down tears and swallowing the intrusive thought that if they just stepped off the platform, it would all stop. The cacophony that had taken over their thoughts was a collection of screaming voices; 'you're too busy for us', 'Daddy says all you care about is your PhD', 'How many hours of teaching are you doing this semester?', 'You haven't filled in this form', 'You will be withdrawn', 'YOU'RE NOT GOOD ENOUGH, WHY CAN'T YOU COPE? YOU'LL NEVER FINISH' …

This person was me.

At this point, you are probably thinking about where this is going, or maybe you are shuffling about uncomfortably because this was also your experience, or just maybe it was so far removed from your own experience that the words you just read are as alien as reading an ancient text. Okay, so where this is going is a reflection, a reflection of one of the toughest years of my life and how this all was intrinsically linked to a choice. My choice. One that I made through necessity and if truth be known by insecurity. The choice to enrol on a partial PhD scholarship. This choice has had far-reaching consequences, and I will carry the scars of this choice with me for the rest of my life. However, it is the scars that I carry that have shaped me, have given me the voice that I use to tell you my secrets, the voice I use to shout about the issues that drive me, and the voice I use to scream into the dark abyss when I attempt to compartmentalise the facets of my life that took me by the hand and led me here.

I am about to drag you with me through some of the most tumultuous times of my adult life. I will trust you with my story in all its gory details and I will write about the aspects of my life that up until now I've been scared to even discuss with the people that I am most intimate with. Interspersed with the words that I share with you now are the real-time Tweets that tell their own story of the mind of a person who had been fractured by expectation, exploitation, and an egotistical desire to prove everybody wrong. I hope that you read my story and rather than it just serving as a cautionary tale, you will walk with me down the bumpy road that I traversed to bring me to the point where I am now. Moreover, with every fibre of my being I hope that any one of you who is travelling the same path as me, realises that I see you, I have been you, and I get where you are. For everyone else, take a deep breath, buckle up and hold on tight, and just as that great late Bill Hicks once spoke to my generation, I now echo his words when I say to you that it's just a ride, man.

Sale of the century: the scholarship

> **The Early Career Academic Serf @EarlySerf**: The universities that help to write the language of emancipation, that fund research into exploitation and teach about the millions of workers whose rights are trampled on in pursuit of profit, hold a murky little secret. Shush, come here let me shout this in your ear … HELP! (9 January 2020)

Before the ink was dry on my undergraduate degree certificate, I decided that I was going to skip straight to PhD and agreed to continue my studies at the same institution that had awarded me my undergraduate degree. This was a partial fee waiver scholarship. This meant that I would agree to undertake six hours of teaching responsibilities in return for my enrolment and supervision. My situation was far from unique, in 2012 a survey conducted by the National Union of Students concluded that many PhD students were expected to teach without any financial recompense. Lynes, Treadwell, and Bavin (2024) articulated that universities were not unlike any other profit-driven corporation and that the insidious exploitation of early-stage researchers had become a necessary component to balance budgets. To ensure that I could keep a roof over my head while I studied, I needed an array of part-time jobs that I had to fit around my teaching commitments. One uniform for the leisure centre, another for the nursery, and another of sorts for the university (although my ripped jeans and slogan tees often caused an unwelcome response from some of the senior management team). As well as these 'jobs' I was a mother to four children, with the youngest living in a joint custody arrangement between me and my ex-husband. I had a house to clean, school uniforms to iron, food to prepare, household finances to worry about, and a menagerie of pets to keep alive. Although highlighted by Toffoletti and Starr (2016) that I was not unique in feeling compromised in my ability to meet the expectations set by my institution alongside my commitment to my family, I felt utterly alone. At the beginning of my first year, I excelled in my balancing act, I juggled my roles with the level finesse of demonstrated by an acrobat from Cirque du Soleil. However, as the next academic year approached, more balls were thrown at me, and I knew something had to drop. It was not long before the cheers within the big top of life had turned to gasps, as the star acrobat sat broken and exhausted with each role that she had seemingly kept from bouncing on the floor, shattered around her. The first to drop was my role as a mother, soon after my role as a wife, and then everything clattered around my feet. However, it was this first loss that became ground zero for the implosion of my entire world, that would usher me down the road toward the worst year of my life.

It's oh so quiet: parental alienation

This section of my story was never going to be easy to write. I spent hours staring at a blank screen, knowing what I needed to write, yet scared to give words to my situation. Scared to reopen the wounds that had never truly healed and scared to be judged. The stigma of a woman being an absent parent, often meant that I would normally shy away from small talk about children. After days of soul searching whether to tell this aspect of my story, I knew that it would be disingenuous of me not to. I also hope that my words cannot only give context to my story but help to heal others who have shared a similar fate to my own. I need to open up about this moment.

This was the moment it all came crashing down, the moment my heart began to break, and I started to lose myself. I had convinced myself that the PhD would be a way of proving that I was worthy and that after years of what Meier (2009) noted as having my inadequacy as a mother showcased in front of my children, no one would ever question my ability to care for them again. After months of balancing my PhD responsibilities, my multiple jobs and caring for my youngest son, he came home from his father's house and told me he no longer wanted to live with me. I tried in vain to placate him; instead, he became more and more withdrawn. Then after a particularly unsettled evening, he told me: 'I was too busy to be his mum'. My heart broke in my chest. Dalton, Carbon, and Olesen (2003) identified a key component of parental alienation was undermining a parent's ability to care for their children – 'she can't look after you she's too busy doing a PhD'. After years of criticising me in front of my son, this was the stick that he had finally managed to subdue me with. Out of fear and desperation, I offered to drop out of the PhD program, but it was too late. There was nothing I could do. I made the decision to let my son live with his father full-time, and I would assume the role of weekend parent. However, it was not long before these weekend visits started to become few and far between.

My inability to manage all the roles that had been handed to me had left me vulnerable and in a cruel twist of fate, attempting to 'better' myself had created the perfect storm to lose everything, and when I lost my son, I lost a part of myself, leaving behind a void that can never be filled, not even with all the box wine you could purchase during the COVID-19 pandemic; I know I tried.

I'm not okay: the deterioration of my mental health

> **The Early Career Academic Serf @EarlySerf**: The stress is so bad that I wander around feeling sick. At the moment my only release is Twitter to vent and see I'm not the only one. Yesterday I realised I was depressed. In debt, barely able to feed myself, relationship in tatters and a whole module to write by Monday … (25 January 2020)

At the end of that first academic year and the start of the next, I threw myself into my work, pretending that everything was okay. After the Christmas, I broke. For weeks I had struggled to leave my house, I felt that I could no longer live with the stigma that I carried. It felt as if it was etched onto my skin like the branding given to criminals to alert others to the stench of their repugnant shame. At the same time my relationship with my then-current partner had broken down, he too was also filled with resentment. I changed, the conversations surrounding my research no longer captivated him, and the hours that I spent working left him feeling abandoned. We had outgrown each other.

As the start of the next semester started, I just wanted to curl up and die, but I could not I had to carry on. By mid-January, I was back at university depressed, drinking too heavily, and desperate for someone to notice that I was on a precipice. During the first week of teaching, I was going through the motions, circling through the masks that I wore to hide my real face (Goffman, 1959, 2002). Like any good entertainer, I delivered the introductory content with enough vigour and vim that the students had no idea that the person in front of them had been reduced to a husk. Then, I delivered the introductory lecture for Transnational Organised Crime, and as I stood in front of a room full of students, hungover from the night before, tired and hungry, as I had not eaten properly in days, inside I started to unravel. The gravity of my situation came closing in. I somehow got through to the last lecture slide, and once the last student left the lecture theatre, I knew that I could no longer fight the overwhelming urge to cry. I sobbed and then I picked up my belongings and walked to the train station.

Panic had begun to take hold of me, I could not deliver this module without rewriting some elements, but when did I have the time? My homelife was unstable, at this point I was sleeping on a yoga mat on the floor of my office, and I was self-medicating with pints of IPA at my local brewery as they helped to dull the pain, and kept me out of the house. I was due to start my second shift of the day at the leisure centre and once off the train I would have to walk the six miles to get there. As I stood on the platform waiting for my train, an announcement was made alerting passengers to stand back from the platform edge as the next train was not stopping. 'You could just step off the platform, Kyla. It would make all this go away', the voice in my head urged me to edge forward. I started to move towards what I thought would be the end of all my troubles, but then in a moment of what had become rare lucidity, I moved back. I then sobbed so hard that a young woman asked if I was okay. I apologised and told her I was just being silly, and with that explanation, she continued on her way.

The following week I wrote an email to the executive dean of the school in which my department was situated. I wanted to make them aware of how the demands of the partial scholarship and the pressures of my life had reduced me to a suicidal wreck. A few months later in an email from the head of the graduate school, the executive dean had confirmed to them that they were aware that that year's workload on the partial scholarship had been 'excessive'.

Bog roll, breakdowns, and boxed wine: COVID-19

By mid-March, there was one word that was dominating conversation both domestically and globally, COVID-19. Stories from Wuhan became so commonplace that I decided to replace the content for my media lecture with a discussion on participatory media and media interpretation of health scares. I chose to focus on the YouTube videos that had been serving as a video diary of the events in China. These videos uploaded by English teacher Ben Kavanagh showed the world what daily life was like living in a city amid a pandemic. This lecture served as a foreshadowing for what was to come. This was to be my last face-to-face lecture with this student cohort. On 23 March Boris Johnson, the then prime minister of the United Kingdom, announced the start of lockdown.

With the COVID-19 pandemic and subsequent lockdown measures that impacted a third of the world's population, inevitably the ramifications began to be felt within the parameters of higher education. Once confined to my home, my academic workload increased. As stated by Weller (2020), the crisis had thrust educational technologies front and centre, and this came with a new set of problems. This paradigm shift within the pedagogical practises meant extra work for academics who were already under pressure to manage student expectations and produce teaching that was of the same standard as campus-based activities. Therefore, justifying the exorbitant student fees that many institutions were hoping not to have to refund. With many institutions feeling the economic pinch due to closed campuses and reduced recruitment capabilities, it fell to the academic staff to manage this transition.

For many academics, myself included, this transition was far from seamless and translated into many hours deciphering new platforms and creating content that is easily accessible and vibrant enough to entice students to engage electronically within an epoch of mass uncertainty. With increased demands on my time, I faced a juggling act between content creation, delivery, meetings, emails about regulation changes, updates, and student enquiries, all while I was supposed to be producing my doctoral thesis. However, it was the student enquiries that demanded the most from me. As Hochschild (1983, 2012) described, this emotional labour is the unpaid invisible work of managing emotions and care, which translated into emails, phone calls, and video conferencing with students who were struggling. They were not only struggling with the new dynamics of the switch from campus-based learning to distance learning but also struggling with the complex situation that COVID-19 had created.

This emotional labour had started for me in the week before the lockdown was announced when a student stood up amid my lecture and disclosed her intention to end her own life. I then spent the next five hours making sure that this student received the help she needed; at the same time, my mental health was in tatters. As I accompanied the student to the local clinic, I could not help but marvel at the irony that the lecturer with whom she had deemed stable enough to disclose her struggles had herself been contemplating suicide only a couple of months earlier. Throughout the first weeks of the UK lockdown, many hours were spent electronically checking on the well-being of this student and many more were spent worrying about her as she was suffering from mental health problems alone within halls of residence with no family or friends that she could call on for help and support. Maybe if I could keep her alive, I could silence my demons. As the weeks rolled into months, the news that she had returned home and had received much-needed support provided me with a momentary sense of quiet. It was not long before the noise returned.

As the weeks dragged on, I spent more and more time in the confines of my office; if I wasn't teaching, I was hiding in the 'World of Warcraft' and a box of Pinot Rouge. The work on my PhD began to grind to a halt. After months of negotiations with my institution's ethics board, I was given the go-ahead to conduct a covert ethnographical study. However, with no sign of the lockdown lifting I had resigned myself to the fact that I needed to change direction. This was when I moved my research online. Unlike the traditional forms of research that offer an escape from the field, with online research, I became saturated. My continuous back and forth between these interconnected realms of the digital and the tangible had blurred the boundaries, summed up by Prince (2019) as 'flow'. My already fragile mind started to become warped by arguments from ideological enemies. This added to my hopelessness. The question of how to untangle myself from these digital battlefields that I had been a tourist in since before my research commenced was replaced with how to repurpose my relationship with it. Moreover, how the hell would I remove myself from my phone, my fifth limb? I knew this was an impossibility, so I stepped back from my PhD for what should have been a short sabbatical, but in reality, it was an emotional disconnect that would take me over a year to reconnect. I made the decision that I could not continue the scholarship. I reasoned that a full-time job and self-funding was the only way that I had any hope of ever limping over the finish line. I quickly became, as Gotye (De Backer, 2011) sang, somebody that my university used to know, and I was left in the wilderness. As I stumbled around in this new post-scholarship wasteland, I became more and more unsure of myself. Imposter syndrome had me in a stranglehold.

I took a job at a local college and convinced myself that I was not good enough. I languished here on the periphery of my chosen discipline, unfulfilled yet scared to knock on the doors of the academy and hope to be let back in.

Imposter syndrome: by design?

> **The Early Career Academic Serf @EarlySerf**: Does imposter syndrome mean that we are more likely to be accepting of exploitation in HE? (14 January 2020)

I think that, as well as sharing the story of one of the hardest years in my life, it is important to understand the factors that led me there, especially as they continue to shape my career as an early career academic and will no doubt impact my future for many years to come. Like the students identified by Nori, Peura, and Jauhiainen (2020), I was a 'non-traditional' student who continues to live with the constant fear of being found out as inferior and utterly incompetent. A first-generation student who started my undergraduate studies in my late thirties. As an undiscovered neurodivergent I left school with a drug and alcohol dependency and three GCSEs I found out that I had almost ten years after leaving school. By the age of 19, I was a single mother living on benefits, that would run from one poor life experience to another. Most of the time I lived in my own head, and when the noise in there became too much to bear, I would drown it out with cocktails of drugs and promiscuous behaviour. At 24, I got clean(er). It was at this point that I began to fully understand how my life choices had shaped not just the lives of myself and my two children, but how I was perceived by the people around me. I went to college and decided that I wanted to go to university. Although I had been the source of constant disappointment to myself and those around me since I had stepped foot in the school system, it was not until I stumbled into academia that I became submerged in my feelings of incompetence and inferiority. I was drowning in imposter syndrome (Clance and Imes, 1978). People who sound and look like me are the subject of academic papers, not the authors.

These feelings of never being enough permeate every aspect of my being, words such as old, common, slut, stupid, bad, and useless that I had spent a lifetime carving into my soul, follow me around like spectres whispering in my ears. The first time that I read Imogen Tyler's (2020) story of how her stigmatisation as a working-class academic drove her work on stigma, it had the 'killing me softly' effect upon me; her words not only resonated, but they also stung. She notes that 'shame lives on the eyelids', and my eyelids are heavy with shame. I also have regret squatting in my psyche, and I wear my perceived working-class inadequacies as a panoply. The choice between assimilation within a milieu that views you as a caricature of fractured working-class identities or becoming the embodiment of that persona is not one to be taken lightly. Each comes with caveats. For me there was no choice, I had to assume the role of the 'social and moral disaster'; which I eventually had tattooed onto my body, wearing my stigma with a heavy dose of chagrin and pride.

It was this imposter syndrome that whispered to my insecurities and pushed me towards the partial scholarship that almost broke me both physically and mentally. It whispered to me that it was a great deal for someone 'like' me and that no other institution would allow me to prove once and for all that I was more than 'this'. Friends, including other academics, told me that I was entering a predatory studentship, but like every other unhealthy relationship I have ever had, I ran straight in with the determination to prove everybody wrong. By 2020, I was asking myself whether this imposter syndrome was an unfortunate by-product of entering the academy, or was it done by design?

Was this the last hurdle for working classes? We can sit at their table but never leave with the same level of satisfaction. Not only do we expect our exploitation in the form of predatory scholarships and precarious contracts, but we are grateful for it.

Those of us who were on precarious contracts live with the constant threat of rejection. Bussotti (1990) identified in their doctoral research that imposter syndrome is often intertwined with people pleasing. Ever amenable, ever available, like a child seeking approval, I know that I, too, fall into this category. In the early months of my scholarship, eager to please, I took on more and more work; I wanted to prove to myself and to the institution that I was worthy. However, extra work such as the weekly quizzes I created, and the guest lectures added up, as Griffiths (1999) postulates, there is more to time than mere clocks, and as a working-class woman who was expected to keep an orderly home, while working two part-time jobs to supplement the income that I was not receiving from my teaching commitments, my time ran through my fingers at incredible speed. I would listen to the stories of other PhD students, who, unlike me, did not have to work two jobs, teach, and balance the emotional labour of being a wife and mother; they would regale me with tails of reading, writing papers with their supervisors, and presenting their fledgling research at conferences. It was another world, one that I longed to be included in. Again, I began to internalise this as my failings. I'm not good enough. I had to earn my seat at the table, and for me, it was never going to be that easy.

Conclusion: A new dawn, a new day and I'm feeling okay

> **Kyla Bavin @KylaBavin** These are the happy faces of three academics who have just finished their book. (30 November 2023)

Two years ago, after yet another setback, I was offered a seat at the table. This seat came in the form of a part-time associate lecturer post at Birmingham City University. Here I met other working-class academics who had overcome their adversity, and I was welcomed. Within 12 months I was in post as a full-time lecturer and had found a cluster of academics that not only had the same research interests, but they also had each other's backs. More than just work colleagues, these kindred spirits became family, my work brothers. I was given new opportunities to collaborate on books such as this, and even more importantly I was given the opportunity to celebrate each of life's milestones together, marriages, engagements, and new life.

Today my PhD is back on track and hopefully will be submitted sometime in the near future. The Twitter account that I created to vent my despair and frustrations at my situation, is redundant; I would also like to think that my writing skills have improved along with my mental health. When asked to write a chapter for this book, I knew that I wanted to write an authentic account of the realities of juggling life and a PhD. While all experiences are different, many of us who are navigating this process are dealing with adversity. Especially working-class women, and in this, I hope that you can find some commonality. Often compared to running a marathon, the PhD process is a hard endurance sport, that most of its competitors have trained vigorously for their entire life, with spectators cheering them on from the sidelines. Others, however, show up late, out of shape and in the wrong shoes. I fall into this bracket.

Putting my story into words for the first time has been an emotional rollercoaster. At points, I realised that I was typing with watery eyes, and when reading extracts to my husband, my voice would start to break a little. Luckily, he's kept me on track with support;, hugs, and mugs of strong black coffee. However, if I were to describe this experience in one word, cathartic would be the one that I would choose. Now, if my story could help just one person who finds themselves struggling throughout this insane process, then I would ask for little more. As my story continues, I know that I have a lot of lost ground to cover and I still have many issues that I need to work through, but I am okay with that. I am okay.

Bloody academia, I made this better.

Summary of reflections

When I wrote this chapter, I had just picked myself up from multiple setbacks; it was my '*let's get this done*' moment. Before I dusted off my thesis for that last push, I wrote this chapter, which was one of the hardest things I have ever written. I put all my demons in a row and then left them on view for all to see. At times, I had to stop typing to cry. There were also times when there was nothing that could have pried my hands from my keyboard as I put into words the pain that I had buried deep inside me that, although on the surface, lay dormant, was actually eating me up from within. Then, once I wrote the last few lines, a sense of closure and relief washed over me, and I realised that I was having one of the most cathartic experiences of my life. Maybe this was the therapy I needed, and hopefully, I can help others in similar situations. After walking what must seem miles in my shoes, there really is not much more that I can say or fit within the word count I was given to reach out to you. Other than telling you that after sharing this chapter with you, I can now move forward with my life, a life in which I want to live in all its scary and magnificent glory. Oh, and I also hope that by the time you read this book, I have once and for all finally finished this PhD.

12

How close is too close? Ethical tensions and reflections in the Breddon Centre

Kavya Padmanabhan
University of Cambridge

Kavya's PhD research is an ethnographic study exploring women's experiences with punishment and care in a women's centre in England.

Introduction

From September 2021 to June 2022, I completed my doctoral fieldwork in a women's centre in England. I had planned to conduct an ethnographic study, relying on participant observations to make sense of the social world in the Breddon Centre. Employing my methodology in practice, however, led to ethical negotiations that reshaped my experience in the Centre. This will be the subject of this chapter. I will reflect on my co-location as researcher and colleague in the Breddon Centre and describe how this unique positionality led a number of ethical tensions and dilemmas. While my commitment to reflexivity may not have resolved these dynamics, it helped me consider the boundaries of my involvement in the organisation, and just how far I would go to understand the Breddon Centre and its inhabitants.

It was late afternoon at the Breddon Centre. I was sitting in the office writing down some of my observations when Abi walked in. 'Hey Kavya. Do you want to come visit a client with me?' I nodded. 'Sure,' I said, gathering my belongings and walking with her to the car park, where we got into Abi's car to visit a 24-year-old client named Thea at her home. Thea met us at the door, her face leached of colour. Her eyes were red. She looked like she had been crying all day. 'Hi darling,' Abi said, reaching out to touch her shoulder. Without a word, Thea turned and ran up the stairs to her bedroom. We followed. Gently closing the door to Thea's room, Abi walked towards Thea and sat beside her on her bed. 'How are you?' she asked. Thea burst into deep, heaving sobs, her hands shaking as she wiped away her tears. 'I'm not okay.' Recently arrested and charged with having an indecent relationship with a minor, Thea was referred to the Breddon

Centre while in police custody. She had been working with Abi to manage the emotional and material consequences of her arrest. Facing a potential prison sentence, Thea was struggling to navigate the fear, deep anxiety, and remorse that she was battling: 'my hair's falling out, and I haven't been keeping any food down. I've lost a stone in the past week', she told us, as she struggled to catch her breath. The air in her room was heavy and intense. It felt inescapably intimate to observe this scene, laden with an emotionality that I had been unprepared for.

I stood near the door, trying to minimize my presence, as Abi placed her hand on Thea's leg. Abi nodded occasionally, listening while Thea processed her grief. Telling Thea to download a mindfulness app on her phone, which Abi felt could help Thea to make sense of what she was feeling, Abi then turned to me. 'What do you think, Kavya? Do you have suggestions on what might help Thea?' With my back leaning against the door, I watched both Thea and Abi turn to look at me. Hesitantly, I cleared my threat. I told Thea, 'I'm so sorry you're feeling low right now. What helps me sometimes is to write some of my thoughts down, just to get them out of my head.' Abi nodded, taking control once again. I stepped back. I had been uncomfortable as an observer of this scene. But this change, being included in the action, felt especially terrifying. Unsure if what I said would help Thea, I felt completely out of my depth.

The Breddon Centre

Every caseworker feels this way, Abi would tell me later. These words framed my role in the Breddon Centre. By the time I had left the field, I had not only conducted research, but I had become a quasi-caseworker as well. Officially labelled a volunteer in the Breddon Centre, I took on a number of tasks during the nine months. I was there working with women one-on-one and leading groups, covering for caseworkers who were on leave, helping to manage crises that came up at the Centre, and sitting on the reception desk for the day. It had not been part of my research plan to become a quasi-caseworker. But, as I immersed myself in the work at the Centre, it began to feel impossibly difficult to isolate myself from the emotional labour that was taking place around me. Like everyone else at the Centre, I absorbed clients' and caseworkers' emotions, becoming a part of the world I sought to describe (Seim, 2021). My very presence in moments where I witnessed clients' emotionally vulnerable moments negated the distance that I had believed that I was meant to cultivate as a researcher. To stay silent and simply observe, without participating, in such scenes felt unfeasible. This initial moment, the choice between offering Thea advice or staying quiet, became an 'ethically important moment', which Guillemin and Gillam describe as 'the difficult, often subtle, and unusually unpredictable situations that arise in the practice of doing research' (Guillemin and Gillam, 2004: 262). Ethically important moments are the micro dimensions of ethical and social interactions researchers may encounter while in the field (Guillemin and Gillam, 2004). Built upon a practice of reflexivity, ethically important moments occur when the researcher must figure out how to address unexpected situations or navigate what they do when there are immediate ethical concerns. They are a product of the messy and dynamic nature of qualitative inquiry.

Leaning into my unique situation, and taking part in the action around me, the slippage from 'observer' to 'participant' inadvertently honed my observations, giving me deep insight and understanding into the unsaid dimensions that characterised the actions of those around me. And through this process, I began to see more, give more, and feel more, building a 'verstehen' (Weber, 1978), an empathetic understanding of the world and actors within it, that drew upon my own reflections of what it felt like to reckon with the same choices that my participants made. While this positionality brought with it a set of ethical tensions, my co-location as a participant and an observer enabled an in-depth and emotionally intuitive view of the environment and actors that I was researching.

Methodological approach and research aims

Influenced by feminist methodologies, I saw a holistic, reflexive approach as essential to my doctoral research. I based this upon Oakley's conceptualisation of 'friendship as method' (Oakley, 2016), which argues that by developing an intimate relationship between the interviewer and the interviewee we can potentially lessen the exploitative nature of the interview setting. And thus, I sought to build relationships with my participants. Relying upon an empathetic methodology that centred building, maintaining, and managing the relationships that I would make in the field, I decided that an ethnographic study would best suit my research aims.

Ethnographies are contextually based methodological tools to explore social behaviour, linking everyday interactions with the macro structures of power that shape it (Burawoy, 1991; Davis and Craven, 2011; Desmond, 2014; Dodworth, 2021; Harvey, 2023). They can provide a relational accounting of why individuals make the choices they do within the environment that ultimately determines the boundaries of action itself (Burawoy, 1991; Desmond, 2014). As such, ethnographies can subvert binary thinking that may solely identify those who have power and those who are without it. Rather, by providing a multiplicity of accounts, such an embedded approach can develop the tangled web of human behaviour, demonstrating *how* and *what* choices each individual has. By providing a necessarily complicated view of the world researchers are immersed in, ethnographic observations can become 'a way of living in and knowing the world' (Ferrell, 2018: 147). There is no denying that the liminal space within which the researcher occupies, 'balancing between distance and involvement ...' (Scheirs and Nuytiens, 2013: 152), is challenging. Nonetheless, by developing relationships and building connections while knowing that they will ultimately leave, the researcher can develop an informed critique of the setting and the actors that mirrors the complexity of the social world itself.

The study

Convinced by this thinking and seeking to immerse myself within a community-based organisation that worked with women, I decided to conduct an ethnographic study in the Breddon Women's Centre in England.

Framed as an alternative to incarceration operating in the community, women's centres are trauma-informed and gender-responsive, working with marginalised women in and out of the criminal legal system. They offer an individualised model of care that is designed to address women's multiple needs by working as a 'one-stop shop': women can get support with housing, substance misuse, domestic abuse, mental health, education, training, and employment, and parenting issues all in one place. However, research has also noted that many women's centres are underfunded, oftentimes operating in a 'chameleon-like' (Gelsthorpe, 2011: 136) manner by altering their service provision to meet the different requirements of various funding streams. Characterised by instability, women's centres rely upon short-term funding provided by a number of organisations such as the Ministry of Justice, local probation, charities, and health services (Howard League for Penal Reform, 2017). Often, such short-term funding can delimit organisations' abilities to provide support, instituting a crisis-driven approach to the environment borne from being under-resourced.

In the Breddon Centre, it was quite clear that there were simply not enough members of staff who could support the rising caseloads. It seemed as if the Breddon Centre caseworkers were at the frontline of an emergency effort to support their clients, many of whom presented with severe, intractable, and totalising needs. The intensity of clients' situations, coupled with this lack of funding, oftentimes meant that the Breddon Centre caseworkers had an unreasonably large number of clients on their caseloads. During one conversation with Liz, Lena, and Audrey, they collectively told me that they felt like they could not give their clients the support that they acknowledged their women needed due to their high caseloads. At one point, each caseworker had around 40–50 women on their client lists. For the type of deep, relational, and intensive care work that caseworkers performed, this was an unsustainable number.

During conversations on gaining access with the research manager at the Centre, I emphasised my desire to volunteer while I was at the Breddon

Centre. I had felt it was my ethical responsibility to ensure that I was not simply extracting resources and data from an underfunded organisation, and had envisioned myself sitting on the reception desk, or co-leading a group. These were situations where I could always maintain my identity, first, as a researcher. As I spent more and more time at the Breddon Centre, however, I soon began to be acknowledged as a 'student' rather than a researcher, similarly situating me with the student social workers who would do their student placements with the Breddon Centre. This was a label that I continuously fought against – being seen as a 'student' not only obscured my positionality as a researcher, but it was a status that I felt bounded my agency. Student social workers were constantly monitored and given 'filler' work such as organising file cabinets. Their time was considered to be less valuable than that of the caseworkers'. While the research manager had clearly understood what my role in the Breddon Centre would be, it did not appear to me that the staff and management in the Centre did. My near-constant and long-term presence at the Breddon Centre placed me as an able body. As I cemented my standing within the Centre, they saw me as more than a 'student' but less than a caseworker.

Marcus and Fischer write that fieldwork can be a 'messy, qualitative experience' (1999: 22), particularly because fieldwork demands an 'immense amount of flexibility' (Moeran, 2009: 17). About a month and a half after I began fieldwork in Breddon, I walked into the office one Monday morning, about ten minutes before Morning Meeting was about to start. Liz was already in. She turned to me and whispered, 'Did you hear the news? Elise was fired on Friday.' Elise had been briefly hired as a perinatal mental health caseworker who, according to gossip in the office, 'never did anything'. While Liz mentioned feeling relieved that Elise was gone, she was concerned about who would have to take on Elise's clients. During this conversation, Abi came over to me. 'Kavya, check your email', she told me. 'I've given you three clients. Reach out to them today, please'. Decisions at the Breddon Centre were often made in this fashion – in that moment, Abi did not see me as a research collaborator. I was a member of staff under her authority. This was not a decision that we made together, but one that, if I chose to fight against, I feared would lose me the depth of access and relationships that I had already garnered. I felt as if I had no choice but to accept this new responsibility. I recognised that this would inevitably muddy my 'researcher' identity, but I saw the high level of need and the increasing number of clients who began to work with the Breddon Centre. Not only did I want to preserve my relationship with the Centre, but I wondered if the most ethical way to conduct research with a severely underfunded organisation was to give back in some meaningful way – in a method that the Centre identified to be useful?

Participant observation and observant participation

Scholars generally consider the central component of ethnographic research to be participant observation, based upon a prolonged time in the field (for example, Keesing, 1981; O'Reilly, 2012). However, 'there seems to be a consensus that essentially all ethnographers are simultaneously participants in and observers of the microcosms they study ...' (Seim, 2021: 2). While there has been acknowledgment that researchers are inescapably linked to the fields that they observe, there is still debate on what constitutes 'going native' (Adler and Adler, 1987; Moeran, 2009; Scheirs and Nuytiens, 2013; Seim, 2021). It is true that there is a line between 'going native' and maintaining adequate distance, but I argue that this line is dependent upon the research context and situation and maintained through a commitment to reflexivity.

Several researchers have noted that the term 'participant observation' can obscure the impact that researchers make in the field that they study (Moeran, 2009; Sufrin, 2015; Seim, 2021). Seim argues that 'essentially all ethnographers exist as people who not only *take from* but *take part* in the social universes they study' (Seim, 2021: 2). By building relationships with the people we desire to know, we are embedding ourselves in their lives, becoming a part of the world they describe to us (Sufrin, 2015). The 'messiness' of conducting fieldwork, coupled with my acknowledgement of how I indelibly altered the Breddon Centre with my presence, led to the 'hybrid' (Seim, 2021) ethnography I ended up employing. There were clear moments where I was a participant observer, watching and noting the interactions that took place around me. After the initial month, all of the staff took my presence for granted. They would often debrief their cases while I was around and talk to me about their experiences in the Centre. Quite often, too, I would sit at the reception desk. Many of the Breddon Centre clients would come and chat with me while they were waiting for their appointments. I became a familiar face to many of them. 'You're always smiling', a client named Marie told me one day. 'It makes me feel so comfortable', she said, chuckling and walking away to sit in the lounge at the bottom of the stairs. My very presence informed the Breddon Centre's environment even in those moments where I attempted to be a 'fly on the wall'.

In an article advocating for an embedded approach to ethnographic research, Loïc Wacquant observes that 'cognition is a situated activity growing out of a tangled dance of body, mind, activity, and world, we can begin to retrieve the tacit knowledge enfolded in cultural and social practices, and thereby enrich our descriptions and deepen our explanations of them' (Wacquant, 2015: 4).

Here, Wacquant finds that simply observing a social environment removes a layer of insight that can only be gleaned by participating in that environment as well. This suggests that a true, empathic sense of the world can only arise from the messy entanglement of the researcher's observation and participation within the environment they are seeking to understand. This is best reflected in observation participation, where Sufrin notes: 'One is already an integral actor in the phenomenon she is studying, making direct contributions in real-time. One is in it and of it' (Sufrin, 2015: 622).

While, as a participant observer, I took note of the environment around me, as an observant participator, I became deeply aware of how the environment was produced and the impact my presence played in this production. I was given some training before beginning to work with clients, but mostly this focused on how to write feedback notes after each meeting with clients and import this into their client files. I was not given training on how to employ a trauma-informed approach to working with clients. Most of the training on how to be a caseworker came from shadowing other caseworkers. For the first one-and-a-half months, I would sit in on caseworker meetings with their clients, go on outreach appointments with them, and watch them lead groups at the Centre. One day, I asked Abi how I should approach working with clients, and she told me, 'Everyone has their own way of doing it'. This response unsettled me. I felt as if I had no knowledge of working with clients, many of whom were emotionally and physically vulnerable. But it was not just me who felt this way. About four months into my time at the Breddon Centre, Kate gathered all members of staff together during our daily morning meeting. In a harsh tone, she told everyone that she was 'really disappointed with the team' because Sofia had told her that she felt as if she had no idea what she was doing.

Sofia had joined the team a few weeks prior, and we had developed a friendship. I asked Sofia about what had happened later that day. Sofia told me that she had gone to Kate a few days earlier because she felt 'overwhelmed and unsupported' by the team. I had noticed that several times prior, during the morning meeting, Sofia would ask to see if she could shadow anyone for the day. Most of the caseworkers would look down or at their phones, and a thick silence would permeate the room. Sofia told me that she had been given 20 clients, but she felt as if she didn't know how to work with them. It seemed, to Sofia, that everyone was too busy or simply unwilling to give her guidance on how to perform her job. Hearing this, I felt relieved. I had thought it was just me, that I was inept, unable to manage the responsibilities required of me. This moment offered me insight into the fears and anxieties that, it appeared, all caseworkers experienced. While it confirmed that I was not alone in feeling unprepared for working with clients, it also allowed me to employ my own reflections, the emotions that I felt while performing my duties as a caseworker, as observations. I was 'in it and of it' (Sufrin, 2015: 622).

Managing my 'selves'

Observant participation, however, was riddled with tensions. At the same time that I saw myself as a researcher, the centre management often saw me as primarily as a member of staff. Quite often, there would not be enough caseworkers in the Breddon Centre – either they were on annual leave or out sick. These staff absences often situated me as someone who could fill in the gaps of the care work at the last minute. On several occasions, Abi would ask me to reschedule or cancel interviews I had planned to conduct with clients and staff so that I could cover an emergent task. In the second month of fieldwork, I walked into Morning Meeting to see Abi's face looking tight and worried. 'Is everything all right', I asked her. 'We don't have anyone to accompany Philippa to her appointment with Turning Point. There aren't enough caseworkers in the Centre today', Abi replied. 'Please can you go with her to the appointment? It's just a ten-minute walk into town'. I nodded my head and said sure. 'What do I have to do?' I asked. Abi looked at me quickly before responding, 'Oh, just go be with her. It's very straightforward'. I walked into the town centre feeling anxious. I felt as if I didn't have enough information about Philippa, her care, or even the appointment that I was supporting her with. I didn't even know what she looked like. All I knew was that Turning Point was a community-based organisation that worked with individuals to manage their substance misuse. Using Google Maps, I navigated to Turning Point and waited outside. A white woman got out of the car and walked towards me. 'Are you from the Breddon Centre?' I nodded my head. 'This is for you'. The woman handed me a note with only one line: 'I can't handle it anymore'. She walked away, and in her place, a Black woman walked to me. 'Hi, I'm Philippa', she said. Philippa told me that the note had been from her mother, whom she was living with. We walked into her appointment together.

Out of my comfort zone, fearful of doing harm, and wanting to make sure that Philippa felt supported, I talked to her as if she was a friend, chatting about the weather and the tv shows we liked to watch. Soon, I could sense Philippa getting comfortable with me. In the waiting room, Philippa told me that she had numerous experiences with trauma, and she used alcohol to cope. I went into the appointment with her, silently sitting next to her while she revealed the most intimate details of her life to the nurse. I left the appointment feeling conflicted. Philippa and her mother had both entrusted me with an intimacy that was borne from my association with the Breddon Centre. Neither had known I was a researcher. Before the appointment began, I could see Philippa's hands trembling. She was visibly terrified. I felt it would have been inappropriate to inform her of my status as a researcher when she was solely seeking emotional validation and comfort from me. And so, I negotiated an ethical line. Moments such as these, when I was being asked to don my 'caseworker' hat and emotionally support women at very vulnerable moments of their lives, would not become part of my analysis. Nonetheless, the production of care that I performed with Philippa informed my sense of the work that caseworkers did: it was highly personal, variable, and emotive. Without embodying caseworkers' perspectives and situating myself within the same worlds I was studying, I would not have understood so intimately the caseworkers' lifeworlds.

My insight in moments such as this gave me access to the 'backstage' (Goffman, 1969) behaviours and thinking that characterised life in the Breddon Centre. I began to understand how caseworkers conceptualised their roles and the emotionality that was intertwined with the care work they performed. I reflected on my own sense of power, helplessness, and ineffectuality, considering how my feelings may very well have been reflected in those of the caseworkers around me. By the end of fieldwork, I had worked with four clients weekly, sat on reception, conducted two psycho-educational groups, and covered for caseworkers in their appointments with clients. I had become equal parts and interchangeably caseworker and researcher.

Ethical dilemmas

Nonetheless, this negotiation did not negate the ethical tensions that inevitably arose within the Breddon Centre. One afternoon, I walked into the office after completing an interview with a participant. The majority of the caseworkers were either out visiting clients on home visits, on annual leave, or sick. I was one of three members of staff in the office, one of whom was the admin and the other, Kate, the interim centre manager was in a meeting. As I was sitting down to write some of my notes, the internal phone line rang. Sharon, the admin, was on the line. 'Hi Kavya, there's a lady saying she's suicidal on the line. Can you speak to her?' I didn't know what to do. I did not feel as if I had the skills or training required to speak to this woman, but to tell Sharon that I would refuse the call seemed equally as impossible. I felt either choice could enact harm. Telling Sharon that I would take the call, I spoke to the client, who was very emotionally distressed. I did not know what to say, or how to go about helping her, but I hoped that my presence, my willingness to listen to her, would help her to feel less alone. Thankfully, ten minutes into the call, Kate walked into the room. Seeing my panicked expression, she took the phone from me and spoke to the client.

Conducting research in an environment where clients regularly expressed past experiences of trauma or mental ill-health, this situation was not abnormal. At least once a week, a client would come into the Centre in crisis, and caseworkers would drop what they were doing to work with her. This was the work of the caseworker. Yet, confronting such moments was always terrifying. I would leave the Centre feeling conflicted, confused, and worried about whether I was acting unethically. I did not feel as if I was best placed to work with women who were emotionally or mentally distressed. While I did not have the required training to know exactly what to say to clients all the time, I did my best to plug the patchwork of care that they had voiced they were experiencing. I became responsive to client's needs, listening closely to attempt to offer them what they said they needed.

I addressed these ethical tensions with my supervisor continuously. We would meet once a week to debrief my findings. She felt, similarly to me, that weighing the situation, it would be more unethical to leave women without any type of care. We acknowledged that I was crisis managing, a situation derived from devising a methodology that could be in flux. Furthermore, we decided that the moments where I was acting to control a crisis would not become part of my ethnographic research, as these were times when I fully donned my 'volunteer' hat, wholly working to aid the Breddon Centre.

While I was not required to revise my ethics application form, this is an instance that could possibly have been supported by a more robust ethics process. As research ethics is quite often negotiated in practice, it is not uncommon to see changes being made to the research study. Thus, a continuous check-in with an ethics board might have given me a firmer grasp on how to manage the situation I was in. There were moments where I hoped I was doing the right thing, and these fears and anxieties could have been allayed by a formalised review. Nonetheless, I was able to effectively manage the ethical questions my research project raised.

Becoming a part of the environment, I sought to observe was an exercise in negotiating ethical tensions. I don't know if I always made the right choices or said the right thing. It's quite likely that I did not. But I stopped seeing my field subjects simply as participants. They were people in need of support. And I was somebody who had the means to help them. There were clear moments when I was conducting research. I conducted interviews with 25 participants. But, while these gave me a formal glimpse into my participants' lives, it was the blurred moments where I became part of the action: by listening to a client reveal a prolonged history of domestic abuse; watching someone marvel over a picture of her foetus; and help another figure out her housing situation that allowed me to not simply hear about women's experiences but feel it. Negotiating ethics in practice requires us to confront the messy terrain of human existence. While ethical principles are important roadmaps to adhere to when working with vulnerable populations, it is inevitable that we will encounter dilemmas that test this narrow definition of ethics.

What do we do in those moments? Yes, we should strive to do no harm in the field. But what if we sought to construct methodologies rooted in care, that gave while it took?

Summary of reflections

The methodology I employed in my PhD project – an 'observant-participation' – gave me deep insights into the social world in which the Breddon Centre was located. At the same time, this methodological choice necessitated flexibility, which was best evidenced by the ways in which my role in the Breddon Centre changed the more embedded I became. While ethical principles can be important roadmaps to understanding what to do in certain situations, they are not exhaustive. There will be moments when the PhD project encounters new scenarios. I suggest we employ our 'ethics in practice' by keeping our focus on human dignity, respect, and researcher accountability. As such, I argue in this chapter that we must focus on 'doing no harm' within the context of the environment in which such harm is located.

13

Methodology unravelled: safely crossing the research minefield

Liam Miles
University of Northampton

Liam's PhD explores how young people in Birmingham are impacted by the cost of living crisis when considering the backdrop of a global risk society.

Introduction

As the global economy faces perpetual collapse with little signs of immediate revival, there is a mutual experience of precarity and risk within all realms of life, ranging from the institutional to the familial. This became rapidly clear to me as I embarked on my PhD journey at Birmingham City University (BCU) in 2021. I first came to BCU in 2017 to begin my undergraduate studies in criminology. My reasonings for studying criminology were not dissimilar from those of the students who I now teach. I wanted to learn more about society and why people committed crime. I wanted to make a difference. I originally wanted to join the police force or prison service upon the completion of my undergraduate studies. It was at this stage of attending university that I became exposed to unique theoretical approaches that awakened my critical consciousness, particularly Critical Criminological and Social Theory which have very much inspired my research interests. This influenced me to abandon my original plans, and excitedly, I decided to pursue a career in academia. Throughout my undergraduate journey, I made life-long friends and had many experiences that shaped who I am today. I also worked in the student union for a year as a sabbatical officer for student academic experience. During this time, I became inspired to develop a safety on-campus campaign in response to growing concerns of violence on and around campus. This motivated me to pursue this topic further in a scholarly capacity. I graduated in the summer of 2021; this was one of the proudest moments in my life. Immediately, I moved upward to my PhD in social sciences in September of the same year after having been interviewed and accepted onto the program. Despite my acceptance and the pride and contentment that encompassed it, I also felt somewhat underserving of my achievement. I felt quite overwhelmed by the self-questioning of 'Am I good enough?' and 'Can I do this?'

This affected me greatly at a time when I should have been overjoyed with the thought of my future career and academic development; as I reflect now, I think this is connected to the fact that I had not completed a master's and most of my competition had just completed theirs. I worried about what people's perspectives of me would be, and through this, I felt a sense of alienation and isolation, and I dwelled upon whether I had earned what I had achieved. Yet I was determined to prove myself wrong and to embrace the PhD journey from the start. I appreciated that this topic differed from what I had been taught in my criminology degree. However, I recognised that this topic contained significant potential to understand better community studies and the political economy. My PhD topic sought to explore how young people in Birmingham participated in activism in their communities in response to an urban and social issue through a youth-led participatory action research methodology (YPAR) that is a method premised on participant observation and ethnographic elements. At the time of writing this chapter, I have completed data collection and analysis and have submitted a first draft of my thesis to my supervisors for review.

Through a participant observation approach, my PhD research is on the cost-of-living crisis (COLC) and how young people in Birmingham have been affected. Halfway through my PhD journey, I changed my topic due to difficulties in obtaining funds for participants and I wrote an extensive report to my supervisors justifying why this conceptual and methodological change was necessary. With this bump in the road, the fundamental necessity was to keep the project on track for completion by considering a fresh approach that would enable data collection. As my PhD was funded by my university, I felt an overwhelming amount of pressure (which I now realise I put upon myself) regarding the timeframe of this substantial reconstruction, however, I was fortunate enough to receive copious amounts of support and assurance from my supervisors that this was the correct decision to take and that I should immediately proceed. My reasonings for this drastic change were underpinned purely by recognition of the structural conditions across the wider higher education sector and communities.

This chapter will draw upon my experiences and challenges in accessing participants through the YPAR approach that compelled me to reconsider a fresh conceptual and methodological approach. It is recognised that YPAR and PAR, more broadly, is an exciting and interactive methodology that historically has served beneficial purposes to the academic community and local communities themselves (Bertrand and Lozenski, 2023). It is equally recognised that YPAR often requires money to incentivise participants, especially if the project is forecast to be long duration, which applied to my PhD project. This chapter emphasises the importance of considering structural (social, political, and economic) conditions when undertaking any research involving other people, particularly within community studies.

Undertaking a methodological U-turn!

Upon starting my PhD, I was always told to ensure the project stays on track to completion as this is essential for funding purposes and desirable for securing full-time jobs at later stages. As much as I am aware that these aspects are of high importance, and part and parcel of the funded PhD journey, this does not mean that the anxiety of the pressure to perform and achieve such aspects does not take over at times. To do a PhD is to be a project manager and to ensure that everything runs smoothly. Akin to this, I was told to make sure I begin talks early with potential gatekeepers, stakeholders, and participants, especially considering the long-term duration intentions of my YPAR methodology. To undertake YPAR or just participatory action research (PAR) means to work 'with' participants to identify an issue and work together for resolution. The role of the researcher here is to identify gatekeepers, stakeholders, and participants, facilitate the process throughout and ensure the project is kept on track. Some consider PAR to be revolutionary in thinking and practice as the researcher moves away from traditional practices in the social sciences that historically were and, in some cases, continue to be today a process of extraction, exploitation, and laden in discourses of power (Kemmis, McTaggart, and Nixon, 2013). These traditional practices saw the participants being researched 'on' rather than 'with', and similarly as a mode of experimentation and observation that was favoured in early anthropological and sociological research (Leavy, 2020).

In recognition of these unethical legacies that still exist across the landscape of research in the social sciences to this day, I was keen to observe good practice by working with young people in their communities through a PAR approach while considering my positionality. The plan of action was to conduct an eight-to-ten-week YPAR approach within which the young people would steer the project to conduct an activist project in response to a socio-political or environmental issue that they mutually identify. Inevitably and unlike traditional modes of qualitative research approaches such as interviews and focus groups, a YPAR approach was of long duration and required commitment from all parties involved. Fundamentally, I believe that if someone undertakes work, they should receive monetary payment or at least some reward and incentive for undertaking the work. Even in the context of research participation, this should remain the case. I hold this view for two key reasons. First, because we are living in a cost-of-living crisis, and time is money. If people are spending their time volunteering and not getting paid, this will inevitably impact their opportunities to make money for their livelihood as their time has been reduced. My doctoral research on the cost-of-living crisis has shed light on the extent of the issue across the country, thus emphasising some of my values. Second, to compensate someone for their time means you are establishing a balancing act of power between yourself as the researcher and the participant, as both parties can benefit. It is recognised, however, that this could equally constitute a reinforcement of power dynamics, although it is arguably less so compared to undertaking free labour, particularly as there is a benefit for all parties. Within long-duration methods such as PAR, these incentives can be negotiated in reflection of the required timescale of commitment.

To further support this, I was looking to work with young people in their communities across East Birmingham, which is categorically considered by Birmingham City Council to be extremely deprived and under-resourced (see Birmingham City Council, 2019). Considering this, I made it a core priority to ensure that funding was secured to incentivise young people to be participants in the study. I reached out to numerous youth-focused organisations across East Birmingham, including youth and sports clubs, cadets, and wider community centres, to gauge responses. I spoke with the centre leaders (gatekeepers), who mutually responded by informing me that they found my project to be of interest. However, they cannot foresee long-term engagement among their young people, who essentially would be asked to volunteer their time with no foreseeable reward. In all honesty, I felt discouraged by this, as I'm sure many PhD researchers would at this stage in their journey. Yet, I tried to not let this impact my progression. And so, I furthered my mission to secure monetary funding for young people to take part. The calculations were based on the number of young people (approximately 16 to 20 splits over two groups) who would be paid up to the minimum wage per hour for the time they commit (approximately two hours per week for eight to ten weeks), and it became clear that the costings would run beyond £1,000. I began by approaching the university for internal funding, and this was approved up to a maximum of £500. I then explored additional internal funding streams and faced little luck. When I considered the ethos of universities that are largely centred around enhancing opportunities for research, particularly those that possess potential for social and community impact, I felt disappointed and let down.

Nonetheless, I then took my quest externally and searched for funding through grant providers such as National Lottery England. I submitted a bid and had no luck. Mentally, I felt drained, especially with the looming realisation that no internal or external funding bodies could not support me. Thankfully, however, I realised that I was not alone. At this time, I joined a national committee dedicated to discussing and collaborating on UK-based PAR research, addressing issues ranging from securing funds to upholding the values of PAR in daily practice. I spoke with an endless number of colleagues both about this issue and who shared similar experiences with me. The general themes of these conversations involved colleagues who set out to undertake PAR and failed to recruit participants due to a lack of incentive. This helped me to feel less isolated during my struggle, and this reassurance, knowing that I was not alone in my pursuit to seek approaches of effectively undertaking YPAR with monetary constraints in mind, enabled me to keep a positive mindset. However, I continued to face rejection from youth organisations who understandably did not want to commit the young people they worked with to a project with no visible and immediate benefit. It has been increasingly noticed that the budgets held within youth centres and wider organisations have been significantly reduced in the wake of austerity politics that accelerated in 2010 (Davies, 2018). The youth organisations were never unwilling to engage in the research itself. However, their mobilities to take part in such a project were hindered by the lack of incentivisation from my side and their own internal funding issues that, under austerity, have had to be rediverted and prioritised. The youth workers whom I negotiated with often said that the project should be shortened to entail a week or two maximum. I knew that this would significantly weaken the impact of the research as less data would be collected. I also considered the validity of a claim to a PhD study, as the data may not have reached the benchmark nor been enriched enough to constitute several discussion chapters. I began to feel immensely anxious about the development and success of my PhD, and the entirety of its existence altogether. These barriers were presented when a youth worker emailed me the following:

> Good afternoon, Liam and apologies, for the radio silence. I did actually bring up your proposal and the documents in our most recent team meeting. Unfortunately, in speaking with the volunteer coordinator and youth lead they believe that the project is too much of an undertaking for our young people who are already finding is challenging with their education/work and committing to the milestones in our programme. I'd be happy to set up another meeting with them if you would like to try and convince them otherwise. Whilst I attempted to mention the mutual benefits and the voucher incentives, I don't think it influenced enough. Apologies and good luck with the work around the research.

This response is reflective not only of the youth workers' willingness to support a research project but also of wider structural conditions within which their hands were tied as barriers became evident. This realisation made me consider to what extent is such research practice feasible in times of economic crisis. I began to recognise the depths of disempowerment facing youth workers across the sector. I equally felt disempowered and helpless in recognising that structural conditions steer much of our everyday life, including how we interact with one another. I was determined to work around this though, and this mindset enabled me to consider alternative paths both to my research delivery and research philosophy. During this time, my PhD project was nearing the end of the first year, and I had no plan to start data collection.

I felt an unsurmountable pressure to keep this project on track, and every spare thought went on how I could make this project happen. One of my key priorities was to ensure that the project remained on track for completion. I have always been interested in learning more about issues of cost-of-living and wider structural inequalities, and it occurred to me that I should change my approach to conduct research that is more targeted and methodologically practical. I engaged in conversations on the cost-of-living crisis and how it can be better understood within a community-based context. The following section will expand on these barriers to research I experienced in the earlier stages of my PhD journey by shedding light on the wider political economy and structural context within which we, as community members and academics, are expected to successfully come together and produce high-impact research. Moreover, research that matters to people and communities, not just for compliance with metric-driven research strategies, is commonly found in neoliberal universities.

What are we up against? High-impact research and neoliberal structural conditions

It is necessary to highlight the background context to the challenges I faced throughout the gatekeeper and stakeholder mapping process. It is no secret that the higher education sector has become increasingly neoliberal in its thinking and practice. Academics are positioned as producers to a consumer body of students whom they teach (Miles, 2023). Fundamental neoliberal characteristics predicated on risk, precarity, self-sufficiency and volunteerism are woven into the fabric of the research field. As discussed earlier, one key challenge I faced was securing university funding for my research. While I recognise the limitations produced through budget constraints, I equally recognise that forecasting such expenditure necessary to conduct participatory action research in communities should have been considered both by me as the researcher and by the institution that accepted my methodology proposal with full acknowledgement that participatory action research often requires incentivisation, particularly through monetary exchanges. Essentially, I was asked to recruit participants for the longevity of this research project with no source of incentivisation for their participation. It is significant here to remember that my participants were young people who lived in Birmingham's East corridor, and according to data from Birmingham City Council's Inclusive Growth Strategy (see Birmingham

City Council, 2021) is one of the most economically deprived and under-resourced wards in the West Midlands.

It is not feasible, therefore, to lean onto the values of volunteerism that I was tacitly encouraged to embrace. This stood entirely against my ethos on exploitation and extractive research that historically has been put onto communities and has rendered community members disenfranchised and sceptical towards the intentions of local authorities, public services, and academic institutions. While some might argue (see Grant and Sugerman, 2004) that it is unethical to offer a monetary incentive for collaboration as it will weaken the participant's integral motivations for taking part and it will establish a hierarchy of power, I argue the contrary, that by offering an incentive and compensation for time, it is a symbolic recognition and respect for the time of the participant whose contributions are so invaluable to our research and our subsequent impact. The news that the university had limited funds for my research produced significant barriers to engaging with youth stakeholders and gatekeepers. Upon engaging in local and national policy-based literature, I realised that this was a testament to the wider neoliberal conditions, particularly those of the Big Society Agenda. In 2010, the Conservatives came to power and established a Coalition with the Liberal Democrats. Core to the agenda was that of the production of a 'Big Society' and 'Small State', as advocated for by Margaret Thatcher in the late 1970s and 1980s (Williams, 2019). Core values involved Active Citizenship, which is predicated on community-based volunteering, and consequentially, money was poured into youth service initiatives such as the National Citizens Service (NCS) and the Duke of Edinburgh Award Scheme (Mills and Waite, 2017).

On the surface, these initiatives appear beneficial for the upskilling of young people. However, the fact is that many people who advocate on behalf of such schemes negate the fact that to participate, you need initial social and economic capital in the first place, not to mention the luxury of time. Many of the young people who I later engaged with as part of my PhD research simply did not possess these capitals and subsequently found themselves increasingly in positions where any spare time away from study was spent working to provide an income for themselves and often for their families. Before I met these young people, however, I had suspicions that these lived realities would exist, particularly when I engaged with fiscal and local economic-based data. Therefore, my motivations for ensuring that no young person participated in my research without reward or real incentive was solidified through the realisation that they would likely face exclusion from schemes such as the NCS and DofE. Therefore, how can these young people participate in my research? All these combined factors provoked me to consider the practices of participatory action-based and community-focused research.

As academics, we ought to consider how we can engage effectively with community members within their communities in reflection of the fact that the cost-of-living crisis has and continues to play such a detrimental role in producing barriers and modes of exclusion away from the government-led goals of 'active citizenship'. Moreover, what role does my positionality play in reproducing some of these barriers and pillars of exclusion? Such thinking led me towards the idea of 'Life Politics' from the perspective of Anthony Giddens (see Giddens, 2005) who advocated for a reflexive turn among researchers and thinkers as late modern conditions and globalising forces influence the everyday constitution of the self and our subsequent positionality. I actively consider my own positionality as a white, heterosexual male from middle-class underpinnings who is attempting to engage with multicultural communities across Birmingham's East corridor. I recognised that I may have faced initial barriers to engagement even with incentivisation and therefore, I strove to ensure that all barriers were quickly identified and mitigated. This account exposes the harsh truth that under neoliberalism, people are increasingly expected to engage in their communities and within wider socio-cultural institutions with little reward or incentive. This triggered me to consider how as academics, we are driven to conduct high-impact community-based research with little monetary capital from both the side of the institution and these communities themselves. I considered the role of the cost-of-living crisis in driving these barriers, particularly concerning young people. Additionally, driven by the requirement to keep my project on track in accordance with its timeline, I opted to drastically change the focus of my PhD to investigate how young people are affected by the cost-of-living crisis in their communities in Birmingham, as opposed to activism and youth and community participation in a broader sense. Although I acknowledged this change was extreme and would come with new barriers to break down, I knew that deep down inside, it would be for the better. And so, I chose to undertake a participant observation research methodology based across youth centres in Birmingham that was met with semi-structured interviews with predominantly young people and supplemented with the voices of youth workers.

I spent a considerable amount of time thinking about the practicalities of such a monumental change. I drafted an extensive document for my supervisors, explaining the rationale behind my motivations for changing my topic. I was fortunate enough to receive ultimate support from my supervisors, who mutually recognised the scale of the challenges I was facing and agreed that a new plan of action was required. I felt an instant sense of relief and immediately after formally receiving their approval, I began the transition process. I felt like I had a new lease of life. I began constructing a new strategy for engaging with gatekeepers and re-writing my methodology chapter, which, at this time, I had completed a full first draft reflective of the YPAR project on activism. So, too, did I begin re-drafting my literature review which again needed to reflect the cost-of-living crisis, specifically within the Birmingham and West Midlands context. Fortunately, I did all these tasks side by side with each other and made it one of my priorities to engage with youth centres in reflection of my new research methodology and focus.

The benefit of participant observation-based research is that it is quite cost-effective, especially when you require no involvement from your participants except for their permission to be in their space. Adjoined to this, I secured £150 from the university to pay for 15 love2shop vouchers at the value of £10 each. This was a fantastic feeling when I considered the struggle that I endured previously. Numerically, this was enough for 15 participants to take part in a semi-structured interview with the incentive of a £10 voucher for an hour of their time. I knew, however, that 15 interview participants were simply not enough for a PhD qualitative study. For example, according to Braun, Clarke, and Gray (2017), an appropriate amount is between 20 and 30 interview participants to validate the research. I knew, therefore, that I needed to secure more funding to reach more young people. Or, I would have to rely on the good faith of young people to be willing to participate with no monetary incentive. I opted to pursue the former option and applied internally and externally for extra funding, with little luck.

This experience alone brought forth the conditions of neoliberalism to my consciousness as the competitive conditions for bidding became increasingly apparent, and it eventually dawned on me that I would need to rely on the goodwill of some young people to partake with little incentive. Surprisingly for some, however, as I spoke with more young people, I quickly realised that they wanted to talk to me with no intention of receiving any reward. I asked these young people why they did not want a voucher for their participation, and although verbalised differently, their responses came under one umbrella reason as to why. This was because their lives had been so negatively affected by the cost-of-living crisis that a £10 love-2-shop voucher possessed limited incentive. Alternatively, they wanted an opportunity to share their lived experience on the cost-of-living crisis with someone they considered to have the power, influence, and capital necessary to pass these lived experiences onto the people in power. This speaks to another tune, particularly around youth voice and political engagement, which, as social thinkers should always be on our radars.

The following section will take these conditions and experiences and inform you as the reader how you can seek new opportunities in response to the socio-economic climate. Moreover, how you can engage with your universities and grant holders to gain the best forms of support that ensure your research is high impact and benefits the communities and social groups we set out to work with and understand.

Responding to structural conditions

This final section will consider ways of seeking new opportunities and methodologies in the face of adversity. Here, I have taken you, the reader, through a journey laden with barriers, obstacles, and arguably little incentive to do research within such community-focused methodologies. However, as I discussed earlier, it is possible to re-adapt your approach in the face of adversity, much of what is required involves support and active involvement from your supervisors. Each PhD student is likely to have a unique relationship with their supervisor that slightly differs from that of their peers. Some students recall horror stories where supervisors have consistently been disengaged, uninterested, and simply too busy to pay their student and their research at the time of day. Meanwhile, other PhD students recall having supervisors who are actively engaged and supportive throughout the journey. I was lucky enough to experience the latter. I had supervisors who were so encouraging and supportive and, moreover, trusted me to do my job to the best of my ability, yet were always there to catch me if I fell off the ladder. I am aware that, unfortunately, not all PhD students are lucky enough to have the positive working relationships with their supervisors that I was fortunate enough to experience. I recognise, therefore, that much of the advice and tales of wisdom in this chapter may not be recognised by all, however as I shall explain, it is not only possible but crucial that if you are reading this as a PhD student, you utilise your own skills and knowledge to keep your project on track and conduct high-impact research that you will later be proud of.

To begin, I believe that it is essential that you consistently keep track of your progress through effective timeline planning. This will help you to see what stage you should be at and if you are in line to complete within the funded period; often this is three years. Even if you are fully funded, it is in your interests to ensure that the project remains on track to completion as so to avoid paying excessive fees. My own PhD was fully funded for three years, and I knew that year two was the ideal time to collect data, enabling me to complete the analysis and write-up in year three.

It was at the end of my first year when I realised that PAR was leading me nowhere and it was at this point where I needed to make the necessary changes. Alongside this, and especially when we conduct social, political, and economic-focused research, it is essential to keep tabs on existing socio-political climates and how ruptures can affect our research. Although the cost-of-living crisis has always existed, particularly under austerity politics, the term cost-of-living crisis did not emerge until national inflation and subsequent accumulations of debt began to affect the middle classes in addition to the working classes who traditionally have always paid the price. It became clear to me that the cost-of-living crisis was bound to impact my research, as increasingly people do not possess the time to participate in research, especially when they are working so hard to feed themselves and, in many cases, their families and keep a roof over their heads. Therefore, by keeping up to date with national and global affairs, I was able to forecast certain ruptures at local levels that, in my case, specifically served to justify the rationale of my topic. It is of crucial importance to actively seek modes of financial support through the universities who employ us and, if necessary, wider and external funding bodies who can see the necessity of our research and support accordingly. Naturally, this requires extensive and consistent engagement and acts of persuasion. The neoliberal climate means that you will be rivalling other researchers for funding and while it is highly likely that their topics will be of equal importance, it is necessary that you make yourself known to those who have the power to pull the purse strings. I maintain here that I do not advocate for nepotism nor neoliberal practices of individualisation, however, it needs to be recognised that you and your research topic are important and worthy of a significant contribution. As such, it deserves the necessary attention and support. As you seek out support and funding, it is important to consider the feasibility of your research and whether it is practical amid the structural conditions under which you operate.

Reflecting upon my research, I should have known better than to assume that the university faculty budget would stretch so far as to fund a YPAR project comprising of 20 young people split into two groups over an eight-to-ten-week period who would be paid the living wage per hour for their time. Upon reflection, I was very naïve and held too high of an expectation to think this was possible. Moving forward from my PhD, I will ensure that all research is met with consideration towards structural conditions. Equally, I will ensure that all talks regarding foreseeable expenditure are extensively discussed with my superiors before setting out to achieve such a goal. This reflexivity is a practice I urge all readers of this chapter to participate in. There is also a bitter truth that exists in that no matter how much we strive to plan and mitigate risk, for as long as neoliberalism exists as our mode of political economy, we will continue to face competition, narrowing opportunities, risk, and rivalry against people who in the absence of neoliberalism could be our counterparts. This leads me onto another theme around working collaboratively and not falling into the neoliberal trap of individualism. For many, the PhD is a lonely journey, particularly as the researcher becomes further engrossed in their work. Often, we forget that others experience the same issues we do. This shouldn't be surprising when one considers the social conditions in which neoliberalism depends upon to thrive. These are driven by hyper-competition, rivalry, and rampant individualism in thinking and practice. Therefore, when we consider issues to be our problem and no one else's, we willingly re-perpetuate such divisive values. It is important to consider, therefore, that as Early Career Researchers and Academics, we are likely to face similar, if not the same, obstacles in our work, although some may experience it more than others. It is imperative, therefore, to establish and nurture cohesive support networks both internally and externally to our institutions to collaborate and share ideas. So too, can we come together to establish new methodologies in research in which the practices are safe, ethical, and manageable. Akin to this is sharing experiences to enable the forecasting of such conditions beforehand. For example, if it is commonly understood that PAR may require a monetary incentive for participation and there is a rising cost of living that is affecting businesses, institutions, and households on national and global scales, perhaps this be food for thought when seeking to undertake research projects at this scale.

The sharing of experiences by colleagues achieves two purposes. First, to resist neoliberal conditions of competitive individualism. Second, to accurately forecast the necessity for expenditure and subsequent planning for the potential for an alternative option. However, this isn't to say that PAR and similar methodologies are not manageable. It is always worth speaking with your university and potential external grant providers to see if they can support your research. It must be reiterated here that a core quality of the researcher is to seek alternative methods in the face of adversity and to identify challenges before they implode. This is to maintain the integrity and time management of the project, which benefits all those involved.

Conclusion

To conclude this chapter, three key take-away points are reiterated to you, the reader. First, whether you are a PhD student or a seasoned academic, it is a normal part of the process to change course with your theoretical and methodological assertions. I call this growth, and my vision is that as Social Researchers, we should never settle for stagnation in our thinking and practices. Throughout the early stages of my PhD journey, I faced these challenges that required a growth mindset in response. Second, a simple truth exists that structural conditions and the wider economy will always play a role in shaping our experiences and responses when conducting research. To conduct research in any discipline is a highly politicised action that we would be ignorant to negate. It is important, therefore, to consider these structural conditions when setting out to conduct academic and community-based/led research. Considering how my research directly explored structural conditions and the cost-of-living crisis, I felt I had a moral duty to consider this in all my research practices. Equally, this aligns with who I am as an advocate for social equality and justice. Understanding structural conditions applies even more so when working with communities and vulnerable social groups. Last, in recognition of structural conditions, we cannot ignore the role played by neoliberalism. It is crucial that we actively abandon politics and social conditions predicated on competitive individualism and see methods of working collaboratively together to share ideas and practices.

Summary of reflections

I hope this chapter has served to benefit all readers from stages of Early Career Researchers to experienced academics in considering the challenges faced when undertaking research and the barriers that can be produced if structural conditions are not considered. As described throughout my chapter, the planning and conducting of a methodology can be like a minefield. You must tread carefully, as there may be threats where you least expect them. However, with thoughtful consideration you can chart a safe path through. The key positive message here is that those around you may struggle with the same issues, so never feel afraid to build and develop working networks where these issues, among others, can be addressed and mitigated. This further serves to present opportunities for us to think creatively, outside of the box, and develop resilience as we navigate the methodological minefield.

Editors' reflections: Part III

As our journey continues through the dense forests of academic exploration, we arrive at our third break – a clearing that provides respite and where we can catch our breath. Given the emotional and, at times, complex topics covered in the preceding chapters, we may be feeling a bit weary by now, but this pause is essential for us to reflect on the ground we have covered so far. Picture this clearing not just as a place to rest but as a crucial overlook where we can see how the terrain we have crossed has shaped our path. Each twist and turn in our recent chapters has forged new trails of understanding, much like a river carving its way through a rugged landscape. Here, we'll take the time to reflect on the intricate patterns and intersections that have emerged in these chapters, concerned with a host of potential dilemmas and challenges that, on first inspection, may be hidden from view.

In Chapter 10, Lisa Edge critically examines PhD students' challenges with complex trauma within the neoliberal university system. Despite the promotion of mental health awareness in higher education, Lisa argues that the structural and cultural barriers in academia can exacerbate the difficulties for students dealing with trauma. We are invited to consider how the competitive, individualistic culture of academia often mirrors the traumatic experiences of these students, making their academic journey particularly precarious. Lisa also critiques the commercialisation of 'trauma-informed' approaches, highlighting the importance of genuine safety and trust in supervisory relationships. Suppose you are a supervisor or considering supervising for the first time. In that case, Lisa also discusses that, by integrating trauma-informed principles, supervisors can create a more supportive environment, helping to mitigate the impact of complex trauma on students' academic and personal lives. Ultimately, in this chapter, Lisa challenges us to rethink the true meaning of inclusion and support within academic institutions.

In Chapter 11, Kyla Bavin shares her harrowing journey through the exploitation and immense pressures faced by postgraduate students, particularly those on partial scholarships. As a first-generation, neurodivergent student, Kyla candidly shares her experience of juggling academic responsibilities, multiple jobs, and parenthood, which led to severe mental health struggles and the eventual alienation from her child. She explores the dark side of academia, where institutions exploit the labour of early-stage researchers, driving them to the brink of collapse. Kyla also delves into the insidious effects of imposter syndrome, which perpetuates a cycle of self-doubt and vulnerability among marginalised students. Through her raw and personal narrative, we are invited to witness the psychological toll of academic exploitation and the profound challenges those striving to prove their worth in an unforgiving system face. Yet, amid the turmoil, Kyla's story is also one of resilience, reminding you that even in the darkest times, there is the possibility of healing and the strength to rise again.

Chapter 12 offers a compelling reflection on the ethical and methodological challenges encountered by Kavya Padmanabhan during her fieldwork. It invites us to delve into the blurred lines between researcher and participant as Kavya navigates her dual roles at the Breddon Centre. Her initial intent to observe gradually morphs into active participation, raising critical questions about the boundaries of involvement, ethical dilemmas, and the impact of her presence on the research environment. Through poignant examples, Kavya illustrates the emotional weight of her work and the necessity of reflexivity in handling ethically important moments. Yet, amidst these challenges, this chapter also carries a message of hope: the deep understanding and empathy she developed highlight the potential for research not just to study but also to contribute to the social world it seeks to understand.

In Chapter 13, Liam Miles chronicles his PhD journey and challenges while transitioning his research focus amid a severe economic crisis. As we navigate this chapter, we discover how Liam's initial ambition to study youth activism through YPAR was stymied by funding issues and structural constraints within academia. His struggle highlights a broader theme: the conflict between idealistic research methodologies and the harsh realities of neoliberal pressures on higher education. Liam's narrative emphasises the impact of the cost-of-living crisis on both participants and researchers, illustrating how financial constraints can hinder plans for community engagement. His experience underscores the need for adaptability in research approaches and highlights the importance of ensuring adequate support. Ultimately, Liam's shift to a more feasible ethnographic approach reflects a pragmatic response to these challenges, showcasing resilience and a commitment to impactful, community-focused research despite systemic obstacles. As you reflect on Liam's journey, remember that overcoming seemingly impossible odds is possible with flexibility, perseverance, and a willingness to adapt your goals to whatever hurdle may present itself on your own PhD journey.

As we pause to reflect on our journey so far, it is important for us to consider the themes that have emerged. We have delved into the complex challenges faced by PhD students, from the exacerbation of trauma by the neoliberal university system to the intense pressures and exploitation experienced by those on partial scholarships. We have also seen how the competitive culture of academia can mirror and intensify personal struggles and how critical it is for supervisors to offer genuine support to mitigate these issues. Additionally, we have explored the ethical dilemmas of fieldwork, where researcher involvement blurs with participant experience, underscoring the need for reflexivity and empathy. Last, the narrative of adapting research goals amid economic constraints highlights the importance of resilience and flexibility. These chapters collectively teach us that while academic and personal obstacles may seem insurmountable, embracing adaptability and support can transform challenges into pathways for growth.

In Chapters 14 through 17, we reach the conclusion of our symbolic PhD journey. However, beyond this point, a vast ocean of possibilities and potential challenges awaits those who have earned the title of Doctor. Chapter 14 features Dr Nick Gibbs, who, having recently defended his thesis, offers insights into the final stretch of the PhD journey and the pivotal decisions that follow its end. Chapter 15, presented by Dr Adam Lynes, reflects on a decade of experience post-PhD, revealing how imposter syndrome can linger despite professional achievements. In Chapter 16, Professor Daniel Briggs discusses the challenges of academic capitalism, balancing a critical view of academia's current state with an encouraging message about the value of the PhD experience. The final chapter, with Professor James Treadwell and his PhD students Chelsea Braithwaite and Owen Hodgkinson, explores the dynamic between supervisor and supervisee, underscoring this crucial relationship's reciprocal and evolving nature.

As one journey ends, another begins, and the lessons learned during the PhD can profoundly shape both post-PhD life and future supervisory roles.

PART IV

14

'Light at the end of the tunnel': the Viva and beyond

Nick Gibbs
Northumbria University

Nick's PhD research explored the use and supply of image and performance-enhancing drugs. Nick developed this thesis into a solo-authored monograph, *The Muscle Trade*, published by Bristol University Press in November 2023.

Introduction: The start of a new journey

The PhD process can sometimes seem interminable. Many post-graduate researchers perform a precarious juggling act throughout their studies, maintaining regular teaching commitments, taking on hourly paid marking, and perhaps orchestrating childcare responsibilities. This means that most full-time post-graduate researchers take around four years to complete, while those in part-time study tend to take approximately five to seven years (depending on funding and interruptions). Research indicates that a whole range of factors can act as roadblocks to completing a PhD, including relationship breakdown, having dependants, practical or bureaucratic issues with data collection, poor supervision, and personal extenuating circumstances (van de Schoot et al, 2013).

However, this chapter will, I hope, serve to leave the reader with some faith that there is *light at the end of the tunnel*. By good grace, I was one of the few who finished the process in three years, thanks in good measure to a fully funded studentship, consistently excellent supervision, and a good helping of privilege. This is something to bear in mind over the following paragraphs, which will first paint a notably optimistic picture of the much-maligned Viva Voce. The work will then offer some advice and reflections on the academic job market in the social sciences before finally emphasising the importance of building a professional network and one's reputation.

I started my PhD in late 2018 in a flurry of nerves, excitement, and a misplaced feeling that I had 'made it' in the world of academia. This latter emotion was soon extinguished when the mountainous task of assembling what became an 85,000-word empirical project dawned on me. Yet, allowing for a handful of existential breakdowns and stumbling blocks, I handed in my completed thesis in September 2021 and faced my Viva Voce panel on 1 December that same year. Ultimately passing with no corrections, I have been lucky enough to find myself in a lectureship at a fantastic research-driven university and, I hope, am well-placed to offer some counsel to any current or prospective PhD students who are concerned about the final hurdle of the PhD race, and what happens when it is all over.

Living la 'Viva Voce'

The Viva Voce, or simply Viva, is the oral examination that appends the PhD journey. Derived from the Latin phrase 'the living voice', the Viva is unlike any other exam that most have encountered or will ever undertake again. This form of PhD examination originated at Oxford University in 1917, and despite coming under some scrutiny from the academy since then (Stephenson, Jackson, and Wilkes, 2023), it remains the standard means of assessing PhD students' suitability to reach the promised land of being a 'Dr'. Often, students describe 'defending' their thesis, arguably the most helpful way of understanding the purpose of this examination. Simply put, the Viva involves a panel of internal and external examiners (all of whom have read the candidate's work) asking questions to establish the following:

- Is the thesis the work of the candidate?
- Is the thesis academically rigorous, ethical, and good enough quality to achieve the award of doctorate?
- Does the thesis make an 'original contribution' to the literature?
- Is the researcher able to justify the methodological and intellectual choices that they have made?

The examination is headed by an independent chair, with the other panel members including the candidate's supervisor, an internal examiner, and an external independent examiner. Typically, while the internal member ought to have at least some expertise in the subject area, it is the external examiner who is the subject specialist. Importantly, the candidate – in conjunction with their supervisor – can choose both the internal and external examiners and can, therefore, deliberately target an expert in the field who can appreciate and critique the thesis in question. The examination generally takes around two to three hours, and a candidate can have one of four outcomes: pass with no corrections, pass with minor corrections, pass with major corrections, and fail.

Like much of 2021, my own Viva experience was touched by the wretched hand of the pandemic. While Viva Voces have traditionally been conducted face-to-face, like many PhD candidates at the time, I had the rather anticlimactic experience of an MS Teams call to decide the fate of my journey. Despite this, though not necessarily 'fun', I found the Viva to be a very positive experience and, as I am ever the optimist, I'd like to share some tips about how to prepare, what to expect, and how to make the most of what should be a very productive dialogue. First, there is no getting around the fact that good preparation involves several meticulous, focused re-readings of your thesis. When the date is set for the examination, it becomes your task to know the document inside out, back to front, and upside down. Ensure that you can justify your methodological choices, that your intellectual arguments are watertight, that you can reel off your findings and analysis, and that you are comfortable detailing your conclusions and how your thesis adds to the existing literature. Depending on your learning style, you might want to write one-page summaries of each chapter or print off a copy and highlight key areas to increase your familiarity. It is also worth conducting post-submission literature searches to ensure that you are up to date with the latest research (sometimes you can wait several months between submission and your Viva, so publications might have come out that you haven't read). More cynically, what have your examiners published? And how might your work relate to their specific interests? This exploration might help pre-empt some obvious questions they might ask. It is also worth (selectively) engaging with the wealth of online Viva preparation videos. One particularly good protagonist of the genre is Tara Brabazon, whose YouTube channel and various publications (see Brabazon, 2016) were instructive in my own Viva preparation. Other sources to engage with include your specific university's guidance (which is usually housed on the website), the various blogs from successful PhD candidates (see Cooper, 2014 and Wood, 2022, for example), and simply asking recent successful candidates about their experiences if this is possible. Although grimacingly corporate in tone, it further pays to develop an 'elevator pitch' for your thesis. Try and distil what I am sure is a nuanced and delicate piece of work into one or two sentences that capture the essence of the project. It may also help to talk to those around you about your thesis. Inevitably, your loved ones will have witnessed you go through the PhD journey and may even be experts by proxy come the end of the process. As a rule, if you can succinctly explain your key points and topic to your family, friends, or colleagues, that is a sign that you are ready to take on your Viva panel.

This advice leads me nicely to the questions themselves. Clearly, there is no 'standard' list of questions, and your examiners will highlight what speaks to them and their expertise. However, from a scan of the literature, coupled with my own experience, there are a core set of questions that are worth specifically preparing for. Crucially, the questions commonly take a tapered approach (Trafford, 2003), starting broad and then homing in on the specifics of the research. Here are some questions (following this 'funnel' approach) that may well arise:

- Tell me what first interested you in your area of study.
- Please give us an overview of your project and the key findings.
- Talk us through your theoretical framework. Why did you choose to employ that perspective and how did it impact your research?
- Please provide an account of your methodology and tell us why you made these choices.
- What is your thesis' original contribution to knowledge and what have you added to the existing literature?
- If appropriate, how will your thesis inform professional practice or make real-world impact?
- What did you find most challenging when undertaking the project?
- What limitations were there with the research, and if you were able to start again, would you do anything differently?

This is far from an exhaustive list and covers just the most generic questions, but as the reader can hopefully discern, your thesis will be interrogated on several levels: from its 'headlines' and bigger picture relevance to the academic minutiae and fine details. Some students, myself included, are lucky enough to have a 'mock' Viva with their supervision team. Taking place a few weeks prior to the formal examination, I found this process extremely reassuring as I had questions fired at me and any weaknesses exposed in time for me to brush up before the day itself. However, if this is not possible, taking the mentioned preparatory steps should deliver you to a place where you feel like the expert that you are and are ready to give an excellent account of yourself. When that day does come around, a well-prepared candidate should be able to fend off any tricky questions (although I'd caution that there will always be one curve ball) and approach the day as an opportunity to learn from some fantastic minds, and ultimately improve your research as a result.

After you have fielded your examiners' questions, the examination group splits as you and your supervisor take some time to reflect while the examiners, overseen by the independent chair, discuss the outcome of the Viva. The good news is that candidates who make it to the Viva mostly gain a PhD. However, this is most commonly subject to minor or major 'corrections', which are essentially the examiners' suggested improvements to make the thesis the requisite quality to gain the doctorate. The verdict is then delivered to the candidate and their supervisor, and the chair draws a close to proceedings. For me, when the Viva was over, it was a rather anticlimactic moment as I sat there in my parent's spare bedroom, decorated in my best suit, as the MS Teams call ended with some hearty congratulations. However, as such COVID-19-secure arrangements are a thing of the past, I sincerely hope that you are able to celebrate, perhaps in the nearest pub, with your supervisor and cap off a monumental journey together.

To bring this section to a close, it is worth imparting some extremely helpful advice that I received in the months leading up to my Viva: your supervisor won't let you submit your thesis if they don't think that you are ready to pass. Despite research noting the lack of training that many supervisors get for steering their charges through the examination (Tonge, 2005), the prevailing wisdom is that if they know, they know. Equally, *nobody on the panel is out to get you*. Good academics are wedded to the continued production of excellent research, and everyone in the room ultimately wants you to do well and showcase the collective efforts of years of post-graduate study. Believe in yourself and enjoy having a room full of people who have read your work and have engaged with your ideas, because it happens less than you think if you become an academic! After all, this is the start – not the end – of your journey as a researcher.

The next steps: negotiating the academic job market

Chapters of this nature have a tendency to offer helpful advice around the Viva examination without addressing the post-Viva period when the successful PhD holder sets out on their voyage of the tempestuous seas of the academic job market. Therefore, it is important to document what lies in store after you have completed the PhD process. The heavily metricised, often exceedingly precarious higher education sector can be daunting for those who have already wrestled through their PhD and, although I would like to paint a picture of a post-Viva Eden, most of us enter something of a dog fight to reach the sanctity of that first secure academic job (Bone, 2020). Thus, I want to offer an optimistic yet realistic account of what to expect, before stressing the importance of building a professional network and 'finding your tribe'.

Like many academics, I began working full time in higher education just prior to handing in my thesis. Through my existing network, I was able to secure a role as a 'teacher in policing', essentially a full-time teaching contract working on the much-critiqued Police Constable Degree Apprenticeship (PCDA) and Degree Holder Entry Programme (DHEP). It is notably rare to enter the job market and immediately secure a full lectureship, and many of us begin life as academics being paid to teach and research 'on the side' (McGregor, 2021). Of course, not every PhD holder wishes to stay in academia (and in some sense, who can blame them, given the backdrop of managerialism, bureaucracy, and high pressure (Winlow, 2022)?), but I am speaking here as someone who is painfully infatuated by the intrinsic worth of knowledge production and cannot, therefore, capture the perspective of those pursuing (often far more lucrative) ventures in the private sector. I personally highly valued the opportunity to be in a classroom during that first role, teaching aspects of what I had studied for so long and would certainly not discourage those in the same position from applying for teaching-focused roles. However, a certain degree of graft is required to hoist oneself from a teaching post (which often do not actually require a PhD) into a role that allows you to flex your intellectual muscles by being research active. This period of your career may well come with sacrifices and some turbulence. Most notably, it is common for early career researchers (those up to seven years post-PhD) to make several moves around the country – and even overseas – in the pursuit of their dream job (McAlpine, 2012). Such marauding took me from my family home in Cheshire up to Leeds and ultimately further north again to Newcastle-upon-Tyne. There is also often a feeling during this period of having to snatch back time to engage in academic research, made more challenging by the busy schedule and energy-sapping nature of long teaching hours. But stick in there, you are building valuable confidence, classroom skills, and resilience that will ultimately serve you well.

Though I took the teaching route, other avenues frequented by early career academics are post-doctoral studies – where you undertake further independent research, commonly funded by one of the many extremely competitive schemes – or working as a research assistant (RA) on a different researcher's project. Though these routes do not give you classroom experience, they are a fantastic way to build your research portfolio, enhance your academic skills (especially as post-docs typically require you to expand your methodological knowledge), and see the inner workings of a funded research project. Again, these opportunities will be advertised and staffed through professional networks and the higher your profile as an aspiring researcher, the more likely you are to find a way into post-PhD research.

The elephant in the room here is that academia is fraught with insecure fixed-term employment, and the burden of this precarity disproportionally falls on early career academics (Enright and Facer, 2017). Often, fixed-term contracts – typically of six months to a year in length – are offered to those having just completed their PhD and, similar to my own experience on a teaching-only contract, you are expected to juggle a heavy teaching allocation (typically, universities look after their full-time staff's workload above that of fixed-term staff) while attempting to produce research and do some future planning. However, if you are an aspiring criminologist, you may well feel the bite of academia's precarity slightly less harshly. Particularly with the recent additions of the PCDA and DHEP policing program, the discipline of criminology is in high demand (Trebilcock and Griffiths, 2022) and therefore, compared to other subjects, is relatively hospitable for early career researchers. With this said, the practices of fixed-term insecure employment have long been noted as a sector-wide issue (Loveday, 2018) and you should be ready for a couple of years of academic entrepreneurship at the beginning of your career.

Conscious that I might be falling foul of the neoliberal dogma of discounting the structural issues with the HE sector and reducing my counsel to 'just work hard', it is also worth noting the role of luck and happenstance in securing a post-PhD position. Though universities are always hiring, you cannot control when that dream position might become available. Similarly, depending on where we are in the Research Excellence Framework (REF) cycle, universities might be more or less inclined to hire an inexperienced and lesser-published scholar and might instead focus their efforts on a tried and tested researcher. This is, of course, a highly cynical and political folly. With my own institution, as the next REF submission was a number of years away at the time, I was recruited along with several other early career researchers, presumably with half an eye on us as 'investments' rather than immediate REF successes. Other examples of luck might include an incidental conversation leading to an opportunity or a post-doc or RA post relating to your research area being advertised at just the right time. You can't control any of this, but you can be ready to take advantage of such opportunities if you are one of the fortunate ones.

My final advice to anyone looking to grab hold of that elusive lectureship is to make a publishing plan. In order to satisfy the entry criteria to most research-intensive universities, you will need at least two peer-reviewed publications as well as a PhD. I secured my current role having published an article from some of the theoretical side of my thesis, as well as collaborating with my former supervisor to write a research-led methodology chapter in a handbook. Though somewhat staggering when one steps back to consider just how much work and expertise this entry requirement actually represents (for a relatively modest starting salary), this is, unfortunately, the current landscape of higher education. Given this, it pays to start thinking about how you want to publish your PhD data, where, and with whom. I have been very lucky in that my thesis lent itself to several papers as well as a monograph (Gibbs, 2023), but this is in part due to a considered approach to how to best use my data to not only produce a reasonable volume of publications but also to say something important about my area of study. Ask yourself the following questions: can you see your thesis being converted into a book? Are there specific arguments or data that lend themselves to an original peer-reviewed journal article? Have you made any theoretical or methodological innovations that are worthy of being published in their own right? This is, again, where it pays to know your literature and to remain a lifelong learner by keeping engaged in your research area even after the PhD process is over. In essence, you are sitting atop a goldmine of some of the most relevant and up-to-date data there is on your topic. You are an expert, so go and show the world what you are all about!

It's what you know *and* who you know: the importance of building a network

Yet another unfortunate reality of contemporary academia is that we are often cast as atomised and symbolically violent agents, competing against one another and frequently reduced to bare-faced self-promotion in order to build our brand and profile (Gibbs, 2021). With an alarming corporate creep, platforms like X (formerly Twitter), LinkedIn, and ResearchGate provide a space for those who shout the loudest to flaunt their latest research, offer their wisdom on current affairs (not even necessarily related to their area of expertise), and aspire to be 'big names' in their discipline. It becomes the job of the newly qualified early career researcher then to balance the need to build a network and establish channels to promote their work, while not falling victim to the riptide of narcissism that has come to characterise this industry. Indeed, the reality of metricised higher education means that we must all develop something of a portfolio and a unique selling point in order to position ourselves as 'impactful' and (more to the point) fundable researchers. But I will argue, you can do this while maintaining some sense of dignity and poise.

First, think strategically about who is well-placed to act as a mentor to you during your early career years. This might be your (former) supervisor, a colleague who is a few years senior to you, someone at the top of their game in a role that you aspire to fulfil, or stakeholders who have an interest in your research area. Once you have identified these people, be bold. Send an email to that professor who you have always admired and tell them. Approach that mid-career researcher who wrote that paper that shaped your PhD and let them know. Crucially though, think about what you can offer them. In some sense, academia runs on goodwill, and it may be that your mentors are happy to altruistically have your back. However, a fantastic skill to develop is to understand how you might offer something mutually beneficial to that person. Do you have an idea for a paper and data ready to go that they could collaborate with you on? Could you be their RA and do an excellent job of their data collection, transcription, or analysis? Could you connect them with another contact or invite them to talk at a strategic event? Similarly, if you see a job opening at a university that you would love to work at, try and establish a connection in that department. Some might say that such tactics are underhand or unfair, but ultimately having well-placed people who think favourably of you will pay dividends. Though extremely cynical to say, much academic networking is that proverbial mutual back-scratching that is often talked about in corporate business. Most importantly though, be genuine and do this because you want to be a fantastic academic and do great work, not simply because you crave status or kudos.

Thinking about academic conferences, my advice will always be to take every opportunity to share your research and network while you are in your early career years. But don't necessarily get drawn in by the bright lights of the big conferences. Yes, for criminologists, the British Society of Criminology conference and Eurocrim are fantastic opportunities to engage with the discipline and meet a wide range of interesting researchers, but often the scale of these events somewhat stifles your opportunity to network effectively. Instead, think critically about which events might deliver the opportunity to have good quality and productive conversations with potential collaborators, mentors, or stakeholders. I am lucky enough to run a modest research cluster at my university and frequently host one-day specialist symposiums and workshops with around 20 subject specialists. Not only are these events the space for cutting-edge research to be shared, but they are also fantastic opportunities to meet those at the forefront of your specialism. Such events are often advertised through professional networks, and therefore, it pays to join all of these that you can. Symposiums of this nature are also often free or at least inexpensive, so you could even do a couple a year! A final note on these conferences is to present if you can. If nothing else, this gives you an identity at the event and should allow you to have something to say to your prospective contacts, who will be able to engage with your work as well as your social interaction. Presenting your findings also gets you into the habit of contributing rather than just observing, which is a must if you want to build a quality research portfolio.

But how can you get your name out there if you are still in the process of writing that first journal article or still building that monograph proposal for your publisher? One excellent solution to this common bind is to produce credible but non-academic outputs. Perhaps the most well-known outlet for research that is in its infancy or aspiring academics is The Conversation. Akin to high-end journalism, platforms like The Conversation, as well as various academic blogs like the British Society of Criminology Blog or various publishers' less formal outputs like Emerald's impact blogs, can be a springboard to getting your work out into the world and, if you pardon the pun, placing yourself in the conversation. With this said, do not feel rushed to publish for publishing's sake. Though paradoxical given the need for peer-reviewed publications in order to secure many academic jobs, afford your data the respect it deserves and be mindful of self-plagiarism with these first forays into the world of publishing. As such, hold a little back when writing such outputs, but give enough to introduce yourself to the reader as a credible and upcoming authority on your subject.

Conclusion

I hope to have painted a hopeful, if not entirely rosy, picture of the final throes of the PhD journey and what lies in store if you do pursue a career in the higher education sector. As a slight rebalance, it is worth stressing that, for me, being an academic is the only job I can ever see myself doing. In few other industries are you allowed the freedom to think, the opportunity to shape people's perceptions and views, and the license to pursue something that you are genuinely interested in. Therefore, while the first steps into post-PhD life can be arduous and testing, it really is worth it in the end. Ultimately, the Viva is rarely as scary as it is billed and should be a rewarding and gratifying experience. Similarly, your trek through the rugged terrain of entry-level academic employment can be made profoundly easier by a supportive and receptive network, an intelligent and forward-facing attitude, a well-formulated publishing plan, and a passion for making your mark and producing excellent work.

Summary of reflections

This chapter aims to provide an optimistic voice to those PhD students nearing the end of their journey, focusing on the much-maligned Viva Voce, the academic job market in the social sciences, and the importance of building a professional network and one's reputation. Based on my experiences of completing a PhD in Criminology, I offer you some pragmatic tips regarding how to approach and ultimately thrive in the Viva, including the appropriate preparations and what to expect during the examination. Following this, I have hopefully set out an optimistic yet realistic account of what to expect from the academic job market as an early career researcher. I touch upon routes into that coveted lecturer role, focusing specifically on teaching contracts, post-doctoral study, and research assistant work. This discussion is underpinned by an acknowledgement of the precarity and insecurity in the sector, as well as the role of luck and happenstance in securing that first full-time academic position. I emphasise the importance of creating a publishing plan as a long-term strategy. Finally, I discuss the importance of networking, encompassing insights on building an online presence and where and how to disseminate your research. My parting message is to hang in there because there is light at the end of the tunnel.

15

The whispers of doubt: ten years after the PhD and pervasive imposter syndrome

Adam Lynes
Birmingham City University

Adam's PhD topic was centred on the occupational choices of British serial murderers, with a particular focus on those who held predominantly driving-focused professions.

Introduction: Where to start?

In attempting to plan and ultimately write this chapter centred on the theme of imposter syndrome post-PhD, my thoughts repeatedly return to my recent attendance at the 2023 European Society of Criminology conference that took place in Florence, Italy. Yes, Florence is as beautiful and vibrant as we are told it is, full of culture, history and, most importantly, mouth-wateringly exquisite food. Looking back as I sit to write this chapter, I cherish the conversations and friendships I was fortunate to have and to build, and the memories that will not quickly fade, including me and a fellow colleagues asking locals if they could help us work out how the cigarette vending machines worked; visiting the local community swimming pool; eating gelato as we admired the beautiful architecture of the Baptistery of St. John and, of course, attending a variety of interesting panels.

On the face of it, this all sounds fantastic, and, indeed, I recognise the extremely lucky situation to be in when my employer funds me to attend such events. However, the lingering, sickening anticipation and dread of my panel talk are splintered deep within such memories – stuck between these moments of joy. I had arrived in Florence on a Tuesday, and unlike some of my more fortunate peers, my panel was not until Friday afternoon. Upon reflection, these positive memories were always corrupted somewhat with this very feeling of terror which, despite all my rationalisations of all the experiences I have since acquired post-PhD, I could never fully quell. I distinctly remember telling myself, 'Stop doubting yourself. Think of all the lectures you have given, look at the books and articles you have published – just stop doubting yourself and enjoy the moment!' Despite all this internal pep-talk, however, the nagging voice would always return, often accompanied by brief visions of some unidentifiable person standing at the back of the room – most likely some distinguished professor – declaring my ideas and work were 'redundant', 'shallow', 'simplistic', and, of course, 'simply wrong'.

As I write this, I picture this voice as dwelling deep within in a cave, occasionally coming up for air and sustenance in the form of my, for lack of a better phrase, positive energy. These visions I mentioned would manifest and take the form relevant to whatever moment I was worried and anxious about, such as, for example, the faceless professor decrying my lack of academic worth, the student laughing as I stumble over the next complex academic terminology, the dean stressing that what I have accomplished the past year just not being good enough and, now the most common, the reviewer who lambasts a paper or research bid I have spent months pouring my heart and soul into. For the last example, the following words are repeatedly stated: 'I just do not see the relevance of this, and it has zero impact'. These voices and accompanying visions would naturally get more frequent and visceral as whatever moment I dreaded drew closer. For instance, while I am, this moment, enjoying writing this chapter, the little pit in my stomach can already be felt: 'Will anyone actually like this?' 'Am I pitching this right?' 'How will my academic peers react? Will they now see me as a fraud?'.

Ultimately, while I know I am not alone in feeling like an imposter weighed down by self-doubt, perhaps my biggest worry comes in the form of a new vision whereby a crowd of academics filled with familiar faces I have come to know and call friends seeing 'behind the curtain', so to speak, and disappearing like the dad wandering into the local for the first-time post-divorce. However, despite these feelings bubbling to the surface, I hope this chapter provides some comfort to those who share similar feelings and to know they are not alone. I will begin this reflection all the way back to 2006 and trace key moments that spring to mind when I think of imposter syndrome. This may be rather chaotic, which I do apologise to the reader for; however, when reflecting on such emotive themes, time and space tend to become jumbled into a cacophony of feelings, faces, and moments.

Tracing the origins of my imposter syndrome

Before university, I was an average student, often receiving positive yet unremarkable reports from teachers who noted I could apply myself more. Like many, I had no clear career path, certainly not in academia or criminology (I wasn't even aware it existed!). Initially, I dreamed of becoming a marine biologist, fuelled by a fascination with sharks after watching

Jaws (1975) with my grandfather. He noticed my enthusiasm and gave me an old book on sharks, which I devoured, captivated by the mysteries of the ocean. However, my dream faded when I realised the top grades in natural sciences required for such a career were out of reach for me. Despite my middling grades, my parents were always supportive, with my dad assuring me, 'Doctor or street-sweeper – we would love you all the same'. I recognise how fortunate I am to have such support, something not everyone has. My grandfather's gift also sparked a love for reading, leading me from the ocean's allure to the fantastical worlds of Charles Dickens, Arthur C. Clarke, Isaac Asimov, and Philip K. Dick, where I found comfort and solace.

After my marine biology dream faded, I had no clear career aspirations. I moved through school without a specific plan, eventually enrolling in my local sixth-form college for A-Levels. When asked about my future, I vaguely responded, 'Not sure, but I'd like to do something that helps people'. Due to my love of reading, I applied to study English Literature at various universities but didn't invest much time researching courses or campuses.

Many can relate to the lack of encouragement to think critically in school, where the focus was on memorising content for exams to boost pass rates for league tables (Leckie and Goldstein, 2017). While I now appreciate teachers' challenges, I believe this approach reduces students to mere statistics, leaving them unprepared for university life and, indeed, the university of life. As I prepared for my A-Levels, the prevailing feeling was one of vagueness, like walking in a direction without a destination.

Everything changed one cold winter night in 2006. I had formed an unlikely friendship with two former secondary school classmates, and we decided to visit a nightclub rumoured not to check IDs. Excitedly, we planned how to get past the bouncers, what drinks to buy with our limited cash, and if there would be girls. The night was mostly uneventful – we got in, had a few beers, and mingled. However, as the night wound down, one of my friends argued with an older, clearly drunk patron. My other friend and I intervened to de-escalate, and it seemed resolved with apologies exchanged. As we left the club near midnight, debating how to get home, I noticed my friends' eyes widen as they stepped back. Before I could react, the drunk customer punched me in the gut. At first, I felt no pain, just a struggle to breathe. Then, one of his friends punched me in the face, knocking out a tooth and dislodging another. The assailants fled into the night. Stunned, I fixated on my mouth, holding my tooth and despairing that I'd only removed my braces a week before. As my adrenaline faded, I noticed a wet spot on my shirt and realised I was bleeding. Panic set in as the intense pain hit me. I will spare further details, but I later discovered that the older guys, angry from the earlier argument, had returned, and I had taken the full brunt of their attack. To this day, I still don't know why they singled me out.

When I think back to that night, I am reminded of the film *Sliding Doors* (1998), a story about parallel universes and how our lives can drastically change and diverge down different paths depending on events and our decisions. What if I decided not to spark a friendship with those two lads? What if I decided not to go out that night? Regardless, the subsequent weeks and months after that night are painful to recall physically and emotionally. I grew up in Handsworth, an area known for significant economic inequality and high crime rates. Yet, this moment completely shattered my sense of security, and I remember being angry that I let this happen. Hospitals and police visits were routine, and all this time, A-Levels became less and less of a priority. Before this took place, I had already applied to several universities based on my predicted grades. Still, if I am being honest, this was done largely because I had no idea what I actually wanted to do, and, naturally, this was not enough for me to keep my studies in mind within the context of what I was going through. I fell behind, was apathetic, and remember drinking more to cope with the pain. I also found solace and peace in my books, in fantastical imaginary worlds where I could temporarily escape.

As months passed, I sat my exams, knowing my heart wasn't in it. While at the airport with my family, my mum handed me her phone with my results. My heart sank as I saw how far I had fallen from my predicted grades. Despite my lack of effort, I hadn't expected to miss my target by such a large margin. My plans for the future were shattered, and my confidence crumbled. Although I was still accepted into Aberystwyth University for English Literature, the experience planted the seeds of imposter syndrome that would follow me for years.

University life and alienation

While I remember being excited at the prospect of leaving Birmingham and moving to the coastal town of Aberystwyth (a population of around 14,000 compared to Birmingham's 1 million), there was a nagging feeling at the back of my mind. From packing my bags and saying goodbye to school friends to being driven by my parents across the Welsh countryside, I distinctly remember thinking that I perhaps did not deserve this opportunity, that the university must have made an administration error, and that I would be sent packing straight back to Birmingham. As we drove towards the campus and up the infamous and locally referred to Cardiac Hill (it is so steep that lorries are advised not to drive on it), I recall that nagging feeling manifesting into palpable sweat. Along with the sense that I did not really belong, I was about to say goodbye to my parents and everything I knew for the past 18 years – my entire life up to that point.

I vividly recall the day my parents dropped me off at university, marking the start of a challenging journey. Soon after they left, I joined fellow students in my residence hall, where names and drinks were exchanged. Among these early encounters, I was nicknamed the 'slow Brummie' by my more southern, 'well-spoken' peers. While I laughed it off, the label deepened my imposter syndrome, making me feel like a fraud among brighter minds.

This insecurity was magnified in my first seminar, where I admittedly struggled to keep up. A friend from halls, who had boasted of being an 'academic prodigy', was in the same seminar, further intensifying my anxiety. The session focused on a Geoffrey Chaucer poem, and as the tutor asked each student for their thoughts, I felt increasingly out of my depth. When my turn finally came, I couldn't even grasp the question until it was rephrased multiple times. My peers' amused and astonished looks made me feel utterly inadequate, reinforcing the 'slow Brummie' label in my mind.

As the semester progressed, winter was accompanied by lots (and lots) of rain and storms that turned the once-calm waves into violent currents that clashed against the pier. Desperate to fit in and block out the sense of inadequacy, I spent much of my time in the local pubs socialising with those in my halls of residence. I had accepted the moniker of the 'slow Brummie' and performed to this label for cheap laughs and a sense of being accepted. I also spent little time studying, as doing so just brought up all the negative feelings I desperately tried to avoid and block out. In creating this what I call 'shield of denial', I infrequently attended my scheduled classes as I could not face the prospect of more laughter or ridicule. Looking back almost 16 years later, I now understand that many of my student peers benefited from private schooling and tuition. My experiences at school and college did not prepare me or give me the necessary skills for individual learning. However, I lacked this perspective and understanding and was afraid to be honest with myself, let alone anyone else, including an authority figure such as a lecturer.

During my first two years of undergraduate study, I barely scraped by, passing most modules but keeping my poor performance a secret from friends and family. I justified my lack of effort with excuses like, 'I don't really study' and 'What do you expect when you go out so much?' This mindset – avoiding effort to avoid disappointment – dominated my early university experience. However, things began to shift in my third year when I chose an optional module on science fiction, a genre I love. The topics excited me, but the module leader and seminar tutor truly changed my approach to academia. In one of the first seminars, we discussed Philip K. Dick's *Do Androids Dream of Electric Sheep?* (1968). I read the assigned book thoroughly for the first time, filling it with notes. While I was nervous in the seminar, the tutor's relaxed and humorous approach put me at ease. When it was my turn to speak, I had a lot to say but was hesitant. The tutor noticed my apprehension, smiled encouragingly, and gave me time to express myself.

Despite my frustration with my delivery, they reassured me with a smile and said, 'Some excellent points there, Adam; good work'.

Once the seminar was over, the tutor walked over to me and said they would like to have a quick meeting in their office. While I was nervous, their tone was positive, so I followed them down the corridor to their office. In this meeting, they noted that they did not recognise me from other modules, and from that, I started to list all the numerous reasons as to why I had been neglecting my studies. I do not know why I felt I could be honest with them. Maybe it was because they were the first lecturer to notice and show interest. Maybe it was because I needed to release all this built-up insecurity and frustration that had been bubbling under the surface over the past three years. They were understanding, and what really sticks with me to this day was when they said, 'Look, you have potential ... keep at it'. While it was not the silver bullet for my insecurities, I left their office feeling like a weight had been lifted. I spent the remainder of the year applying myself to my studies, and, to my surprise, I enjoyed it. I spent less and less time going out with friends and drinking, so I decided to go to the gym and spend my time in the university library. I could not completely reverse the damage done over the past couple of years, but I completed my degree with a 2.1 in English Literature.

A return to academia and the resurgence of imposter syndrome

I returned to Birmingham with my degree certificate in English Literature and a renewed sense of optimism. To be clear, at this point, I had no interest or inclination to continue in academia, having instead decided to pursue a career in the police. As I mentioned earlier, I had always wanted to work in a profession that helped others. As I reflect on that fateful night in West Bromwich, I think I wanted to help others who lived through similar experiences or, ideally, prevent it from happening to them. However, this was in 2010, and due to the new coalition government's approach to cuts to public spending (Disney and Simpson, 2017), there was a freeze on recruitment. 'Never mind', I remember thinking; I could instead join the Specials on a volunteer basis and gain the necessary experience. I took part in the assessment process but was informed that despite doing well, they could not even provide uniforms due to budget constraints. I resolved to see this through, so I decided to try to wait for this pause in recruitment to end. In the meantime, I applied for countless jobs ranging from a library assistant (at Birmingham City University, no less) to a security guard, but I received no responses.

With no job prospects, I searched for a qualification that might improve my chances of joining the police once recruitment resumed. Living close to BCU's Perry Barr campus, I found a criminology master's program that seemed perfect for policing and affordable with my criminal compensation money. Accepted into the course due to my degree classification, I felt optimistic – things were finally moving forward. I also cannot recall the usual imposter syndrome feelings during my master's. The lecturers were supportive, and I connected with the discipline in a way I hadn't during my undergraduate years. I was no longer labelled the 'slow Brummie', and my lack of criminology background wasn't criticised. In one of my first essays, a professor's feedback changed my life; they noted I had a 'nice writing style'. This shocked me, and encouraged by this feedback, I started attending morning breakfast sessions with the faculty, eager to learn as much as possible. This experience starkly contrasted with my undergraduate years, and I made sure to seize every opportunity to grow academically.

As my master's program neared its end, the professor who had praised my writing suggested I consider a PhD, expanding on my dissertation project. This suggestion was a pivotal moment for me, presenting two possible paths: academia or joining the police. I often wondered where I would be if I had chosen the latter, especially during challenging times like heavy marking seasons or paper rejections. Despite my excitement and acceptance of the opportunity, old insecurities resurfaced. Why pursue a PhD when I was so close to realising my long-standing goal of joining the police? This question often troubled me, and my answer would vary depending on my mood. Reflecting now, I realise that the professor's belief in my potential was crucial to my decision. Additionally, the desire to make my family proud influenced me. As a first-generation university graduate, I was motivated by my father's unfulfilled dream of further education, which his parents had discouraged in favour of immediate employment. The professor's encouragement opened up new possibilities for me, suggesting that I could achieve more and, perhaps, finally, overcome my inner doubts. Unfortunately, my struggle with imposter syndrome continued despite this encouragement, and my expectations were not fully met.

Adam Lynes, Associate Professor in Criminology and impostor

Apologies for the abrupt time jump; the preceding chapters have all done a far better job explaining the numerous and complex challenges one can face when undertaking a PhD in the Social Sciences. Instead, given my rather unique position of completing my PhD ten years ago, I wished to explore the origins of my imposter syndrome. My relationship with this feeling, I hope I have demonstrated, is a long and complicated one based on a myriad of decisions and life events – some I could control and others not so much. As will likely be no surprise, my imposter syndrome returned and was further compounded during my PhD. Looking back to this time, almost every facet of my experience only nourished those cave-dwelling voices. From the high standards and expectations, constant evaluations (in terms of research and teaching), and lack of clear guidelines to the overwhelming sense of isolation – when meshed together, you have a very potent environment for imposter syndrome to flourish. This is before even getting into the ever-increasing neo-liberalisation of higher education (Winlow, 2022), whereby academic community and intellectual curiosity have been supplanted with intense competition, ego, and the return to the dreaded league tables such as in the form of the National Student Survey, Teaching Excellence Framework, and the Research Excellence Framework. I am by no means immune to these cultural changes. The irony is not lost on me when teaching students the concept of *amour propre* (simply put, a sense of one's worth) and how our current political economy means this is now predicated on the downfall and failures of others (Rousseau, 1990; see also Hall, Winlow, and Ancrum, 2008). During my PhD years, I recall the distinctly mixed emotions of seeing others flourish and struggle and how I felt bad at the former and better at the latter when comparing my progress. It is important to stress here that this is a feeling that still exists even all these years later, and while I do my best to rationalise and quieten such thoughts, that voice in my head that tells me I am not good enough still fuels those knee-jerk reactions and emotions. I would not readily admit this in person and around my colleagues and peers, but to ignore it would be disingenuous of me and unfair to those reading this.

Reflecting on both the PhD journey and the years since passing the viva, I think another important factor I have only begun to understand is the relationship between my sense of self-worth and external validation. I believe that the need for others to recognise our potential or work is universal and extends beyond the walls of academia. However, I can now more clearly see how the nature of higher education only exacerbated my insecurities and need for validation from outside sources. If I chart the defining moments of my career, I can recall a familiar mantra I remember telling myself repeatedly: 'Once I get X, I will have made it, and I will finally believe in myself'. This mantra would naturally evolve over the years, including obtaining my Doctorate, getting my first peer-reviewed article accepted, getting promoted, having my monograph published, and, most recently, attempting to secure my first grant (at the time of writing this one is still eluding me). Each success, I thought, would be accompanied by the retreat and banishment of my insecurities and feelings of being an imposter. Unfortunately, these successes only seemed to make them worse, that I was, in fact, only making it more difficult for myself to hide and conceal my flaws as I moved from being an early career academic and into more senior roles with more significant responsibilities. If I were to close my eyes and visualise this process, it would not be so far removed from a gladiator about to step out into a Roman Colosseum. Each achievement was a vital piece of my armour as I would prepare for battle against my enemies – in this case, the aggressive peer-reviewer, disgruntled student, and faceless professor. The mid-module student feedback was my braces; the glowing peer review was my chest plate; my monograph was my helmet; and my PhD certificate was my trusty shield. Of course, no Roman Colosseum would be complete without the all-powerful Emperor observing from up high, dispensing either life to those who impress or death to those who failed to excite or win over the crowd's adoration. This important figure, naturally, would be the dean. However, in reality, by holding such an external endorsement so highly yet my own internal validation so low, I was, in fact, not building up my defences but instead making myself far more vulnerable than I realised at the time.

Only ten years after the PhD have I finally begun to reflect on what motivates me and why I struggle to feel a sense of belonging in academia. I believe I better understand the key moments that fuelled such sentiments, yet much work remains to be done. I am still susceptible to seeking external validation and need to remind myself that any feedback, good or bad, is not reflective of me as a person. I also need to remind myself that all of the feelings associated with feeling like an imposter will never be quelled while I continue to seek validation beyond myself. I think I can confidently state that if I were to secure a significant grant or be published in the highest-ranking journal in the discipline, these feelings would not only remain but only get worse! In many ways, I suppose writing this is a meaningful step in the right direction. Perhaps embracing vulnerability and lowering the proverbial shield I usually hold high when I write anything related to academia is the path towards embracing imperfection instead of the perfectionism we crave and are taught to achieve.

The one thing I do hope for is to use my experiences to help others. In discussing my plans for this chapter, one of my PhD students and co-editors for this book, Sarah Jones, pointed out that she has observed how I often approach students who are perhaps not engaging or talking in seminars and workshops. She explained how I would 'see the 18-year-old Adam who needed support and encouragement'. This was somewhat revelatory to me when she said this and, if I am being honest, emotional. However, it made perfect sense, and I suppose I ended up in a profession in a roundabout way that provided me with the means to help others. Perhaps imposter syndrome does not always have to be negative and, if understood and channelled in the right direction, can instead be an empowering means to relate and ultimately aid others on their own journeys, including pursuing their own PhD.

Remember, you are not alone

In bringing this chapter to a close, I always fear still being that mortified 18-year-old who messed up their A-Levels and the 'slow Brummie' who expected to be removed from university and who never really felt like they fitted in with the other, well-spoken, and better-educated students. To say I have, ten years after the PhD, the answers to overcoming imposter syndrome would be a lie. If I were asked to write on this topic only a couple of years ago, I would have attempted to convey a sense of overcoming such concerns and a series of well-ordered recommendations on how to incorporate them into the lives of others. However, as hopefully demonstrated via this brief journey into my imposter syndrome, each person's story and relationship with such feelings are unique, and each person needs to find ways that support their ability to navigate the academic environment – both during and after the PhD. If there is one morsel of guidance based on my experiences, it is that you have to come to terms with and accept that such feelings are likely not to go away anytime soon and that seeking external validation – be it via passing the PhD or becoming a professor – will likely not be the elixir we may be led to believe. To demonstrate this, we must return to where this all began: Florence, Italy.

Friday, the day of my talk, finally arrived. The voices that dwelt in the back of my mind had only intensified, and the visions of the faceless professor at the back of the room lambasting my presentation had only become more lucid and visceral. I contemplated pretending to be sick, that 'I really want to deliver my talk but just not feeling well'. To pass the time, a couple of the academics I had met invited me to have a coffee at one of the local restaurants. Seeing the look of worry on my face, one of these academics, renowned professor Daniel Briggs, whom I had only met a couple of days before, asked if I was all right, and that 'I looked like I was staring into some abyss'. I brushed off their question and attempted to portray the sense of confidence I had learned to emulate in my early PhD years – to mask the imperfections. They took a sip of their espresso and simply replied, 'You know what, Adam, I often feel at these conferences like I don't belong … like I'm not smart enough or well-published to be in the same room as some of these people'. As I have previously stated, I am aware that many of the feelings I have discussed are not unique to me, but it was the way this professor, someone whom I had idolised from reading their work, opened up at that moment. This individual, who could have easily been the faceless professor who haunted my visions, told me about their background, their sense of alienation at various universities, and feelings of never quite living up to standards that, as they explained, were put on themselves. We spoke for at least an hour about how neither of us felt like we belonged and shared similar nerves and anxieties about various academic scenarios, especially conferences. We finished our drinks, and I returned to the conference venue off the back of this heart-to-heart. My talk was not perfect; I suffered from the dreaded 'dry mouth' and had to rush through my slides due to the timing, but I enjoyed it all the same.

I suppose the message is clear here: most, if not all, of us — regardless of our respective stages of career or experience — have this shared imposter syndrome. However, I think the more important message is that it is okay to talk about this with others and occasionally let the guard or, more aptly, shield down. Perhaps if we did, we would no longer feel like imposters.

Summary of reflections

As you navigate your PhD journey and beyond, you may often feel like an imposter, doubting your place among a sea of highly accomplished individuals. This chapter, rooted in my personal experiences, hopefully serves as a reminder that you are not alone in these feelings. Whether surrounded by peers who seem more knowledgeable, facing critical feedback from supervisors, or dreading the scrutiny of an external examiner, it is important to recognise that even those who appear confident have likely felt the same at some point in their own academic journey. Imposter syndrome is a universal experience that affects not just students but also established academics and even seasoned professors with years of experience. As you progress in your academic career or decide to enter other fields, remember that self-doubt is a common thread that binds us all. Embrace it as part of your journey, knowing that your peers and mentors have often felt similarly out of their depth. Ultimately, we are all doing the best job we can, which is all we can hope for, and that is enough.

16

Fifteen years later, at the moral crossroads: retaining purpose and direction in the face of academic capitalism

Daniel Briggs
Northumbria University

Daniel's PhD in Sociology made use of ethnographic methods with crack cocaine users in South London over a period of 12 months. The PhD was undertaken part time over a period of five years as Daniel worked as a contract researcher in the London area.

Introduction: The status quo of academic life for the foreseeable future

So, you got your PhD well done. No small feat. You beat the odds; you defeated the isolation and inevitable lack of support on top of other personal stuff you may have had going on for you at the time. You probably took on exploitative teaching and admin responsibilities and buttered up senior academics in the process to get yourself into some temporary academic position. Well done. You bided your time, took on the extra favours like doing the seniors' jobs at times, flattered them, and cited their publications. You came across as 'the future', someone 'breaking through' who had immense potential to … just continue this ridiculous cycle just to get noticed in academia.

In these early exploitative roles in which you could not stop saying 'yes' to more work, you were encouraged to do the leg work for aimless and almost inevitably flawed research proposals which were either destined to be rejected or change almost nothing in society. The research seemed to have a good moral and social purpose, but the funder rarely seemed to shortlist your team. You reasoned you were unlucky and spent months rejigging your proposal only to receive bad news once again. Still, you convinced yourself to plough on and continue to submit proposals to be able to do social research, despite your elite intellectual and methodological training and drive and ability to do it without research funding.

Knowing what is expected of you as an early career researcher (ECR), post-PhD, you rigorously and admirably submitted articles to the most prestigious journals, awaiting glowing reviews from your peers who anonymously evaluated your knowledge contribution to the world. While a few publications came off after lengthy revision processes, you started to feel somewhat disheartened when some reviewers wrote so crudely and offensively about your work. Such comments from peers seemed unfair, almost irrational given how you had told yourself how 'the shared goal was to produce new knowledge'. It felt like some of these people were just taking their shit out on you incognito and that they had no vested interest in aiding your work with its potential to threaten their already-established knowledge hierarchies. But this was why you studied a PhD, right?

The teaching loads were heavy, and student numbers were high, but all this was worthwhile, you reasoned, given you had just started out. Eager to impress but also still committed to investing the same energy in every class and in every student. This was your duty, remember. There were a few successful instances in which this paid off when you saw the benefits of what happens when a minority of students blossomed and flourished. The majority, however, showed patchy interest and looked for shortcuts by plagiarising, getting help from Chat GPT or handing in idle contributions, which, when you juxtaposed it against the commitment you had given towards your own studies, made you start to feel aggrieved toward some of them. You figured times were changing, perhaps aloof to the magnitude of the general uptake in consumer hedonism and the general downturn in intellectual commitment and educational ability. This generation had begun to heavily commit to digital distractions and didn't even seem that bothered about meeting up to have sex with each other unless it was through an app, a trend further aggravated by questionable COVID-19 policies, which exacerbated already embryonic anti-social tendencies (Winlow and Hall, 2013; Briggs et al, 2021). Still – and even if it started to drain you – you were continually made to feel it was your responsibility to 'listen' to these students, 'engage', 'inspire', 'guide', 'support', and 'mentor' them: generally, do anything it took to make sure they graduated one way or another.

You started to get an early clue about how this may be playing out medium-to-long term but began to continually deny its impact on you, even if these experiences went against why you did your PhD in the first place. Institutional pressure in the form of 'performance reviews' and a general chase for academic kudos and personal recognition seemed to propel you on to continue to submit research proposals, strive for impeccable student survey evaluations, throw your publications at the highest impact factor journals, and juggle all this with insane amounts of pointless administrative duties. Instead, you began to disavow it all, craving the inconsequential yet newfound escapisms like a funded conference (aka 'academic holiday'): the paid trip, the new destination, the expenses to run up and claim, the event's grandeur, the dull and lengthy plenary rewarded by the free wine on the welcome night. Life was good. The PhD was worth it, remember?

And this is how it continued for a few years. And your ambition was compensated with promotion and a wage increase. You got a few citations. There was intermittent media interest in your work, and you did a few interviews albeit resulting in poorly contextualised soundbites in the end. It was worth it, wasn't it, even if some seniors still looked down on you? There was general support for you coming through the ranks because you were considered to be someone who could reproduce the same institutional antagonisms by slotting yourself into the problematic hegemony of 'competitive knowledge construction', even if a few tried to stifle your ascent. In any case, you wanted to continue to progress and so you had to master the tricks of the trade, looking for shortcuts in the admin, dodging alternate meetings and seeking ways to streamline marking time. Anything, just anything to be able to nail another research proposal and/or deliver findings from a snapshot study to a funder who was unlikely to act on the results or have a direct influence on social change. It had to be worth it, that PhD, wasn't it?

Academic capitalism

In this respect, I shouldn't be surprised that this was my initial experience during my early career since I was in the midst of a process which had ensnared the university in neoliberal principles of marketisation and profit maximisation. All these manoeuvres that you now find yourself flirting with relate to the intrinsic presence of 'academic capitalism' and how the modern university has become a hotbed for neoliberal capitalist principles: it has become an *economic entity*, driven by *income generation*, maximising *revenue streams* and *economic competition* (Jessop, 2018). To endure, this entity is required to act as a *business* and is compelled to annually secure large amounts of cash as a means of growing its customer base – aka 'students' – to survive in a competitive market determined by other metric obscurities in the national university league tables (Cribb and Gewirtz, 2013). For us, this means satisfying both employer (university) and customer (students) with the performance of an array of administrative tasks, marketing activities, pastoral care and support, classroom teaching, grant applications and publications ... as well as striving for 'social impact' and generally save the world simultaneously (see Briggs et al, 2018).

All this places substantial demand on time that is probably better spent prioritised doing problem-led and socially significant research that can enrich and inspire the student experience and instead channels academics into constrained forms of funded research, into backward administrative processes to satisfy internal outcome and compliance procedures, and before evidencing it on social media. The 'income generation' agenda, in particular, pervades discussions of research, with academic time increasingly only allotted to research activity where external funding is provided. Academic research is thus now recast through a corporate or governmental lens whereby funding priorities determine what should be researched and simultaneously establish intense competition to only commit to study discrete and preordained challenges or issues, often at the expense of individual research interests and agendas (Edwards, 2020) that have often organically evolved from PhD study (Briggs, 2020). And you are tasked with sharing knowledge from these compromised projects – if they come off – to your 'customer base', sorry, I mean 'student base'. The neoliberal university is subsequently loaded with marketing strategies around 'value for money' and 'customer service', which have significant implications for students who, perhaps understandably, believe they are *buying a service* rather than *getting an education*. This was crudely made clear to me when, after failing a student for an assignment recently, she approached me publicly in front of a class and said, 'It was worth a pass; come on, I pay your wages'. Tuition fees, therefore, create an 'internal market' whereby institutions compete for students because *instead of looking up to you as inspirational knowledge acquirers at the frontier of their fields*, they tend to *look down on you as the human-shaped formalism* which stands between them and a pass.

Once upon a time ...

All this was what I was thinking and experiencing, having completed my PhD and got my first track tenure position in a low-ranked university in London. So, if any, or at least some of this resonates with you, then please read on and let me share the secret of why the PhD was worth it. And for me to arrive at revealing this treasured knowledge – so you hopefully avoid feeling disoriented, pessimistic, jaded, and/or burned out by higher education – I must share further secrets related to how and why I myself came to study a PhD. Make no mistake, this is not some vanity exercise, nor is it a platform to feed my own ego. You just need a little more context.

I am an ethnographer, so I seek to try to immerse myself within different social groups to try to understand their situations and outlooks, their behaviours and their treatment. I have to be empathetic and sensitive to many facets of human behaviour and avoid imprinting my own bias and conceptions of reality on those I study. If I am to do this with any success, I must also listen and make no judgements about the people I am with. I must learn from them. I must look for things I have in common with them to build rapport and get their trust. In the main, I work as much with violent and risky social groups as I do with the vulnerable.

Such training I inherited from having a dad who ran a centre for vulnerable children. During the summer holidays, when I was young, he would take me along to the centre where I would play with the other children, many of whom had learning difficulties, had developed erratic, often violent behaviours and had mental health issues. Home Office Place of Safety Orders allowed authorised people like my dad to remove a child or children from their if they were exposed to serious risks (such as harm or abuse). In my eyes, I didn't see their 'difference' or their 'suffering' so much, only that they were other children like me. Such ability I also reconcile comes from having a mum who was an occupational therapist. My mum supported all sorts of people, from those who had had life-changing accidents to the elderly. Very often, after picking me up from school, we would do extra 'check-up' trips on some of these people because my mum's day job didn't permit enough time to support them emotionally. I'd go into these peoples' houses and help my mum, help these people. In my eyes, I saw that it was more than a job; it was a duty.

My mum and dad had got these jobs in a rural part of England, having left South London in the mid-1980s where increased racial tension, violence, and chronic unemployment were all around us. We were to return to where my dad grew up even if his whole family had ostracised him for marrying my mum, 'an orphaned woman of colour'. The other children in my new primary school thought I was different because of my colour. 'Fucking Paki' and 'Paki cunt' were playtime taunts which were often followed by beatings. I fought back as best I could but lost many more than I won. This quickly became the norm for me, and my behaviour started to become challenging; I became angry and challenged the authority of the teachers. I was often sent to the headmaster's office: 'You are the bane of my life, Daniel Briggs', he would shout while banging the table. The only way for me to navigate the beatings was to become friends with my enemies, even if that meant involving myself in their activities. Numerous parent/teaching meetings and suspensions followed, but, in my eyes, I had enough of a rapport with my adversaries to avoid being beaten up.

Reluctant for me to go to the local secondary comprehensive and perhaps forecasting inevitable delinquency, my mum and dad sent me to attend church, where I sang in the choir. Regular attendance helped me get into a poorly achieving Catholic school where many of the same problems resurfaced for me. Of the 1,200 students, I was one of two kids who weren't white. Clinton, the other 'non-white kid', quickly acknowledged the imbalance, and we became friends for a few years. He never made it to his GCSEs, though, dropped out, fought in Iraq, and lost a leg in a mine before becoming a disabled alcoholic. At secondary school, I saw a different landscape. I reasoned that, by comparison, the racism and beatings I'd received were nothing by comparison to some of the problems some of my friends were developing. One drifted into heroin addiction and homelessness by the age of 14; another became involved in drug dealing and quickly came into regular contact with the criminal justice system at age 15, and another committed suicide at the age of 16.

After attaining six GCSEs and even failing a whole A level, I finished school and worked in numerous unskilled jobs in factories, warehouses, and construction sites. The majority of people with whom I worked had long dropped out of school; some had learning difficulties, while others had pronounced mental health issues. I saw hardship and misery and continued to see where people end up if they 'fall short' in life and slip through the cracks of the education system. I then ended up working for a year in a retail shop where most of the missing stock could be traced back to the staff more so than the infrequent shoplifter. The limited work progression and poor wages motivated me to try and find a way to return to education. Yet when making applications for university, because of my low grades, I only received one offer: to study Criminology and Media & Cultural Studies at Middlesex University in north London. That was the only opportunity I needed.

A long shot at university and a longer shot at PhD study

I missed the last year of free university education because, at the time, in the late 1990s, higher education became a fee-based system. So, by working evenings and weekends at a north London branch of another exploitative retail shop, I was able to fund my undergraduate studies. I found criminology fascinating, so much so I was generally the first person to arrive in the lecture halls. The academic expectation was challenging, and I remember reading basic texts several times, having with me alongside a dictionary to look up the long words. In my first year, I just about passed. My marks were low because my writing quality was so poor. I attended and completed an evening journalism course, and in my second year, my marks started to improve. Around me, the general university experience of leaving home and partying had started to affect the motivation of some of my student friends, some of whom fell into massive debt and dropped out with drug problems. I kept my focus, having had a firsthand taste of the kind of work that awaited me if I didn't make the most of this opportunity. In my final undergraduate year, aged 20, I managed to pick up some data entry work at the Institute of Psychiatry. Though statistics were way beyond my mathematical capacity, I endeavoured to put it right since I failed it at GCSE. The one-day-a-week job became two, and while completing my dissertation, I speculatively sent my CV to several institutions.

Somehow, a research team from Imperial College picked up my CV and invited me to assist on a project interviewing drug-offending prisoners.

I began work over the summer of 2001 and visited over 25 prisons in England and Wales, interviewing more than 100 people put in prison for drug-related offences. It was fascinating, and within a month of working, I had signed up for a part-time master's in criminology. When my contract ended at Imperial College and my master's began, an open invitation was placed to the new cohort of postgraduate students to work at the Centre for Criminology as research assistants. The chance to work alongside some of the great Criminologists like Jock Young, Roger Matthews, John Lea, and Vincenzo Ruggiero inspired me, and thereafter, I became involved in further prison and criminal justice-related studies funded by the Home Office and Youth Justice Board. Most of these research projects were heavily quantitative, and while it was good experience, what I didn't like was trying to fit peoples' responses into boxes. I remember on one visit to a secure unit, I was to interview 15-year-old Deanne, who, prior to my visit, had already been in prison four times for various violent crimes. I remember thinking about how she carried the image of those offences when she walked towards me. The way in which she answered my questions made me feel like she had told so many people the same thing so many times. The interview ended with her verbal protests and the guard came over to chaperone her away to her cell. There was then a flurry of exchanges on the guard's radio, and we entered a prison lockdown. I stood around looking for things to entertain me while Deanne lingered on the second floor and looked down at me for a minute or two. She shouted down, 'Oi mister, you wanna see my cell?' I leapt up the two levels of stairs while the guard rolled her eyes and followed. As I pushed open the door to her cell while Deanne jumped on the bed. 'Look, this is my mum and my sister', she said as she waved a picture of her family at me. As I smiled, looking at the picture, my eyes diverted to the damp and mouldy wall, which was littered with drawings, poems, and letters; they came alive in the breeze, as did the cutout paper angels flapping from one of the prison bars. She continued to jump around, showing me moments from her life. She grabbed a letter from her mum and shoved it in my hand: 'dis one is my favourite': 'We will always love you. Come home soon' it read.

The other way in which I was involved in these studies made me uneasy because, at their conclusion, and in the months and years that followed, the circumstances of the people I had researched didn't seem to change. The policy recommendations we made in the reports seemed to make no difference to the circumstances of the people. I felt at the time a more intimate, in-depth study of a social issue could offer more value, and without knowing it completely, I became more interested in qualitative methodologies, particularly ethnography.

By the age of 24, criminality stemming from crack cocaine addiction had consumed many UK cities and had appeared as frequent explanations for the problems of the increasing prison population. So, I configured a research proposal to study crack cocaine lifestyles on the streets. When I approached two different university departments and their respective ethics committees about an ethnographic study in South London, they quickly rendered the idea impossible. I left Middlesex University and instead found work at a private drug and alcohol company, determined to get funding for such a study to form the basis for a PhD. Now, I hadn't even set out to study for a PhD but found it to be the most natural next step if I were to pursue social change. I approached nine different London boroughs, all suffering high levels of crack cocaine use, and the tenth agreed to fund the study. However, the 12-month ethnographic project could only take place if I signed an insurance liability waiver, essentially making me responsible for myself. I moved to the area and rented a cheap flat before immersing myself in the volatile street crack cocaine scene. When I re-emerged with my data, the University of London were more than happy to take forward my PhD application and even accepted my ethics application because I already had my data.

This crude experience of being with people ensnared in a cycle of homelessness, addiction, and crime transformed my life and the way I undertook research. The PhD marked not only a commitment to ethnography but to researching and helping people in vulnerable situations and converting those studies into accessible means for people to learn about them. However, I wasn't impressed as I started to do the things expected of me as a PhD student. At postgraduate meetings at the British Society of Criminology, where I sat alongside a lean and vociferous James Treadwell, the people I came to know didn't seem to be doing a PhD for the same reasons I was. In one post-meeting conversation, one young woman told me she was going to 'be a Dr by the age of 25'. To me the title never even crossed my mind.

Much to my disappointment, as I began writing up, the novelty of my topic area, research method, and potential findings seemed to generate more frowns than encouragement. Roger Matthews, who had initially employed me at Middlesex University and then at London South Bank University as a contract researcher was a great mentor, exposed like so many senior academics do, an insecurity about their own intellectual capacity. When we were fully immersed in a project funded by the Home Office on football hooliganism at the Portugal Euro 2004 competition, he said in front of four senior colleagues, 'Dan, you shouldn't be doing a PhD; you're just a researcher'. All I did was just use those words to take my PhD forward. In later meetings where I approached him to discuss my findings, he batted me off: 'You can't take this seriously, Dan; stick to interviewing people, trust me'.

Red-brick rejections = post-92 pathway

But I did take it seriously. With six months left on my contract at London South Bank University, I sent my CV to the faculty asking for some teaching.

I took on every module possible and worked out of hours on the research projects to make it possible. The students – most of whom were from the local area – liked my approach; I was talking about issues relative to them, about the poverty and deprivation from which many had come, about the violence many had seen and even about the criminality in which some had been active themselves. I loved teaching them and found great meaning in helping some of them come out of very dark personal places and blossom as individuals. As I handed the results of one of my last projects to Roger, he looked at it with mild interest. 'It's quite good, Dan; there is a paper in this', he said to his surprise. But I had to move on and made numerous applications to red-brick universities, perhaps convinced that if I worked in an institution with a superior league-table position, things could be better.

I never got that opportunity in a red-brick institution and, to this day, haven't had it. I reduced my expectations and made applications to post-92 lower-league universities, getting a job as a Senior Lecturer in Criminology and Criminal Justice at the University of East London. It had to be worth it, that PhD? This was the question I was asking myself, having gotten set in my first track tenure job. My motivation and energy didn't seem to be that welcome in a department where the general attitude was sedentarily committed to *do the minimum* and *keep things how they were*. On induction, during which I had to sit in on other staff teaching, I observed how some of the academics relished the power and their automatic status as knowledge imparters. Was this what was expected of me?

I worked hard for the students and co-founded a student society. The society received institutional awards, and as I won more regional and local research grants, I got promoted quickly to Reader, much to the disdain of some colleagues who had become bitter and jaded by their jobs for some years. The Dean of the School started to circulate news of my success by means of motivating other staff, but it instead did the opposite and created resentment. One evening, while working late, one esteemed colleague burst into my office and said to me, 'I don't like you mate, you better watch out what you're doing here, coming in here, stirring it up, you fucking cunt'. The only thing I could think of was to work even harder so that within a year, he would be in the shadows. But if I were to move up, promotions were attached to fully engaging with the expectations of academic capitalism: winning the university grant money, publishing in high-quality journals, marketing the university, and so on. The university just wanted to look good so it could improve its kudos and general academic 'excellence', which it could then celebrate in glossy publications and social media updates to capture more students.

But as I committed myself to this project, my relations became further fractured with colleagues and I started looking for new opportunities. Maybe the velocity of how I was working had meant I, too, started getting ahead of myself, feeling consumed by the idea of pursuing a six-figure grant, thought I deserved a 'better place to work', perhaps I thought I deserved to be a professor much like that young woman had done when she told me she would have a PhD by the age of 25. Now in my early 30s, I had acquired a decent academic profile with numerous publications and research grants, but this was not to be enough. This time, my applications resulted in interviews, which didn't result in job offers. Before one panel, I was told I was 'too young' to be a professor even before the interview had started. In another, which composed of three separate break-off interviews with three panels made up of colleagues at different levels, I was asked in each one if I would take on the Head of Department role. 'But that wasn't the job I applied for', I said. I didn't get the job.

At the time, however, my wife developed psychological and neurological difficulties stemming from working in a soulless corporate environment, which undervalued women made worse when she was told she couldn't have children. It radically affected her and negatively impacted our relationship. She decided she wanted to return to Spain which was where I redirected my energies and started to learn Spanish. If I was to research in Spain, I needed to speak the language. I took up a project looking at gypsy marginalisation and drug markets in the northeast of the country, while at the same time, began a three-year study of problematic British tourism in Ibiza. I was sure that someone of my profile could get work in Spain, particularly if I could evidence my interest in projects about the kinds of challenges the country faces.

Academic cul-de-sac, Spain, and the moral crossroads

Once again, I made numerous job applications. This time, to Spanish institutions, perhaps without knowing that nepotism was even more powerfully present in the public university systems. After speaking with some Spanish colleagues, they rated my chances slim since I needed to essentially *start again from the bottom* as a research assistant. It wasn't as if I was unprepared to do it, only that the wages were meagre, and career progression was so slow. Then, by some miracle, my wife fell pregnant. Things continued like this until the birth of my daughter in London when I suddenly got an interview at a private university in Madrid. I remember at the time feeling quite desperate, and after a broken conversation in Spanish, they offered me a job at half the wage I was receiving. On reflection, I felt that this was my only choice and so we moved to Madrid. I reasoned that my priority was my wife and family and that my career needed to take the back seat.

I quickly discovered new levels of painful and unnecessarily slow bureaucracy. My place of work had the hallmarks of a five-star hotel but the personable treatment of an understaffed and overworked doctor's surgery.

The campus was spotless, and the cleaning staff seemed to follow people around, attending to rubbish and fingerprints. My shared office was entirely dedicated to hotdesking, and each employee was required to clock in and out to complete their contracted hours at the university campus. There was literally no escape, for if I didn't register my hours on the system, it would activate an automated warning from Human Resources and trigger a meeting with the faculty seniors. None of my colleagues spoke English, and I was thrust into teaching complex criminological theory 20 hours a week in Spanish to, as I was to discover, droves of mostly self-entitled and wealthy Spanish students who cared very little for their studies.

I remember coming home exhausted, my brain frazzled by having to communicate all day in Spanish at such an intense level. Because I was thrown into this high teaching load, the research team I was promised and even the space to carve out my own research didn't materialise. Instead, I was asked to write proposal after proposal to national governmental calls to plug the funding gap in the doctoral department. But with no time during the day, this was only reserved for evenings and weekends. I was just a small cog in the academic capitalist machinery, but every time I submitted failed proposal after failed proposal, I felt myself sink deeper and deeper into a depression. Rest assured I was producing the necessary metrics for the faculty seniors to look industrious.

My wife's personal situation deteriorated, and even though I had done my best to help her, I myself had become run down, and we separated. I had become lost for many reasons and started to mentally implode, manifested mainly by repelling the pressure generated by the university – perhaps as I had done when I was younger at school. On one occasion, for example, all faculty staff were sent on an obligatory five-hour training course on 'personal marketing'. At the end, we were obliged to open a social media account, have a photo taken of ourselves with the university in the background, and make updates about our general activity. I didn't seem to get many followers when I took photos of the pitch black and said I was walking to work. I was summoned to the faculty senior's office and told to delete the account. In my defence, I said I was committed to the university as I was reporting about my 'general activity', and I considered walking to work as something that exemplified my commitment to the university, to sustainability, and to the environment, so in my view, I was ticking more than one box. As punishment, my boss told me I had to accompany her and represent the faculty at an international OECD event looking at the future of student markets. At the event, I asked a few challenging questions about corporate plans for new 'student markets' and was then subjected to another 30 minutes of shouting in her office; 'Daniel, I believe in freedom of expression, but you cannot ask those things', she berated.

I was told to then report every morning at 9 am to her without fail and sit in my place. Instead, I started working in the Sports Faculty, but she found out and ordered me to her office the next day. I was due, once again, to be humiliated that morning but, by some miracle, when I came into the office, two security guards were standing around her as she was tearfully packing her things into a box. She had been fired for harassment, bullying, and mismanagement of the faculty's funds. I suddenly felt mentally lighter as she was marched out of the faculty, all the while colleagues whispering and doing their best to hide their elation. Later that day, I got drunk and, under the stars, made a promise to myself to resurrect my research career and reverse myself out of the professional and personal cul-de-sac into which I had somehow driven. Why? Because that night, the clearness of the sky merged with a clearness of my conscience, and I vowed to return to the original foundations which had led me into this line of work: I remembered why I studied for a PhD.

(A) Discussion (for both of us)

When I went to work the next day, each of us were required to meet with an interim line manager. I requested a reduction in my hours so I could start up my own 'self-funded' studies. Why did I need to waste time pursuing money just to undertake a research study? This was benefitting no one, really. I was more than equipped to research reality in a non-judgemental and objective manner. After all, I had a PhD. Not one funded study I had done or been involved with seemed to have resulted in significant change, and this was a philosophy inherent to me as much as my academic profile. I started up ethnographic studies on Spain's largest ghetto, on the refugee crisis across Europe, and even worked for 18 months in a luxury brothel. I was next to people who were dying of overdoses among the rats and rubbish, was watching young children and babies catch diseases in decrepit and overcrowded refugee camps, and befriended the manager of three lucrative venues dedicated to the 24/7 sale of luxurious sexual experiences. No permission, no ethics approval, no meetings. The general situation of most of the people I studied tended not to change. Still, in all these studies, I went about my studies in an ethically diligent manner and went out of my way to help the people under study. I felt it was my duty and the least I could do rather than just using them for my own career gain.

When COVID-19 came along, the vast majority of university colleagues in the social sciences blindly accepted the lockdowns, worked at home, and waited for the funding calls to emerge post-COVID. But within two weeks of the lockdowns, I had started up my own online survey. No permission, no ethics approval, no meetings, and the survey took only half a day to configure. When nearly 1,000 people completed it from 59 different countries, the project evolved into a mixed-methods, three-year study of the different phases of the pandemic. It made a critical assessment of the impact COVID-19 policies had on the poor and excluded. Having seen refugees die and fight for food in squalid camps, I opened my doors to a family of four Ukrainians who stayed with me early in their conflict with Russia. This is because, likely thanks to my mum and dad, I have come to see people as equal, regardless of their personal history and difficulties. I realised that contentment and reward at a time of philosophical decline in our industry rely on us putting aside our egos and initiating a moral obligation to help people.

Having seen the cost-of-living increase so and my wage stay stagnant in Spain, I have since returned to work in the UK. Having had the blessing of time to instigate pressing and important studies which are at the pulse of social change, I was shocked to return to a higher education industry on the brink of economic and logistical collapse. The expanding presence and control of faculty execs and pro-vice chancellors were forcing through budgetary cuts due to strains pertaining to the once-lucrative international student market. Once again, higher education and its precious market of student client/customers had created funding schisms – in the main by the very model which purported to boast its success and 'excellence'. And people like me now in senior positions were charged with motivating ECRs towards the very flawed pursuit I have described in this chapter: grant accumulation, 4★ publications, high-scoring student survey returns, and so on. And for what?

Fifteen years later, I've learnt that we work within an academic system that is very distant from the brutal real-life experiences I've described and researched and instead encourages us to focus on ourselves and our achievement. This is because the system promotes an obsession with citations, grants, and academic status. I have watched many colleagues become unhappy, succumbing to such direction, and lose sight of why they may have done a PhD or even embarked on a career in education and research. Fifteen years later, I've learnt that no university is better or worse because they all have that same focus: their own 'excellence' at your expense. This means that the grass isn't necessarily greener on the other side. It's just grass. Fifteen years later, I've found a healthy relationship between prioritising socially relevant research over the impossible pursuit of student satisfaction and the mind-numbing chore of emailing. It's one of the few things you will likely take to your senior years as a measurement of your contribution to society. Fifteen years later, I've come to realise that everything I learnt and experienced during my childhood came to fruition with my PhD study. The moral of the story is that the story is the moral. Just remember, the PhD was worth it. Remember.

Summary of reflections

This chapter is a reflexive account of academic life 15 years post-PhD. Having negotiated the doctorate and early exploitative and precarious work positions in higher education institutions, the chapter offers a moral pathway for readers which can help them navigate the increased banality of university administrative processes and the crude consequences of the commodification of everything about academic life. The reflections reveal how the false allure of academic capitalism is competitively programming ECRs into conceiving that the be-all-and-end-all of their careers is about the accumulation of personal kudos and the acquisition of institutional 'excellence' through big-buck research grants, 4★ Research Excellence Framework publications and being a teacher, inspiration instiller, mentor, shoulder-to-cry-on-provider and general hand-holder to a cohort of students who increasingly undervalue the *modus operandi* for their own studies and futures. A commitment to this cause, I believe, drains the newly fledged academic wayfarer of their ambition and instead progressively and cancerously replaces it with feelings of distance and disavowal. From personal and firsthand observations of academic life, I show how this can jade colleagues into feeling and behaving enviously and resentfully as they irreversibly morph into disoriented and burned-out 'end products'. There is an alternative, however, and these reflections are a testament to it.

17

Mentoring moments: a collaborative reflection on supervision

Chelsea Braithwaite, Owen Hodgkinson, and James Treadwell
Staffordshire University

Chelsea's PhD research examines the social, cultural, and economic implications of the COVID-19 lockdowns on young people in Stoke-on-Trent.

Owen's PhD research explores hedonism within Stoke-on-Trent's night-time economies through the use of ethnographic methodology.

James' PhD research, inspired by the changes in the scene that arose out of the socio-economic culture of football in the early 1990s, involved extensive study of a football hooligan group in the North of England using ethnography in the form of participant observation.

Introduction

This chapter is borne out of an unusual collaboration and role reversal in academia, the conventional norm being that academic staff school PhD students and guide them through the process. In contrast, reversing these norms' role, we considered the frustrations and challenges of the PhD from the point of view of two doctoral candidates, Chelsea and Owen, and one supervisor, James, both sides trying to be honest. The conventional story of the PhD, of course, is that of the 'academic apprenticeship' served by candidates where the master draws on their extensive subject area expertise and knowledge of the subject, knowledge of research methods, and skills to see the PhD successfully completed, learning from an established supervisor who is the senior and expert. In reality, the truth is that the process is one of collaboration, where all learn from one another and find their way through imperfectly. This is as much the process of candidates learning to manage supervisors and shape them to the role. If, as one of the authors here is frequently heard to suggest, 'managing academics is like herding cats', then handling the academic supervisor and moulding them as a good mentor is partly the candidate's role. That, of course, also requires established academics who are willing to learn and grow and relinquish their expert status. In essence, drawing on all our relationships working together on two PhD candidates and one supervisor, we hope to have an honest and frank discussion about the PhD process and do so in a way and manner that is not usual in the textbook accounts of the process.

Getting a PhD – the academic golden ticket

Today, the most common pathway into an academic career and the often-sought permanent lecturer post is often (though not always) getting a PhD. Most job advertisements in higher education (HE) stipulate it as a requirement, and it can be challenging to break into the 'industry' (although we dislike that term and see that as part of the Marketisation of British Universities, see Winlow, 2022) without that qualification. Obtaining a PhD or a Doctorate of Philosophy in Social Science and cogent subjects such as criminology (although we recognise the problem of framing that field, Sparks, 2020) typically involves students independently conducting an original and significant project of empirical research before producing a publication-worthy thesis usually around 80,000–100,000 words. This is then followed by passing an oral Viva Voce exam with a normal period of registration being three years (full-time) and an expectation of full-time study that the thesis will be submitted within four years of initial registration. The significance of obtaining a PhD in pursuing an academic career cannot be overstated, and we hope to reassure our readers of this fact.

Part of the first year is spent undertaking research training. The second and third years usually involve full-time research on the topic. Undertaking a PhD enables candidates to become experts in their chosen subject and explore the topic's intricacies. Normally, to satisfy the examiners, you must demonstrate originality of thought, detailed analysis, and the production of a document that meets a publishable standard. The process is often (in the plethora of advisory textbooks) now described as more a marathon than a sprint, often with heavy use of quite unoriginal travel metaphors.

Suppose it goes to plan as conventional accounts would suggest. In that case, it should start with a willing student and an enthusiastic, learned academic supervisor (or two) planning and collaborating on a project that takes the candidate from an inexperienced dilettante to a research master ready for an academic career. Yet, while the process is guided, it is also supposed to be founded on the growth of academic 'independence' that may not be apparent initially. In many of the guidance books, the PhD becomes a process whereby the kindly and good PhD supervisor, well versed and experienced in overseeing their students through to completion, is selected by virtue of their strong and respected publication record, is active in their research field, has enough time to provide adequate supervision, is genuinely interested in your project, and can provide supportive mentorship.

While many advisory texts tend to present straightforward and familiar information, they often focus on standard methods without delving deeply into the real challenges or frustrations that can arise during field research. Additionally, these texts may not always explore the moral, practical, and ethical considerations that researchers might encounter. However, there are exceptions that provide valuable insights into the realities of fieldwork, such as the works by Hobbs and May (1993), Hamm and Ferrell (1998), and Rice and Maltz (2018). Criminological research methods texts can be informative, though some may lack engaging content and often do not fully capture the challenges of working in academia. While guidance texts for PhD students might carry titles like 'The PhD Survival Guide', it's worth noting that academia, unlike fields such as farm work or industrial engineering, is generally not hazardous and usually involves less physical hardship, though it can lead to some frustration and complaints.

However, what often is not stated in such texts is that the relationships between students and supervisors, and vice versa, are often complex and often made harder by the flaws and faults that exist on both sides. The reality in praxis is vastly more complex than is presented in many of the textbooks. Relationships, of course, are, to some extent, shaped by variation in status, experience, knowledge, and power, and for the most part, the established academic will often have more. In PhDs, like life in general, the power imbalance in relationships needs to be recognised and acknowledged. The PhD process usually involves imperfect candidates and supervisors working together to develop a functional and effective collaborative relationship. Ideally, this partnership avoids descending into a cycle of recriminations and counterclaims, although such situations occur more often than expected.

It is also important for us to consider the wider context in which this supervisor/supervisee relationship takes place. Although there has been a significant increase in resources designed to support postgraduate researchers, problems often stem from factors beyond just relationship dynamics. With this in mind, it is important to note that the current state of HE is far from ideal. As Winlow (2022: 479) notes, 'The university's traditional telos [or ethos] was tied to the pursuit of truth and the expansion of human knowledge. However, only vague traces of the university's grand ideals can now be found throughout large expanses of Britain's university system'. Financial pressures have intensified due to frozen tuition fees, high inflation, and declining international student numbers. Over the past decade, government funding for teaching has been cut by 78 per cent, and student loans have been capped at £9,250, resulting in a significant drop in domestic fee income for UK universities. In just the last three years, inflation has eroded university resources by 20 per cent. This has led to increased pressure on academics to 'do more for less', fostering a competitive culture that creates high-pressure workplaces. Meanwhile, prospective PhD students are often told that their future success hinges on the relationship they build with their academic supervisors. However, many established academics, including some contributors to this book, have experienced poor relationships with their supervisors.

In this chapter, we aim to provide a nuanced and honest reflexive account, arguing that strong relationships are more likely to develop when all parties involved acknowledge their strengths and limitations and approach each other with realism and tolerance. While many current discussions of the PhD process focus heavily on relationships, they also often overlook the importance of the enabling and framing environment, which, where relevant, will also be considered.

Why do a PhD? Supervisor and supervisees' reflections

In a world increasingly shaped by artificial intelligence, the process and value of pursuing a PhD may need to be reconsidered. It's possible that AI-generated documents could eventually replace traditional PhD writing, rendering current discussions obsolete, but that time has not yet come. Traditionally, a PhD was expected to make a significant and original contribution to knowledge. However, many higher education institutions (HEIs) have moved away from this requirement. In current HE landscapes, expertise is often linked to an activist stance and the identity of the researcher, where expertise is less about impartial evaluation of evidence and more about promoting one's existing views to an audience that already shares those beliefs. This aligns with what Jonathan Haidt and Greg Lukianoff describe as the increasingly narrow and 'protective mission' of universities, where students are seen as vulnerable consumers (Haidt and Lukianoff, 2018).

PhD holders, now often regarded as professional academics, are increasingly encouraged to produce work of publishable quality. In some contexts, obtaining a PhD requires a thesis and a certain number of publications in peer-reviewed journals. This shift in focus from the learning process to measurable outputs has reduced the time PhD students spend on reading and deepening their knowledge. Additionally, much of the social science research being published today is criticised for lacking meaningful insights and rarely reaching an audience beyond academia. While many acknowledge that the current state of academia is problematic, this is closely linked to what Winlow (2022) describes as the 'marketisation of universities' and the rise of careerism, factionalism, empiricism, and conformism (p 479). Alongside this, we have also witnessed:

> the swift decline of creativity, curiosity, intellectual ambition, and our willingness to stand apart from the crowd (Winlow, 2022: 479) where being a successful academic criminologist is less about producing

important ideas that can illuminate the causes of crime and harm, and more about selling ideas to funders, filling our CVs with details of large research grants, and suppressing awareness that we often work well within our capabilities [with] many of our proposed projects are of only limited intellectual value. (p 486)

Therefore, the decision to pursue a PhD is increasingly driven by career ambitions and the desire for long-term financial security. While it's understandable that PhD students seek stable and well-paying jobs – benefits that previous generations of academics have enjoyed – the nature of PhD projects has become more constrained and less connected to the student's intellectual curiosity. As a result, the system may prioritise factors other than a candidate's genuine inquisitiveness. This shift is reflected in a growing trend where academics offer paid study guides on using tools like ChatGPT. This environment highlights that the definition of what constitutes valuable 'skills' for a PhD candidate is still evolving.

As for the reasons for undertaking a PhD, while books may talk about the inspiration that is found in one's (non-red flag) inspiring teachers, perhaps as honest a rationale is that a PhD may present simply as the easiest and best option that is there at the time for the candidate. Owen can relate to this perspective. This isn't to say that he wasn't genuinely interested in ethnography and criminology. However, upon reflection, it was perceived by Owen as a way to extend the student lifestyle for a few more years, avoiding formal responsibilities while justifying it as research (see Hobbs, 1988; Armstrong, 1999). For Chelsea, on the other hand, they initially expressed doubts about her suitability for a PhD and felt she was better suited to a practitioner role. However, a mixture of limited opportunities combined with some words of encouragement by James, who eventually became their supervisor, ultimately changed their perspective. In one of the discussions that helped shape this chapter, Chelsea admitted that James's strong belief in her abilities played a crucial role in her decision to pursue a PhD. However, she also noted that this kind of encouragement might be a tactic sometimes employed by a 'red flag' supervisor, which will now be discussed in greater detail.

The red flag supervisor: supervisee perspectives

Academic ego aside, what makes for red warning flags and signs to avoid when it comes to PhD supervision? For this chapter, we at least thought it worth reversing some orthodoxies and considering what makes a good PhD supervisor by reflecting honestly on what might make a flawed one. Then we realised that we might have to write about our supervisor's flaws, which might not be a good idea. Our supervisor, James (and the third author of this chapter), encouraged us to list his flaws and faults in texts and emails. If we are being honest, it was not too hard. We made a very long list. He went through and crossed many things off, then reluctantly admitted that most of them were pretty fair. We cross-referenced these with several websites that advised on red flags with PhD supervisors and realised that we should, by all accounts, be in pretty dire straits.

James might be a notable ethnographer, a well-known subject expert, and a fairly approachable sort of person (well, when you can get him, and not usually by email). However, he is far from faultless, and there are a lot of red flags. Advice like 'If they have a poor work-life balance and sacrifice everything for their career, they will expect you to do the same, avoid' might seem fine, but criminological ethnographers can tend to be that sort of person. So, too, delayed response to emails/text communication – tick; has fallen out with former PhDs – tick; they do not have any active research council project funding in the last few years – tick; and are disorganised and chaotic – tick.

Nevertheless, when we look over the full vista of all those in social sciences and, particularly, fields such as criminology, there can be a great deal that is wholly subjective when it comes to what constitutes good supervision. There will not likely be a standard one-size-fits-all. Some supervisors may work brilliantly with some students and be terrible with others, and there is likely an array of ways that supervision can work out or not. From the supervisor's point of view, doctorates are also hard to supervise.

Few academics are willing to admit, as one has in the Guardian, that 'I was an utterly appalling supervisor, and I did not even realise it' (Townson, 2016). Perhaps most academics are fallible and imperfect. Perhaps so, too, are most PhD students. Is there really such a thing as a red flag for PhD supervisors? Well, maybe there is. Not all are good, and certainly, you will not have to be a PhD student for long to hear rumours, gossip, and gripes that you may not have previously heard about a supervisor. There are also, if you look widely enough, plenty of examples of supervisors who have exhibited far worse behaviour than that, which is often listed as red flags, from taking advantage of the vulnerabilities of PhD students and stealing their ideas to taking advantage of them in sexual relationships. You could come to believe that the corridors of the university are not dissimilar to the experiences of a fresh and inexperienced prisoner, and the choice of 'protection' may merely be the best short-term option. By now, you may be reading this thinking you have given up on the idea of a PhD, which is not our intent. However, while there might be some truth to the suggestions of red flags in guidance, do not believe all you read. Hopefully, this can be somewhat explained by the brief overviews provided by two of the authors and current PhD students, Chelsea and Owen, in the following.

Reflections on a 'red flag' supervisor – Chelsea

Like any other relationship, the supervisory relationship can be difficult to manage. At the start, one of my biggest challenges was managing my own expectations of the level of support a candidate can expect from a supervisor. However, with hindsight, I became slightly over-reliant on their validation and reassurance from James when, in fact, asking for his input merely fed into the very insecurity I initially felt. James would be honest in saying he remains 'crap' at reassurance at times and still need to be reflexive about responding with reassurance better (another red flag, maybe, but at least there is reflection and recognition here).

Now past the data collection stage, my PhD is taking shape as an ethnographically informed qualitative study of the harm experienced by emerging adults in Stoke-on-Trent due to the COVID-19 pandemic. More specifically, the study examines how the implementation of neoliberally informed non-pharmaceutical interventions, such as lockdowns, mask-wearing, and social distancing measures, created both new harms and heightened the existing harms experienced by emerging adults living in the 'forgotten city' of Stoke-on-Trent.

After it became clear a youth prison ethnography would not happen, early failures to secure access meant that instead of feeling reassured, I often came out of supervision meetings feeling deflated after getting hung up on small details. Sometimes, questions like 'Why have you taken that approach?', 'Why have you put this in here?', or 'Have you thought of this perspective instead?' became obstacles and barriers and sometimes greater objects of doubt than they needed to be. However, it is the job of your supervisor to offer alternative perspectives and point out the flaws in your work because if they do not, someone else will at a later date (perhaps at a conference or, worse still, during the Viva), then perhaps there is the red flag of the over supportive or protective mentor. If the academic is supposed to be a critical friend that supports and helps the candidate to succeed and produce work at a PhD level, they will have to, at some point, let the candidate own their work. Yet, nonetheless, every piece of advice and constructive criticism can sometimes feel like a personal attack on your work and capabilities. The hardest lesson, then, on reflection, is that you learn to trust the process and trust your own abilities and instincts. By doing so, you eventually learn that you can often work through the flaws, doubts and challenges without anyone really knowing they existed in the first place.

In the end, despite my earlier frustrations with the 'hands-off' approach taken by my primary supervisor, James, I have come to enjoy and even thrive within the space afforded. I may have sometimes felt that it took a lot longer to develop a relationship with James than it did with others, and that might be because he is a difficult character who is, at times, quite frustrating (perhaps the red flags are right). However, upon reflection, I am grateful that my PhD went through all of the bumps, false starts, and problems that it did. Perhaps without such challenges, the project would not be what it is now, and they would not have grown into the independent and resilient researcher that I am today.

Reflections on a 'red flag' supervisor – Owen

I commenced my PhD in September 2021 and am scheduled to complete it in September 2024. My PhD employed ethnographic methods (long-form unstructured interviews and longitudinal fieldwork via participant observation) to research the lives of those who were currently or previously engaged consumers of Stoke-on-Trent's night-time economy (NTE). This study aimed to uncover people's motivations for engaging with the NTE while also assessing the state of the city's nightlife from the 1970s to the present. This has thus far unveiled an NTE that is in permanent decline, increasingly unable to fulfil the hedonistic drives of its consumers who want their need for sex, drugs, alcohol, violence, and socialisation to be fulfilled. It was in part inspired by similar works and ethnographies that members of the supervisory team, including James, had undertaken.

When I first encountered James' work, I was captivated. His ethnographies had set a high bar for research in our field, and I vividly remember reading his past research with enthusiasm. However, as I began my journey, I became increasingly disillusioned. My attempts to seek guidance through emails went unanswered, and scheduled meetings were repeatedly postponed. Deadlines for feedback were missed, leaving me stranded in uncertainty. All worrying signs of the red flag supervisor and, if I am being honest, caused many a moment of self-doubt as to whether this was going to work. Yet, over time, I came to understand the immense pressure James was under juggling research bids, writing books, publishing papers, and managing a heavy teaching load. I realised he was but a small cog in the vast machinery of the university system. As I progressed through my studies, the wider context of the university environment and its potential to impact this supervisor relationship began to reveal itself to me in surprising and alarming ways.

Of course, when entering a PhD, students are often outsiders still and lack knowledge of the university system and all of its disappointing and frustrating realities. For instance, one of my central challenges was that of dealing with several PhD supervisors entering and exiting at various stages of my journey. Over the three years, I have witnessed three separate supervisors leaving the university for other institutions (including one forced by their new institution to completely drop out of the supervisory team), which had a negative impact on the consistency of advice I received. There were indeed those moments of receiving conflicting and contradictory advice, the challenges of building a new supervisor relationship from scratch, and the déjà vu sensation of having to explain my PhD as though back in my first year for those supervisors just joining and needing a much-needed orientation. This is not a poor reflection on the supervisors; it is far from it. It merely reflects the neoliberal university that pressures staff with unmanageable workloads and continual job insecurity.

Yet that backdrop has built a degree of resilience as, in this time, I have managed to secure and hold down work at a well-regarded local HEI, have produced publications subject to peer review and have gained a good relationship and reputation among colleagues. Perhaps in adversity, there can sometimes be the confidence, determination and self-reliance that should be the hallmarks of an apprentice showing a growing mastery of the craft. What is increasingly lost and undervalued is the love of reading, the ability to think about or discuss a subject in a detailed and intelligent way, and the ability to enthuse students and teaching with research findings. Simply, the process of undertaking research becomes equated to an early expectation that a PhD candidate will face the requirement to pass a Viva with as few corrections as possible early in their career and continue to research and produce in a similar vein on the back of that experience in a linear and simple way. However, despite this rather bleak outlook, James – despite his many faults – has always been one to keep the flame of reading and lively debate alive. Between the exiting of supervisors and the withering capacity to engage in genuine intellectual curiosity, James has been a guiding light, and despite these drawbacks, I will prevail.

Twenty years later: reflecting on my journey from PhD student to supervisor – James

When I was asked to contribute to this collection, I reminisced about my own PhD journey all those years ago, when I undertook a large-scale ethnographic research study with a group of football hooligans. It made me ponder my own supervisor relationship and whether or not I may have been, in fact, a red flag supervisee. I distinctly remember failing to meet deadlines, missing meetings, and challenging some of the supervisor's ideas and suggestions (including when I was ready to submit the thesis!). Upon reflection, maybe, just maybe, I have carried some of these traits over the past 20-odd years and into my role as supervisor. However, are these traits really that bad? Are they worthy of the dreaded 'red flag' status?

What do we learn from this process of reflection, then? These so-called 'red flags' might not be just that. There is not a perfect supervisor, and students are not perfect either. Well, on reflection, the process of writing this chapter with my two current PhD students may have revealed some basic and simple rules. Be nice to each other; for students, it is sometimes good to get reassurance and a speedy response, but what a student wants and needs may not be the same. None of this seems shockingly revelatory, but we know that supervisors can have the candidate's best interests at heart but do not always show it, and maybe we need to both recognise and honestly confront one another's strengths, faults, and limitations if we really are a team.

Additionally, the point may be that supervisors are not chosen as often as they are stumbled upon. Then, they assume a range of duties in this role; for example, providing feedback on the candidate's work and being a good academic does not make them good at these. Feedback, for example, can range from giving some general comments and encouragement to close editing (and re-editing) of sentence constructions and grammar. Simply put, it can take many forms, from useful constructive feedback for improvement to demoralising and repetitive reworking that demoralises and demotivates. An honest conversation can help and usually does if you are both on the same page. Unfortunately, as the reflections on the higher education environment have demonstrated, getting the right people together might be more down to luck than planning.

At this stage, with input from Chelsea and Owen, I would like to offer our own set of red flags that are perhaps omitted from most textbooks and websites. There are bad supervisors who, in some instances, will financially or sexually manipulate students. Some supervisors are abusive in a plethora of ways, but not all are known about. Sometimes, the seemingly nicest people can be the worst abusers, especially if cultures of complicity and hypocrisy hide those whose conduct is the worst but whose presentation is the most polished. It should be no shock that some who present the best impression may have the worst records of conduct, just as those whose reputation may be criticised may not be as suggested. There is also the supervisor who is controlling and expects the candidate to replicate the field in their image. There is the supervisor who sees the candidate as a sponge who should only absorb the same worldview similar to that of theirs. There is the supervisor who expects the candidate to solely research and write peer-reviewed articles, only to later take credit for all their hard work. There is the supervisor who is largely absent and is present only occasionally and rarely has any understanding of the student's needs or their project. All of these are, arguably, ever more likely encountered in a highly dysfunctional and marketised system. A system that stresses ever more competition and commercialisation as the solution to the very woes it creates.

Of course, not all PhD students will reject that philosophy of competition and self-interest either, because as competition comes to define the experiences of HEIs more, increasingly it may be that self-funded student consumers undertaking self-funded studies may come to hold ever greater expectations of academic supervisors and their role. Just as some supervisors may show oddly obsessive and controlling behaviour to students, so too sometimes students can form unhealthy and unrequited obsessions with the established academics. Some may also come to expect more than pastoral care from their supervisors, who are charged with dealing with the sometimes complex and emotional or affective issues, including the mental health of students that they are not equipped or qualified to take on. Just as there can be a rescue industry in some aspects of the social sciences and the good intent of scholar-activists, the real-world complexities of people with all their flaws, faults, and limitations should not be overlooked.

Conclusion

So, what have we learned? Well, perhaps there is nothing that is revelatory, but supervisors should have candidates' best interests at heart. They should be able to rely on them to provide the best advice they can possibly give, both on a personal level and in a professional capacity. Supervisors and supervisees are people with all the frustrations and faults that come with that. Good supervisors will hold candidates as colleagues, treat them as equals and, where needed, provide training to help build them into collegiate and professional academics. They might seek to exploit your IT skills a bit, but they are there to do the best for you and try to ensure your work is held in respect. Supervisors or advisors should reflect on and recognise that their role is to guide their charges through the morass of regulation and requirements and that they, too, have flaws and are very far from perfect. They should offer suggestions (even when they are busy) and be sensitive to the life cycle of the PhD process. Another important lesson to remember is that, if you are also a supervisor currently facing challenges with a supervisee, remember that you once stood in their shoes, to remember that not every day was perfect and that you likely also needed to find support, solace, and hear words of encouragement from others with more experience. Given all the pressures and workloads that amount to plate-spinning, it is easy in academia to perhaps forget these experiences. However, taking the time to reflect on your past experiences may hold the key to ensuring the success of those under your proverbial wing. However, the most important thing is that the real red flag supervisor that we have outlined is no more common than the red flag student. This is only further reinforced when we consider that a supposed 'red flag' supervisor was one of the authors of this chapter.

Summary of reflections

These reflections on supervision show that managing expectations and insecurities is crucial. Early reliance on your supervisor's reassurance can hinder your independence, but you can grow to trust your abilities and the process over time. Your supervisors should foster your development into a resilient researcher. If you encounter delays, conflicting advice, and multiple supervisor changes, the pressures of academia do not always have to be a burden, and you can grow stronger through adversity. While your supervisor may have their faults, the hardships that you may experience can, in fact, help you become a more independent scholar. If you, the reader, happen to be a supervisor, it is important to remember that your role is to have your supervisee's best interests at heart, to guide them professionally and personally through the PhD process. Treat candidates as colleagues and support them as they grow into independent academics. While frustrations and imperfections exist on both sides, good supervisors offer support, even when busy, and must respect the emotional demands of the process. Remember that you were once in their shoes and that reflection on your past experiences can provide valuable insights.

Editors' reflections: Part IV

As we approach this final break in our PhD journey, we find ourselves at the last overlook before the path ahead disappears into the horizon. This is not just a moment to rest, but a place to recognise that although this leg of our journey is coming to an end, it is also the beginning of something new. The chapters we have just traversed have shown us that the end of the PhD is not a final destination, but a gateway to new explorations. The knowledge and skills we have gained continue to evolve, guiding us on uncharted paths. As we pause here, let us reflect on how far we have come and how the journey of learning and discovery stretches beyond the confines of the doctoral experience. This is our last pitstop, but far from the end of our expedition.

In Chapter 14, Nick Gibbs explores the final stages of a PhD journey, focusing on the Viva Voce examination and the challenges of navigating the academic job market. Nick reflects on his own experience, emphasising the importance of thorough preparation for the Viva and offering practical advice for handling its rigorous demands. He also addresses the often-precarious nature of early academic careers, stressing the need to build a robust professional network and strategically approach opportunities. Despite the challenges, Nick encourages readers to stay resilient, believe in their expertise, and view the Viva as a stepping stone toward a rewarding academic career. Nick's chapter is particularly valuable not only for those navigating academia but also for those considering a transition out of it. Themes of resilience, adaptability, and leveraging personal strengths are universally applicable, and whether pursuing a career in industry, entrepreneurship, or other sectors, the insights shared may assist you in identifying your own unique value as you navigate the challenges of any new environment both within and outside of academia.

Chapter 15, by Adam Lynes, delves into his persistent battle with imposter syndrome that has shadowed his academic journey. He recounts how his early education and personal experiences, including a traumatic assault, sowed the seeds of self-doubt that followed him through university and beyond. Despite achieving many of his academic goals, Adam consistently questioned his worth, grappling with the fear of being exposed as a fraud. His reflections underscore how the pressures of academia – exacerbated by the neoliberal focus on competition and external validation – nurtured these insecurities. However, by sharing his story, Adam aims to reassure others facing similar challenges that they are not alone, encouraging them to find strength in their accomplishments and in their ongoing struggles. Ultimately, Adam argues that imposter syndrome is not something to be conquered. Accepting it as a part of one's experience can actually be beneficial, transforming the feeling into a tool for growth and empathy.

In Chapter 16, Daniel Briggs reflects on 15 years in academia, revealing the challenges faced in a market-driven higher education system. After completing his PhD and navigating exploitative early roles, he encountered the harsh realities of academic capitalism, where the pursuit of funding, prestigious publications, and high student satisfaction overshadowed meaningful research and genuine teaching. As Daniel explains, this environment often left academics disillusioned, burned out, and disconnected from their original passions. Despite the pressures and setbacks, Daniel shares a personal journey of resilience, emphasising the importance of staying true to one's initial motivations and values. His story underscores that while academic capitalism can be disheartening, focusing on genuine research impact and personal commitment can reignite purpose and fulfilment. It is vital for us all, whether staying in academia or moving on, to remember that dedication to meaningful work is crucial. Amid bureaucracy and competition, maintaining your passion and integrity is key. Embrace your journey with a commitment to what truly matters to you.

Chapter 17, by Chelsea Braithwaite, Owen Hodgkinson, and James Treadwell, explores the dynamic of PhD supervision from both student and supervisor perspectives. Traditionally, PhD candidates are seen as apprentices to expert supervisors, but this chapter highlights the collaborative nature of the process. The authors discuss how PhD supervision often involves managing imperfections on both sides, with supervisors and candidates learning from each other. They address common challenges, such as the impact of financial pressures on academia and the evolving expectations of PhD research. Through honest reflections, Chelsea and Owen share experiences of navigating complex supervisory relationships and the impact of their supervisor's perceived flaws. James, their supervisor, reflects on his own journey and acknowledges that perfect supervision is elusive. The chapter concludes on a positive note, emphasising that understanding and collaboration, despite flaws, are key to a successful PhD experience. We can perhaps also draw from this chapter that embracing imperfections is not just integral to the PhD process but also a valuable part of navigating life's broader challenges.

Reflecting on this collection of chapters concerning life post-PhD, it becomes clear that we are not at a conclusion but at the cusp of new beginnings. This stage represents a reflective pause rather than an end, marking the transition from the structured path of academia to broader horizons. The experiences shared highlight that the culmination of a PhD is not a final destination but an entryway to ongoing discovery and growth. This journey through academia post-PhD has imparted valuable lessons about resilience, adaptability, and accepting imperfections. These insights remain crucial as we move forward, whether within academia or beyond.

As we reach the end of this diverse collection of voices and experiences from those who have experienced life as a PhD student in the social sciences, we find ourselves at the final vista of our shared exploration. We have wandered through varied paths, each offering unique insights and lessons. This moment invites us to reflect on the winding trails we have traversed and the myriad perspectives that have shaped our understanding. Now, as we prepare to draw our conclusion, we will weave together the rich tapestry of experiences and discoveries, illuminating the common threads that unite our journeys, and the collective insight gained along the way.

Conclusion

Sarah Jones, Mikahil Azad, Liam Miles, and Adam Lynes

To bring this book to a close, we would like to take a minute to address you, the reader. If we were able to speak to you now, we would want to ask you how you are feeling now you have absorbed the stories of the authors? Have any chapters spoken to you personally? Have any experiences surprised you? Have you found solace in reading these stories? And finally, do you feel a sense of catharsis now you have reached the end of this collection of diverse narratives of PhD life?

While we are unable to ask you these questions directly, we do hope that we have been able to offer some reassurance and, if possible, some support, regardless of where you are within your PhD journey. Whether you are still debating to undertake a PhD or not, struggling to connect with your project, finding it difficult to navigate a fraught supervisor/supervisee relationship, grappling with your work-life balance, facing the daunting task of moving country to pursue your academic dreams, dealing with an unexpected life event, or wresting with your inner saboteur, our intention was to provide you, whatever your situation may be, with some words of reassurance from those who have walked or are currently walking a similar path.

If we were to take stock of some of the central themes that have appeared throughout this collection, words such as self-doubt, lack of ability, fear of external criticism, isolation and loneliness, stress, mental health struggles, financial difficulties, academic pressures, hyper-competition, and career uncertainty may well be conjured. This is, indeed, a sobering and, if we are honest, a rather depressing picture of PhD life. However, within this sea of negativity, there is a light in the distance beckoning us to safer shores. While there is indeed a host of potential challenges, there are, in fact, as demonstrated via the stories within this collection, many more positive themes that have been uncovered. Words such as perseverance, motivation, passion, strength, resilience, friendship, purpose, self-belief, self-advocacy, empowerment, self-care, support, accomplishment, reflection, and growth. Within each of the stories shared, regardless of the challenges and struggles conveyed, the light prevails against the dark.

We would also like to take this moment to speak to each individual who contributed to this collection, as without you, this book would not have been possible and would have remained a fantasy and a talking point within our fleeting coffee breaks. From first-year PhD students to experienced professors, we are aware that sharing your thoughts, reflections, and fears is not an easy task, to say the least. We are in an industry by which we are increasingly judged on our carefully crafted academic profiles, and to show any form of weakness or, dare we say it, humanity is often frowned upon. With that in mind, we sincerely thank you for not only taking the time out of your busy schedules to compose your chapters but also believing in this very unconventional book. Your stories have inspired us and will no doubt inspire others in the future.

As conveyed throughout the myriad of stories within this collection, the road to a PhD is, in many ways, inherently unknown. It is a voyage cloaked in mystery, risk, and adversity. Some obstacles may slowly reveal themselves in time, while others may appear right before your eyes. However, as hopefully demonstrated throughout, no matter the circumstances or challenges, there are ways to navigate and stay the course of your PhD. While each journey is unique, as is each person's life, this does not mean that you need to feel adrift or isolated. It was mentioned in the introduction to this book that the contributors felt a renewed sense of community and belonging when writing their chapters. We hope that, in reading and connecting with these stories, you now feel like you, too, belong within this community, and we hope that you feel like you can continue to embrace the unknown.

YOU ARE NOT ALONE.

References

Abdellatif, A. and Gatto, M. (2020) It's OK not to be OK: Shared reflections from two PhD parents in a time of pandemic. *Gender, Work and Organization* 27: 723–733.

Abdelnoor, A. and Hollins, S. (2004) The effect of childhood bereavement on secondary school performance. *Educational Psychology in Practice*, 20(1): 43–54.

Adler, P. and Adler, P.A. (1987) *Membership Roles in Field Research*. Newbury Park, CA: SAGE Publications Ltd.

AdvanceHE. (2024) *Lesbian, gay and bisexual people.* [Online] Available at: https://www.advance-he.ac.uk/guidance/equality-diversity-and-inclusion/creating-inclusive-environment/lesbian-gay-and-bisexual-people

Altbach, P.G. (2014) India's higher education challenges. *Asia Pacific Education Review*, 15(4): 503–510. https://doi.org/10.1007/s12564-014-9335-8.

Altbach, P.G. and Mathews, E. (2015) India's need for higher education internationalization. *International Higher Education*, (82): 23. https://doi.org/10.6017/ihe.2015.82.8874.

Altbach, P.G. and Mathews, E. (2020) Is Indian higher education finally waking up? *Change: The Magazine of Higher Learning*, 52(3): 54–60. https://doi.org/10.1080/00091383.2020.1745602.

Armstrong, G. (1999) *Football Hooligans: Knowing the Score*. Oxford: Berg.

Awan, I. (2018) 'I never did anything wrong' – Trojan Horse: A qualitative study uncovering the impact in Birmingham. *British Journal of Sociology of Education*, 39(2): 197–211.

Awan, I. and Zempi, I. (2020) *Islamophobic Hate Crime*. Oxon: Routledge.

Bachmann, C.L. and Gooch, B. (2018) *LGBT in Britain: Universities Report*. Stonewall. Available at: https://www.stonewall.org.uk/system/files/lgbt_in_britain_universities_report.pdf

Baptista, A., Frick, L., Holley, K., Remmik, M., Tesch, J., and Åkerlind, G. (2015) The Doctorate as an Original Contribution to Knowledge: Considering Relationships between Originality, Creativity, and Innovation. *Frontline Learning Research*, 3(3): 55–67. Available at: https://files.eric.ed.gov/fulltext/EJ1091022.pdf

Barbieri, P., Elia, S., Fratocchi, L., and Golini, R. (2019) Relocation of second degree: moving towards a new place or returning home? *Journal of purchasing and supply management*, 25(3): 100525.

Battle, C. (2012) The café culture of mainland Europe. *The Oxford Student*, 19 September. Available at: https://www.oxfordstudent.com/2012/09/19/the-cafe-culture-of-mainland-europe/

Baumeister, R.F., Shapiro, J.P., and Tice, D.M. (1985) Two kinds of identity crisis. *Journal of Personality*, 53(3): 407–424.

Beasy, K., Emery, S., and Crawford, J. (2019) Drowning in the shallows: An Australian study of the PhD experience of well-being. *Teaching in Higher Education*, 26(4): 602–618. https://doi.org/10.1080/13562517.2019.1669014.

Becker, H.S. (1963) *The Outsiders: Studies in the Sociology of Deviance*. New York: Free Press.

Bertrand, M. and Lozenski, B.D. (2023) YPAR dreams deferred? Examining power bases for YPAR to impact policy and practice. *Educational Policy*, 37(2): 437–462. https://doi.org/10.1177/08959048211019975.

Bhagat, M., Kahalkar, H., Salampuriya, R., Salampuriya, R., and Padiya, S. (2022) Analysis of problems faced by the Indian students to apply for higher education at foreign universities. *International Journal of Advanced Research in Science, Communication and Technology*, 2(4): 463–468. https://doi.org/10.48175/ijarsct-3956.

Brimingham City Council (2019) Index of Deprivation 2019 [Online] Available at: https://www.birmingham.gov.uk/downloads/file/2533/index_of_deprivation_2019

Birmingham City Council (2021) East Birmingham Inclusive Growth Strategy. Available at: https://www.birmingham.gov.uk/info/20054/local_plan_documents/2048/east_birmingham_inclusive_growth_strategy

Block, P. (2023) The dropout crisis of mature part-time doctoral students: a critique of the insufficient support and supervision provided by UK university doctoral schools. https://doi.org/10.13140/RG.2.2.20480.61447.

Blomberg, T.G. (2019) Making a difference in criminology: Past, present, and future. *American Journal of Criminal Justice*, 44(4): 670–688. https://doi.org/10.1007/s12103-019-09484-6.

Bone, K.D. (2021) Cruel optimism and precarious employment: The crisis ordinariness of academic work. *Journal of Business Ethics*, 174: 275–290. Available at: https://link.springer.com/article/10.1007/s10551-020-04605-2

Boss, P. (2016) The context and process of theory development: The story of ambiguous loss. *Journal of Family Theory & Review*, 8(3): 269–286.

Bourdieu, P. (1986) The Forms of Capital. In Richardson, J. (ed) *Handbook of Theory and Research for the Sociology of Education*. California: Greenwood Publishing Group, pp 241–258.

Bourdieu, P. (1999) *The Weight of the World: Social Suffering in Contemporary Society*. Cambridge: Polity Press.

Brabazon, T. (2016) Winter is coming: Doctoral supervision in the neoliberal university. *International Journal of Social Sciences & Educational Studies*, 3(1): 14–34. Available at: http://ijsses.org/wp-content/uploads/2016/09/Volume-3-Issue-1.pdf

Braun, V., Clarke, V., and Gray, D. (2017) *Collecting Qualitative Data: A practical Guide to Textual, Media and Virtual Techniques*. Cambridge: Cambridge University Press.

Brewer-Smyth, K. (2022) *Adverse Childhood Experience: The Neuroscience of Trauma, Resilience and Healing Throughout the Life Course*. New York: Springer.

Briggs, D. (2020) *Climate Changed: Refugee Border Stories and the Business of Misery*. London: Routledge.

Briggs, D., Cordero, R., and Pérez Suárez, J. (2018) From crime science to the crime of science. *Safer Communities*, 17(1): 22–32.

Briggs, D. Ellis, A., Lloyd, A., Telford, L., and Kotzé, J. (2021) *Lockdown: Social Harm in the Covid-19 Era*. London: Palgrave MacMillan.

British Dyslexia Association, The (2019) *About dyslexia*. [Online] Available at: https://www.bdadyslexia.org.uk/dyslexia/about-dyslexia/what-is-dyslexia

Brown, L. and Holloway, I. (2008) The adjustment journey of international postgraduate students at an English university: An ethnographic study. *Journal of research in International Education*, 7(2): 232–249.

Brunton, R. and Dryer, R. (2023) Theoretical perspectives of child abuse. In Brunton, R. and Dyer, R. (eds) *Perinatal Care and Considerations for Survivors of Child Abuse: Challenges and Opportunities*. Cham: Springer International Publishing, pp 29–48.

Burawoy, M. (ed) (1991) *Ethnography Unbound: Power and Resistance in the Modern Metropolis*. Berkeley: University of California Press.

Bussotti, C. (1990) The imposter phenomenon: Family roles and environment (Doctoral dissertation, Georgia State University). Dissertation Abstracts International, 51, 4041 B.

Campbell, D. (2022) Lockdown drinking increase could cause 25,000 excess deaths in England. *The Guardian*, 26 July. Available at: https://www.theguardian.com/society/2022/jul/26/lockdown-drinking-increase-could-cause-25000-excess-deaths-in-england

Clance, P.R. and Imes, S.A. (1978) The imposter phenomenon in high achieving women: Dynamics and therapeutic intervention. *Psychotherapy: Theory, Research & Practice*, 15(3): 241.

Cooper, E. (2014) *'Demystifying the Viva': Some Reflections on my Experience*. Dr Emily Cooper. [Online] Available at: https://ecooper2site.wordpress.com/2014/06/06/de-mystifying-the-viva-some-reflections-on-my-experience/

Cornell, B. (2020a) PhD Life: The UK student experience: HEPI Report 131. *Higher Education Policy Institute*. Available at: https://eric.ed.gov/?id=ED607599

Cornell, B. (2020b) PhD students and their careers. *Higher Education Policy Institute*. Available at: https://www.hepi.ac.uk/wp-content/uploads/2020/07/HEPI-Policy-Note-25_PhD-students-careers_FINAL.pdf

Cribb, A. and Gewirtz, S. (2013) The hollowed-out university? A critical analysis of changing institutional and academic norms in UK higher education. *Discourse: Studies in the Cultural Politics of Education*, 34(3): 338–350.

Dalton, C., Carbon, J.S., and Olesen, N. (2003) High conflict divorce, violence, and abuse: Implications for custody and visitation decisions. *Juvenile and Family Court Journal*, 54(4): 11–33.

Davies, B. (2018) *Austerity, Youth Policy and the Deconstruction of the Youth Service in England*. Cham: Palgrave Macmillan.

Davies, W. (2020) How the humanities became the enemy within. *The Guardian*, 28 February. Available at: https://www.theguardian.com/commentisfree/2020/feb/28/humanities-british-government-culture

Davis, N. (2021) Surge in alcohol-related deaths during England lockdown, report finds. *The Guardian*, 15 July. Available at: https://www.theguardian.com/society/2021/jul/15/surge-in-alcohol-related-deaths-in-england-during-lockdown-report-finds

Davis, D.-A. and Craven, C. (2011) Revisiting feminist ethnography: Methods and activism at the intersection of neoliberal policy. *Feminist Formations*, 23(2): 190–208.

De Backer, W.A. (2011) Somebody I Used to Know [CD] *Making Mirrors*. London: Universal Music Group Global.

Department for Education (DfE) (2024) Widening participation in higher education. Available at: https://explore-education-statistics.service.gov.uk/find-statistics/widening-participation-in-higher-education#releaseHeadlines-summary

Department of Health and Social Care (2022) Working definition of trauma-informed practice. Available at: https://www.gov.uk/government/publications/working-definition-of-trauma-informed-practice/working-definition-of-trauma-informed-practice#working-definition-of-trauma-informed-practice

Department of Work and Pensions (DWP) (2013) Free school meals entitlement and child poverty in England. Available at: https://assets.publishing.service.gov.uk/media/5a7baa50e5274a7318b90202/free-school-meals-and-poverty.pdf

Desmond, M. (2014) Relational ethnography. *Theory and Society*, 43(5): 47–579. https://doi.org/10.1007/s11186-014-9232-5.

Dick, P.K. (1968) *Do Androids Dream of Electric Sheep?* New York: Doubleday.

Dinh, H., Strazdins, L., and Welsh, J. (2017) Hour-glass ceilings: Work-hour thresholds, gendered health inequities. *Social Science & Medicine*, 176: 42–51.

Disney, R. and Simpson, P. (2017) Police workforce and funding in England and Wales. *Institute for Fiscal Studies*. Available at: https://ifs.org.uk/sites/default/files/output_url_files/bn208.pdf

Dodworth, K. (2021) 'A real African woman!' Multipositionality and its effects in the field. *Ethnography*, 22(2): 164–183.

Dumitrescu, I. (2020) Heroism should not be part of the academic job description. [Online] Available at: https://www.timeshighereducation.com/opinion/heroism-should-not-be-part-academic-job-description

Dunleavy, P. (2003) *Authoring a PhD: How to Plan, Draft, Write and Finish a Doctoral Thesis or Dissertation*. London: Bloomsbury Publishing.

Dye, H. (2018) The impact and long-term effects of childhood trauma. *Journal of Human Behavior in the Social Environment*, 28(3): 381–392.

Dyregrov, A., Lytje, M., and Rex Christensen, S. (2022) The price of loss: How childhood bereavement impacts education. *Bereavement: Journal of Grief and Responses to Death*, 1.

Edwards, R. (2020) Why do academics do unfunded research? Resistance, compliance and identity in the UK neo-liberal university. *Studies in Higher Education*, 47(4): 904–914. https://doi.org/10.1080/03075079.2020.1817891

Enright, B. and Facer, K. (2017) Developing reflexive identities through collaborative, interdisciplinary and precarious work: The experience of early career researchers. *Globalisation, Societies and Education*, 15(5): 621–634. https://doi.org/10.1080/14767724.2016.1199319.

Etherington, K. (2004) *Becoming a Reflexive Researcher: Using Our Selves in Research*. London: Jessica Kingsley Publishers.

Ferrell, J. (2018) Criminological ethnography: Living and knowing. In Rice, S.K. and Maltz, M.D. (eds) *Doing Ethnography in Criminology: Discovery Through Fieldwork*. Cham, Switzerland: Springer, pp 147–161.

Firth, J.W. (2022) Understanding the human mind: a foundation for self-regulated study. *Journal of the Chartered College of Teaching*, 14: 6–9. Available at: https://pureportal.strath.ac.uk/en/publications/understanding-the-human-mind-a-foundation-for-self-regulated-stud

Forrester, N. (2023) Fed up and burnt out: 'Quiet quitting' hits academia. *Nature*, 615(79531): 751–753.

Forster, J., Petrie, M., and Crowther, J. (2018) Deindustrialisation, community, and adult education: The north east England experience. *Social Sciences*, 7(11): 210.

Ganesha, H.R. and Aithal, P.S. (2022) How to complete the Ph.D. program in time and without complications in India? *Zenodo (CERN European Organization for Nuclear Research)*. https://doi.org/10.5281/zenodo.7308315.

Garlick, S. (2003) What is a man? Heterosexuality and the technology of masculinity. *Men and Masculinities*, 6(2): 156–172. [Online] Available at: https://journals.sagepub.com/doi/epdf/10.1177/1097184X03255851

Gaw, K.F. (2000) Reverse culture shock in students returning from overseas. *International Journal of Intercultural Relations*, 24(1): 83–104.

Gelsthorpe, L. (2011) Working with women offenders in the community: a view from England and Wales. In Sheehan, R., McIvor, G. and Trotter, C. (eds) *Working with women offenders in the community*. London: Willian.

Gibbs, N. (2021) *'Mum, I got the job! Check my LinkedIn for the details...': Self-branding and unpaid labour on LinkedIn*. Emerald Publishing. Available at: https://www.emeraldgrouppublishing.com/opinion-and-blog/mum-i-got-job-check-my-linkedin-details-self-branding-and-unpaid-labour-linkedin

Gibbs, N. (2023) *The Muscle Trade*. Bristol: Bristol University Press.

Giddens, A. (2005) The emergence of life politics. In Hier, S.P. (ed) *Contemporary Sociological Thought: Themes and Theories*. Toronto: Canadian Scholars Press, pp 347–356.

Gilovich, T., Medvec, V.H., and Savitsky, K. (2000) The spotlight effect in social judgment. *Journal of Personality and Social Psychology*, 78(2): 211–222. https://doi.org/10.1037/0022-3514.78.2.211.

Goffman, E. (1959) *The Presentation of Self in Everyday Life*. New York: Doubleday.

Gov.UK (2013) *Higher Education Funding Council for England annual report and accounts from 2012 to 2013*. Available at: https://www.gov.uk/government/publications/higher-education-funding-council-for-england-annual-report-and-accounts-2012-to-2013

Grant, R. and Sugerman, J. (2004) Ethics in human subjects research: Do incentives matter? *The Journal of Medicine & Philosophy*, 29(6): 717–738. https://doi.org/10.1080/03605310490883046.

Green, T. (2015) *The Fear of Islam: An Introduction to Islamophobia in the West*. Minneapolis: Fortress Press.

Griffin, G. (2022) The 'work-work balance' in higher education: Between over-work, falling short and the pleasures of multiplicity. *Studies in Higher Education*, 47(11): 2190–2203.

Griffiths, J. (1999) *Pip pip: A sideways look at time*. London: Flamingo.

Gu, Q., Schweisfurth, M., and Day, C. (2010) Learning and growing in a 'foreign' context: Intercultural experiences of international students. *Compare*, 40: 7–23.

Guillemin, M. and Gillam, L. (2004) Ethics, reflexivity, and 'ethically important moments' in research. *Qualitative Inquiry*, 10(2): 261–280.

Haidt, J. and Lukianoff, G. (2018) *The Coddling of the American Mind: How Good Intention and Bad Ideas are setting up a Generation for Failure*. London: Penguin UK.

Hall, S. and Winlow, S. (2015) *Revitalizing Criminological Theory: Towards a New Ultra-realism*. Oxon: Routledge.

Hall, S. and Winlow, S. (2018) Ultra-realism. In DeKeseredy, W.S. and Dragiewicz, M. (eds) *Routledge Handbook of Critical Criminology*. 2nd ed. London: Routledge, pp 43–56.

Hall, S., Winlow, S., and Ancrum, C. (2008) *Criminal Identities and Consumer Culture: Crime, Exclusion and the New Culture of Narcissism*. Abingdon: Routledge.

Hamm, M. and Ferrell, J. (1998) *Ethnography at the Edge*. Boston: Northeastern University Press.

Harris, M. and Fallot, R.D. (2001) Envisioning a trauma-informed service system: A vital paradigm shift. *New Directions for Mental Health Services*, 2001(89): 3–22. https://doi.org/10.1002/yd.23320018903.

Harrison, S. (2010) *How to Write a PhD in Less Than 3 Years: A Practical Guide*. Milton Keynes: Authorhouse Ltd.

Harvey, L. (2023) Editorial: Critical social research. *Quality in Higher Education*, 29(3): 280–283. https://doi.org/10.1080/13538322.2022.2154139.

Hayes, N. and Introna, L.D. (2005) Cultural values, plagiarism, and fairness: When plagiarism gets in the way of learning. *Ethics and Behavior*, 15(3): 213–231. https://doi.org/10.1207/s15327019eb1503_2.

Hazell, C.M. and Berry, C. (2022) Is doing a PhD bad for your mental health? *Impact of Social Sciences* [Blog] 12 January. Available at: https://eprints.lse.ac.uk/114173/

Healey, M. (2005) Linking research and teaching to benefit student learning. *Journal of Geography in Higher Education*, 29(2): 183–201. https://doi.org/10.1080/03098260500130387.

Hercog, M. and van de Laar, M. (2016) Motivations and constraints of moving abroad for Indian students. *Journal of International Migration and Integration*, 18(3): 749–770. https://doi.org/10.1007/s12134-016-0499-4.

Higher Education Statistics Agency (2023) *Higher Education Student Statistics: UK 2021/22 released*. Available at: https://www.hesa.ac.uk/news/19-01-2023/higher-education-student-statistics-uk-202122-released

Hillman, N. (2016) The coalition's higher education reform in England. *Oxford Review of Education*, 42(3): 330–345. https://doi.org/10.1080/03054985.2016.1184870.

Hobbs, D. (1988) *Doing the Business: Entrepreneurship, the Working Class, and Detectives in the East End of London*. Oxford: Clarendon Press.

Hobbs, D. and May, T. (1993) *Interpreting the Field: Accounts of Ethnography*. Oxford: Oxford University Press.

Hochschild, A. (1987, 2012) *The Managed Heart*. Berkeley, CA: University of California Press.

Hockey, J. and Gupta, S. (2019) *PhD 101: The Manual to Academia*. USA: Independently Published.

Holden, C., Wright, L., and Sims, P. (2021) Imposter syndrome among first and continuing generation college students: The roles of perfectionism and stress. *Journal of College Student Retention: Research, Theory & Practice*, 25(4): 726–740.

Holt, S., Buckley, H., and Whelan, S. (2008) The impact of exposure to domestic violence on children and young people: A review of the literature. *Child Abuse & Neglect*, 32(8): 797–810.

Hoque, J. (2018) Quality concern in higher education in India. *UGC Journal Serial Number*, 7(13): 662–668.

Howard League for Penal Reform (2017) *Is this the End of Women's Centres?* All Party Parliamentary Group for Women in the Penal System. London: Howard League for Penal Reform.

Jack, P. (2023) PhDs and masters 'overwhelmingly slanted' to wealthy Students. *Times Higher Education*, 12 September. Available at: https://www.timeshighereducation.com/news/phds-and-masters-overwhelmingly-slanted-wealthy-students

Jackson, L. (2018) *Islamophobia in Britain: The Making of a Muslim Enemy*. Switzerland: Palgrave Macmillan.

Jaws (1975) [film] Dir. Steven Spielberg. United States: Universal Pictures.

Jepsen, D.M., Varhegyi, M.M., and Edwards, D. (2012) Academics' attitudes towards PhD students' teaching: Preparing research higher degree students for an academic career. *Journal of Higher Education Policy and Management*, 34(6): 629–645. https://www.tandfonline.com/doi/full/10.1080/1360080X.2012.727706.

Jessop, B. (2018) On academic capitalism. *Critical Policy Studies*, 12(1): 104–109.

Johnson, K. (2019) Chronic poverty: The implications of bullying, trauma, and the education of the poverty-stricken population. *The European Journal of Educational Sciences*, 6. https://doi.org/10.19044/ejes.s.v6a6.

Johnstone, D.B. (2004) The economics and politics of cost sharing in higher education: Comparative perspectives. *Economics of Education Research*, 23(4): 403–410. Available at: https://www.sciencedirect.com/science/article/pii/S0272775703001171

Joshi, A. and Mangette, H. (2018) Unmasking of impostor syndrome. *Journal of Research, Assessment, and Practice in Higher Education*, 3(1): 1–9. Available at: https://ecommons.udayton.edu/cgi/viewcontent.cgi?article=1021&context=jraphe

Jouhki, H. and Oksanen, A. (2022) To get high or to get out? Examining the link between addictive behaviors and escapism. *Substance Use & Misuse*, 57(2): 202–211.

Jump, P. (2013) PhD completion rates, 2013. *Times Higher Education*. [Online] Available at: https://www.timeshighereducation.com/news/phd-completion-rates-2013/2006040.article

Keesing, R.M. (1981) *Cultural Anthropology: A Contemporary Perspective*. 2nd ed. Fort Worth: Harcourt Brace College Publishers.

Kemmis, S., McTaggart, R., and Nixon, R. (2013) *The Action Research Planner: Doing Critical Participatory Action Research*. Singapore: Springer.

King, E.A. (2017) Outcomes of trauma-informed interventions for incarcerated women. *International Journal of Offender Therapy and Comparative Criminology*, 61(6): 667–688. https://doi.org/10.1177/0306624X15603082.

King, R. and Sondhi, G. (2017) International student migration: A comparison of UK and Indian students' motivations for studying abroad. *Globalisation, Societies and Education*, 16(2): 176–191. https://doi.org/10.1080/14767724.2017.1405244.

Kinman, G. and Jones, F. (2008) A life beyond work? Job demands, work-life balance and wellbeing in UK academics. *Journal of Human Behaviour in the Social Environment*, 17(1): 41–60.

Kljakovic, M., Kelly, A., and Richardson, A. (2021) School refusal and isolation: The perspectives of five adolescent school refusers in London, UK. *Clin Child Psychol Psychiatry*, 4(26): 1089–1101.

Kolomitro, K., Kenny, N., and Le-May Sheffield, S. (2019) A call to action: Exploring and responding to educational developer's workplace burnout and well-being in higher education. *International Journal for Academic Development*, 25(1): 5–18. https://doi.org/10.1080/1360144X.2019.1705303.

Lawson, D.M., Davis, D., and Brandon, S. (2013) Treating complex trauma: Critical interventions with adults who experienced ongoing trauma in childhood. *Psychotherapy*, 50(3): 331–335. https://doi.org/10.1037/a0032677.

Leavy, P. (2020) *The Oxford Handbook of Qualitative Research*. 2nd edn. New York: Oxford University Press.

Leckie, G. and Goldstein, H. (2017) The evolution of school league tables in England 1992–2016: 'Contextual value-added', 'expected progress' and 'progress 8'. *British Educational Research Journal*, 43(2): 193–212.

LeFebvre, L., LeFebvre, L.E., Allen, M., Buckner, M.M., and Griffin, D. (2019) Metamorphosis of public speaking anxiety: Student fear transformation throughout the introductory communication course. *Communication Studies*, 71(1): 98–111. https://www.tandfonline.com/doi/abs/10.1080/10510974.2019.1661867.

Loveday, V. (2018) The neurotic academic: Anxiety, casualisation, and governance in the neoliberalising university. *Journal of Cultural Economy*, 11(2): 154–166. https://doi.org/10.1080/17530350.2018.1426032.

Lynam, S., Lafarge, C., and Milani, R.M. (2024) Exploring the experiences of ethnic minority postgraduate researchers in the UK. *Educational Review*, 76(7). https://doi.org/10.1080/00131911.2024.2316614.

Lynes, A., Treadwell, J., and Bavin, K. (2024) *Crimes of the Powerful and the Contemporary Condition: The Democratic Republic of Capitalism*. Bristol: Bristol University Press.

Lytje, M. and Dyregrov, A. (2019) The price of loss: A literature review of the psycho social and health consequences of childhood bereavement. *Bereavement Care*, 38(1): 13–22.

Marcus, G.E. and Fischer, M.M.J. (1999) *Anthropology as Cultural Critique: An Experimental Moment in the Human Sciences*. 2nd edn. Chicago, IL: University of Chicago Press. Available at: https://press.uchicago.edu/ucp/books/book/chicago/A/bo3613216.html

Matthews, G. and Clance, P. (1985) Treatment of the impostor phenomenon in psychotherapy clients. *Psychotherapy Private Practice*, 3(1): 71–81.

Mazzarol, T. and Soutar, G.N. (2002) 'Push-pull' factors influencing international student destination choice. *International Journal of Educational Management*, 16(2): 82–90. https://doi.org/10.1108/09513540210418403.

McAlpine, L. (2012) Academic work and careers: Relocation, relocation, relocation. *Higher Education Quarterly*, 66(2): 174–188. https://doi.org/10.1111/j.1468-2273.2012.00514.x.

McCann, C. (2018) *The Prevent Strategy and Right-Wing Extremism*. Oxon: Routledge.

McCarthy, R. (2022) Birmingham armed response gang: Everything we know about notorious group. Available at: https://www.birminghammail.co.uk/news/midlands-news/birmingham-armed-response-gang-everything-24651764

McGregor, R. (2021) Making ends meet. Available at: https://bscpostgrads.wordpress.com/2021/10/08/making-ends-meet/

McLaughlin, C., Lytje, M., and Holliday, C. (2019) *Consequences of childhood bereavement in the context of the British school system*. Cambridge: Faculty of Education, University of Cambridge.

McLeod, M. (2022) *Informal Exclusions from School: A ROTA Research Report*. London: Race on the Agenda.

Meier, J.S. (2009) A historical perspective on parental alienation syndrome and parental alienation. *Journal of Child Custody*, 6(3–4): 232–257. https://doi.org/10.1080/15379410903084681.

Meredith, M. (ed) (2024) *Universities and Epistemic Justice in a Plural World*. New York: Springer.

Miles, L. (2023) Understanding violence on British university campuses through the lens of the deviant leisure perspective. *Journal of Consumer Culture*, 24(1): 64–81. https://doi.org/10.1177/14695405231186471.

Milicev, J., McCann, M., Simpson, S.A., Biello, S.M., and Gardani, M. (2023) Evaluating mental health and well-being of post-graduate research: Prevalence and contributing factors. *Current Psychology*, 42: 12267–12280. https://link.springer.com/article/10.1007/s12144-021-02309-y.

Miller, E.V. (2018) Trauma and Sexual Violence. In Kurtz, J.R. (ed) *Trauma and Literature*. Cambridge: Cambridge University Press, pp 226–238.

Mills, S. and Waite, C. (2017) From big society to shared society? Geographies of social cohesion and encounter in the UK's National Citizen Service. *Geografiska Annaler: Series B- Human Geography*, 100(2): 131–148. https://doi.org/10.1080/04353684.2017.1392229.

Mirick, R.G. and Wladkowski, S.P. (2018) Pregnancy, motherhood, and academic career goals: Doctoral students' perspectives. *Affilia: Journal of Women and Social Work*, 33(2): 253–269.

Moeran, B. (2009) From participant observation to observant participation. In Ybema, S., Yanow, D., Wells, H., and Kamsteeg, F. *Organizational Ethnography: Studying the Complexities of Everyday Life*. London: SAGE Publications Ltd, pp 139–155. https://doi.org/10.4135/9781446278925.n8.

Moffitt, T.E. (2013) Childhood exposure to violence and lifelong health: Clinical intervention science and stress-biology research join forces. *Development and Psychopathology*, 25(4 pt 2): 1619–1634.

Montacute, R. and Cullinane, C. (2023) 25 years of university access. The Sutton Trust. Available at: https://www.suttontrust.com/wp-content/uploads/2023/10/25-Years-of-University-Access.pdf

Morris, S. (2022) Bristol University found guilty of failings over death of student. *The Guardian*, 20 May. Available at: https://www.theguardian.com/education/2022/may/20/bristol-university-found-guilty-of-failings-over-death-of-student-natasha-abrahart

Munro, E. (2023) Postgraduate Researchers and the Cost-of-Living Crisis: UCU Submission to the APPG for Students Inquiry into the Impact of the Cost-of-Living Crisis, March 2023. [Online] Available at: https://www.ucu.org.uk/media/13627/Postgraduate-researchers-and-the-cost-of-living-crisis/pdf/UCU_APPG_submission_March_2023.pdf

Myers, W. and Lantz, B. (2020) Reporting racist hate crime victimization to the police in the United States and the United Kingdom: A cross-national comparison. *The British Journal of Criminology*, 60(4): 1034–1055. https://doi.org/10.1093/bjc/azaa008.

Newsome, L.K. and Cooper, P. (2016) International students' cultural and social experiences in a British university: 'Such a hard life [it] is here'. *Journal of International Students*, 6(1): 195–215.

NHS (2022) *Dyslexia*. [Online] Available at: https://www.nhs.uk/conditions/dyslexia/

Nori, H., Peura, M.H., and Jauhiainen, A. (2020) From imposter syndrome to heroic tales: Doctoral students' backgrounds, study aims, and experiences. *International Journal of Doctoral Studies*, 15: 517.

Oakley, A. (2016) Interviewing women again: Power, time and the gift. *Sociology*, 50(1): 195–213. https://doi.org/10.1177/0038038515580253.

Oberg, K. (1954) *Culture Shock*. Indianapolis: Bobbs-Merrill.

O'Brien, J. (2010) Building understanding: Sensitive issues and putting the researcher in the research. *Anthropology Matters*, 12(1): 1–16. [Online] Available at: https://www.anthropologymatters.com/index.php/anth_matters/article/view/188

Office for National Statistics (2023) Birth characteristics in England and Wales: 2021. Available at: https://www.ons.gov.uk/peoplepopulationandcommunity/birthsdeathsandmarriages/livebirths/bulletins/birthcharacteristicsinenglandandwales/2021

O'Reilly, K. (2012) *Ethnographic Methods*. 2nd edn. Abingdon, Oxon: Routledge.

Pallela, K. and Talari, S. (2016) Plagiarism: A serious ethical issue for Indian students. *2016 IEEE International Symposium on Technology and Society (ISTAS)* [Preprint]. https://doi.org/10.1109/istas.2016.7764048.

Pollitt, A.M., Mernitz, S.E., Russell, S.T., Curran, M.A., and Toomey, R.B. (2021) Heteronormativity in the lives of lesbian, gay, bisexual, and queer young people. *Journal of Homosexuality*, 68(3): 522–544. Available at: https://www.ncbi.nlm.nih.gov/pmc/articles/PMC7035158/pdf/nihms-1047896.pdf

Porges, S.W. (2001) The polyvagal theory: Phylogenetic substrates of a social nervous system. *International Journal of Psychophysiology*, 42(2): 123–146. https://doi.org/10.1016/S0167-8760(01)00162-3.

Prince, S. (2019) (Re) Tracing the everyday 'sitings': A conceptual review of internet research 15 years later. *Issues and Trends in Educational Technology*, 7(1).

Quinn, B. and Khalaf, L. (2020) Regent's Park mosque prayer leader returns day after being stabbed. *The Guardian: UK Politics*, 21 February, p 4.

Raey, D. (2021) The working classes and higher education: Meritocratic fallacies of upward mobility in the United Kingdom. *European Journal of Education*, 56(1): 53–64.

Rajan, S.I. and Wadhawan, N. (2014) Future diasporas? International student migration from India to the UK. In Rajan, S.I. (ed) *Indian migration report 2014*. London: Routledge India, pp 171–189. https://doi.org/10.4324/9781315656342-22.

Raymen, T. (2022) *The Enigma of Social Harm: The Problem of Liberalisation*. London: Sage.

Regehr, C., Alaggia, R., Dennis, J., Pitts, A., and Saini, M. (2013) Interventions to reduce distress in adult victims of sexual violence and rape: A systematic review. *Campbell Systematic Reviews*, 9(1): 1–133. Available at: https://onlinelibrary.wiley.com/doi/pdf/10.4073/csr.2013.3

Rice, S. and Maltz, M. (2018) *Doing Ethnography in Criminology; Discovery through Fieldwork*. New York: Springer.

Robertson, M.J. (2022) Surviving and thriving: Doing a doctorate as a way of healing imposter syndrome. In Addison, M., Breeze, M., and Taylor, Y. (eds) *The Palgrave Handbook of Imposter Syndrome in Higher Education*. Cham: Springer International Publishing, pp 277–291.

Rodden, J. (2021) What is executive dysfunction? Signs and symptoms of EFD. [Online] Available at: https://www.additudemag.com/what-is-executive-function-disorder/#:~:text=Executive%20function%20skills%20enable%20us,Reviewed%20on%20January%2014%2C%202021

Roseby, S. and Gascoigne, M. (2021) A systematic review on the impact of trauma-informed education programs on academic and academic-related functioning for students who have experienced childhood adversity. *Traumatology (Tallahassee, Fla.)*, 27(2): 149–167. https://doi.org/10.1037/trm0000276.

Rosenbaum, A.T. (2015) Leisure travel and real existing socialism: New research on tourism in the Soviet Union and communist Eastern Europe. *Journal of Tourism History*, 7(1–2): 157–176.

Rousseau, J.J. (1990) *Rousseau, Judge of Jean-Jacques*. Hanover, NH: Dartmouth College Press.

Sahay, A. (2015) Doctoral degree in India: The need for transformation. In Lal, H. (ed) *Transforming Indian Higher Education*. New Delhi: Bloomsbury, pp 235–255.

SAMHSA. (2014) SAMHSA's Concept of Trauma and Guidance for a Trauma-Informed Approach. Available at: https://store.samhsa.gov/product/samhsas-concept-trauma-and-guidance-TI-approach/sma14-4884

Santos, G. and Cabral-Cardoso, C. (2008) Work-family culture in academia: A gendered view of work-family conflict and coping strategies. *Gender in Management: An International Journal*, 23(6): 442–457.

Scarpa, A. (2003) Community violence exposure in young adults. *Trauma, Violence, & Abuse*, 4(3): 210–227.

Scheirs, V. and Nuytiens, A. (2013) Ethnography and emotions. The myth of the cold and objective scientist. In Beyens, K., Christiaens, J., and Claes, B. (eds) *Pains of Doing Criminological Research*. Bruxelles: ASP, pp 141–160.

Seim, J. (2021) Participant observation, observant participation, and hybrid ethnography. *Sociological Methods & Research*, 53(1): 121–152.

Sherry, E. (2013) The vulnerable researcher: Facing the challenges of sensitive research. *Qualitative Research Journal*, 13(3): 278–288. Available at: https://www.emerald.com/insight/content/doi/10.1108/QRJ-10-2012-0007/full/html

Siegel, D.J. (1999) *The Developing Mind: Toward a Neurobiology of Interpersonal Experience*. New York: Guilford Press.

Singh, J.D. (2011) Higher education in India–Issues, challenges and suggestions. *Higher education*, 1(1): 93–103.

Sivasubramanian, R., Sridharan, R., and Saravanan, S.S. (2013) Indian Higher Education: A students' perspective. *2013 IEEE International Conference in MOOC, Innovation and Technology in Education (MITE)*. https://doi.org/10.1109/mite.2013.6756367.

Sliding Doors (1998) [film] Dir. Peter Howitt. United Kingdom: Paramount Pictures.

Sparks, R. (2020) Crime and justice research: The current landscape and future possibilities. *Criminology & Criminal Justice*, 20(4): 471–482. https://doi.org/10.1177/1748895820949297F.

Stephenson, Z., Jackson, A., and Wilkes, V. (2023) Student experiences of the 'closed-door' PhD and doctorate level viva voce: A systematic review of the literature. *Assessment & Evaluation in Higher Education*, 45(5): 601–615. https://doi.org/10.1080/02602938.2023.2282941.

Stergiopoulos, V., Gozdzik, A., Misir, V., Skosireva, A., Connelly, J., Sarang, A., Whisler, A., Hwang, S.W., O'Campo, P., and McKenzie, K. (2015) Effectiveness of housing first with intensive case management in an ethnically diverse sample of homeless adults with mental illness: A randomized controlled trial. *PLoS ONE*, 10(7): e0130281–e0130281. https://doi.org/10.1371/journal.pone.0130281.

Sufrin, C. (2015) 'Doctor, why didn't you adopt my baby?' Observant participation, care, and the simultaneous practice of medicine and anthropology. *Culture, Medicine, and Psychiatry*, 39(4): 614–633. https://doi.org/10.1007/s11013-015-9435-x.

Thakre, A. and Jaishankar, K. (2018) Whither Indian criminology? *International Journal of Criminal Justice Sciences*, 13(2): 247–263. https://doi.org/10.5281/zenodo.2647852.

Toffoletti, K. and Starr, K. (2016) Women academics and work–life balance: Gendered discourses of work and care. *Gender, Work & Organization*, 23(5): 489–504.

Tomlinson, J. (2021) Deindustrialisation and 'Thatcherism': Moral economy and unintended consequences. *Contemporary British History*, 35(4): 620–642.

Tonge, J. (2005) The last bastion of ad hocery? Research supervision from idea to viva. *European Political Science*, 4(2): 230–237. https://doi.org/10.1057/palgrave.eps.2210020.

Touma, R. (2023) Cozzie livs: Light-hearted term for cost-of-living crisis named Macquarie dictionary word of the year. *The Guardian*. [Online] Available at: https://www.theguardian.com/australia-news/2023/nov/28/cozzie-livs-light-hearted-term-for-cost-of-living-crisis-named-macquarie-dictionary-word-of-the-year

Townson, S. (2016) I was a terrible PhD supervisor. Don't make the same mistakes I did. *The Guardian*, 24 March [Online] Available at: https://www.theguardian.com/higher-education-network/2016/mar/24/i-was-a-terrible-phd-supervisor-dont-make-the-same-mistakes-i-did

Trafford, V. (2003) Questions in doctoral vivas: Views from the inside. *Quality Assurance in Education*, 11(2): 114–122. https://doi.org/10.1108/09684880310471542.

Trebilcock, J. and Griffiths, C. (2022) Student motivations for studying criminology: A narrative inquiry. *Criminology & Criminal Justice*, 22(3): 480–497. https://doi.org/10.1177/1748895821993843.

Tyler, I. (2020) *Stigma; The Machinery of Inequality*. London: Zed Books Ltd.

UCU (2022) UK higher education: A workforce in crisis. [Online] Available at: https://www.ucu.org.uk/media/12532/UK-higher-education---a-workforce-in-crisis/pdf/UK_HE_Report_24_Mar22.pdf

Van Bueren, G. (2021) Universities must embrace working-class academics, students and culture. [Online] Available at: https://www.timeshighereducation.com/blog/universities-must-embrace-working-class-academics-students-and-culture

Vance, T. (2019) Addressing mental health in the Black community. [Online] Available at: https://www.columbiapsychiatry.org/news/addressing-mental-health-black-community

Van Der Kolk, B.A. (2005) Developmental trauma disorder. *Psychiatric Annals*, 35(5): 401–408. https://doi.org/10.3928/00485713-20050501-06.

van de Schoot, R., Yerkes, M.A., Mouw, J.M., and Sonneveld, H. (2013) What took them so long? Explaining PhD delays among doctoral candidates. *PLoS ONE*, 8(7): e68839. https://doi.org/10.1371/journal.pone.0068839.

Wacquant, L. (2015) For a sociology of flesh and blood. *Qualitative Sociology*, 38(1): 1–11. https://doi.org/10.1007/s11133-014-9291-y.

Waters, H.R., Hyder, A.A., Rajkotia, Y., Basu, S., and Butchart, A. (2005) The costs of interpersonal violence: An international review. *Health Policy*, 73(3): 303–315. [Online] Available at: https://www.sciencedirect.com/science/article/pii/S0168851004002805

Weber, M. (1978) *Economy and Society: An Outline of Interpretive Sociology*. Berkeley, CA: University of California Press.

Webster, A. (2018) Student revolt: Voices of the austerity generation. *Social Movement Studies*, 17(6): 756–757.

Weinstein, N., Haddock, G., Chubb, J., Wilsdon, J., and Manville, C. (2023) Supported or stressed while being assessed? How motivational climates in UK University workplaces promote or inhibit researcher well-being. *Higher Education Quarterly*, 77: 537–557.

Weller, M. (2020) The COVID-19 online pivot: Adapting university teaching to social distancing. [Blog] LSE Blogs. Available at: https://blogs.lse.ac.uk/impactofsocialsciences/2020/03/12/the-covid-19-online-pivot-adapting-university-teaching-to-social-distancing/

Williams, B. (2019) The big society: Ten years on. *Political Insight*, 10(4): 22–25. https://doi.org/10.1177/2041905819891369.

Wilson, D.B., Yardley, E., and Lynes, A. (2015) *Serial Killers and the Phenomenon of Serial Murder: A Student Textbook*. Hampshire: Waterside Press.

Winlow, S. (2022) Beyond measure: On the marketization of British universities, and the domestication of academic criminology. *Critical Criminology*, 30(3): 479–494. https://doi.org/10.1007/s10612-022-09643-y.

Winlow, S. and Hall, S. (2013) *Rethinking Social Exclusion: The End of the Social?* London: Sage.

Wood, E. (2022) *My viva (and how I prepared for it) – Ellie Wood*. [Online] Available at: https://blogs.ed.ac.uk/ellie-wood/2022/08/22/my-viva-and-how-i-prepared-for-it/

Woodward, K.P., Yu, Z., Chen, W., Chen, T., Jackson, D.B., Powell, T.W., and Wang L. (2023) Childhood bereavement, adverse and positive childhood experiences, and flourishing among Chinese Young Adults. *International Journal of Environmental Research and Public Health*, 20(5): 4631.

Zempi, I. and Awan, I. (2016) *Islamophobia. Lived Experiences of online and offline victimisation*. Bristol: Bristol Policy Press.

Zempi, I. and Chakraborti, N. (2014) *Islamophobia, Victimisation, and the Veil*. Hampshire: Palgrave Macmillan.

Zhao, N., Zhang, X., Noah, A., Tiede, M., and Hirsch, J. (2023) Separable processes for live 'in-person' and live 'zoom-like' faces. *Imaging Neuroscience*, 1: 1–17. https://doi.org/10.1162/imag_a_00027.

Index

A

academic capitalism 198–199, 204
academic culture 87–88
academic identity 84, 149
academic job markets 179–181
academic writing skills 48, 52, 58
accepting help 100
Access to Higher Education courses 19, 74, 111
accommodation, finding 51
accountability 86, 89
Active Citizenship 162, 163
ADHD 114
adversarial working conditions 125
adverse childhood experiences 16, 105–116, 124, 129
advice before starting a PhD 23, 39
affinity spaces 115
age profiles 3
ageism 32–33
AI 213, 214
alcohol 79, 138–139, 141, 142
A-level results 19, 45, 187–188, 201
annual leave 85, 88
anxiety
  about studying 19
  choosing a topic 37
  'culture shock' 47
  and grief 18
  and overwhelm 107, 113, 127, 151
  public speaking 31
  statistics on PhD students suffering 4
application processes 61, 62–66
archives, accessing 86
associate lecturer roles 95, 143
Associate Professorships 191–193

B

Beasy, K. 3
belonging, sense of 49, 50, 54
Berry, C. 3
Big Society Agenda 162
Block, P. 101
blogs 183
boundaries 84–86
Bourdieu, P. 84
Brabazon, T. 177
Braun, V. 164
bureaucracy 46–47
burnout/stress 80, 85, 87–88, 102, 114, 125
Bussotti, C. 143

C

capitalism 28, 129, 198–199, 204
  see also neoliberalism
career goals 38, 58, 59, 65, 96
careers after PhDs 4, 176, 179–181, 191, 204
caring responsibilities
  elderly relatives 21, 24
  parenthood 74, 75, 93–104, 111–112, 137–138, 205
casualisation 4
childcare availability 99
childcare costs 95, 97
chunking of work 91
Clance, P.R. 90
class, as barrier to entry 3
  see also working class academics
coaching 102
colonialism 62
comfort zone, exceeding one's 24, 52, 55, 113, 152
community, importance of 11, 50
commuting 86
competition/competitiveness
  career paths 192
  friends 38
  hyper-competitiveness of academia 26–34
  neoliberalism 213
  supervision 219
  taking account of structural conditions 164, 166
  and trauma-informed approaches 125, 128
  Viva 182
complex trauma/post-traumatic stress disorder 124
conceptualising a PhD topic 35–44
conditional offers 32
conferences 99, 100, 125, 182–183, 185, 194, 197
constructive feedback, seeking 41, 65
Conversation, The 183
Cooper, P. 48
Cornell, B. 4
'corrections' 178
cost-of-living crisis 83, 84, 157, 163, 164, 208
counselling 81
COVID-19
  additional emotional labour 139–141
  effect on data collection 86
  encouraging anti-social tendencies 197
  ethics 42, 207–208

and grief 20, 79
health risks 27
positive benefits on online events 99
and Vivas 176
working from home 97
criminology 6, 38, 60, 180, 211
critical conversations 42
critical thinking 58, 59, 156, 183, 187
criticism, receiving 127–128
cultural capital 84
cultural identity 47, 53
'culture shock' 45, 46–48, 67

D

Dalton, C. 138
data collection
  building a professional network as a research assistant 182
  changing methodology 157, 159–160, 164, 165
  choosing methods of 40–41
  COVID-19 86
  funding 54
  shortage of data 160
  while working full-time 86
data integrity issues 60
deadlines 80, 90–91
deaths 16–17
  see also grief
dedications 77
'defending' the thesis see Viva
depression 4, 18, 65, 66, 127, 138–139
desk space at home 97
Disabled Student Allowance 112
diversity 5
  see also equality, diversity, and inclusion (EDI)
domestic labour 99, 137
downtime 86
  see also rest and relaxation
dropping out 3, 87, 101, 141
Dumitrescu, I. 89
Dyregrov, A. 16–17, 18
dyslexia 107–108, 112

E

early career academics 4, 24, 180, 182–183, 192, 197, 208
emails 85–86, 126–127, 215, 217
emotional costs 46, 50
emotional fatigue 31
emotional labour 140, 143, 146, 152–154
emotional recognition 30–31
emotional regulation 113–116
emotional support from supervisors 50, 54
equality, diversity and inclusion (EDI) 123, 130
escapism 111–112
essay writing skills 48, 52

ethics
  academic integrity 58
  complexities of conducting in another country 50
  COVID-19 42
  fieldwork 145, 150–153, 158–159
  Indian PhD system 60
  resolving ethical tensions 145–155, 203, 207
  supervision 212
ethnicity 3–4
ethnography 41, 42, 64, 141, 145–155, 199–200, 202
exercise 80, 102
exploitation 135–144, 162, 196
extensions 95, 97
extenuating circumstances 97

F

Fallout, R.D. 128, 129
family
  financial support from 64, 66
  leaving to move abroad 46
  mental health 97
  parenthood 74, 75, 93–104, 111–112, 137–138, 205
  support from 24, 64, 66, 89, 115, 187
  see also partners
fear of failure 20, 90
feedback
  on applications 62–63, 65
  receiving negative feedback 41–42, 48, 63, 90
  seeking constructive feedback 41, 65
  soliciting 62
  supervisors' duties 219
fees for studying 4
  see also tuition fees
fellowships 61
Ferrell, J. 147
fieldwork
  compensation for participants 158–159
  complexities of conducting in another country 50, 54, 64
  in cost-of-living crisis 160
  ethics 145, 150–153, 158–159
  incentives for participation 159–160, 161–162
  interruptions to 151
  as 'messy, qualitative' experience 149, 150, 154
  observant participation 151
  shortage of data 160
  see also data collection
finalising topic after enrolment 42–43
finances
  costs of second degrees 63
  experiencing problems with 64
  rent deposits 46
  see also funding; part-time work

'finding your tribe' 179
first generation students 84, 90, 91, 141–142, 191
Fischer, M.M.J. 149
fixed-term contracts 180
Free School Meals 83–84
friends
  competitiveness 38
  maintaining friendships 87–89
  making new 49, 50, 143
  support from 18, 20, 24
'friendship as a method' 147
full-time job, PhD as 88
full-time lecturing 83–92
full-time versus part-time study 23, 94–95
funded PhDs
  applications 62
  see also partially-funded PhDs; self-funding
  applying for funding 26–34
  changing methodology 158–161
  making the decision to go for 23
  'pre-defined' PhD programmes 37
funding
  applying for research grants 192, 203, 206
  changing methodology 157, 158–161
  for fieldwork 54, 159–160, 161–162, 166
  for fieldwork abroad 54
  incentives for participation 164
  Indian PhD system 59–60
  international students 61
  participant-observer research method 164
  part-time work 51
  tied-in teaching roles 95
  timeline planning 165

G

gaps in the literature, finding 39–40, 42, 53
gatekeepers 50, 54, 55, 158, 159, 161
GCSE results 17, 19, 73–74, 142, 201
gender identity 4
gender roles 99
getting the work done 79–80
Giddens, A. 163
Gillam, L. 146–147
global South 57–68
Goffman, E. 153
grief 15, 16–18, 24–25, 78–80
Griffiths, J. 143
guidance/advisory texts 211–212
Guillemin, M. 146–147
guilt 81, 86, 89, 91

H

Haidt, J. 213
Harris, M. 128
Hazell, C.M. 3
healing 53, 81
hobbies and interests, keeping up 95

Hochschild, A. 140
'home,' sense of 47–48, 53
homesickness 47, 49
homophobia 32–33
hourly-paid contracts 84
hours per week 95
household management 99, 137
hyper-competitiveness of academia 23, 26–34

I

identity
  academic identity 84, 149
  cultural identity 47, 53
  gender identity 4
  personal identity 28, 29, 31
  researcher identity 84, 149
  spatial identity 55
  'student' identity 149
identity politics 130
IELTS tests 46, 61
Imes, S.A. 90
impact 38–39, 40, 64, 182, 186, 198
imposter syndrome
  ageism 32
  channelled 193
  comparison with peers 50
  designed-in 141–143
  handling workloads 52
  managing 89–92
  nervousness 31–32
  origins of 17, 186–187, 191–192
  and people-pleasing 143
  pervasive after PhD 185–195
  research proposals 29
  senior academics 194, 203
  strategies to overcome 80
  in those with trauma backgrounds 113, 127
Indian education system 57–58
individualism 125, 134, 166, 167
inequalities 130
insurance liability waivers 203
international students 45–56, 57–68
interpersonal hypervigilance 125–127, 133
interruptions 97, 175
interviews 65, 66–67
Islamophobia 38–39, 40, 43
isolation/loneliness 4, 27, 127, 225

J

jargon 51, 85
job markets 179–181

K

Kemmis, S. 158

L

language
  IELTS tests 46, 61
  PhD in a foreign 46, 48–49

league tables 192, 198
learning about how to do a PhD 84–85, 211–212
learning difficulties 105–116
lecturer roles 179, 181, 211
LGBTQIA+ community 32
'Life Politics' 163
'life stuff,' unexpected 97
  see also grief
literature reviews 39
lived experience 28, 29, 30, 31, 53
living costs 46, 51, 66, 83
  see also cost-of-living crisis
living standards 46, 51
loans 4, 66
loneliness 27, 127, 225
Lukianoff, G. 213
Lynam, S. 4
Lynes, A. 22, 23, 42, 136
Lytje, M. 17, 18

M

Marcus, G.E. 149
marketisation of universities 4, 5, 198, 211, 213, 219
Master's level study
  applying for a PhD without 157
  choosing a PhD topic 36–37, 41–42, 44, 191
  hyper-competitiveness of academia 27–29
  imposter syndrome 190–191
  as research training 58, 59, 60, 61, 65, 202
  second master's degrees 63
  self-doubt 20
  statistics on socioeconomic backgrounds 3
  tailoring to specific needs 113–114
'mature' students 19
McLeod, M. 106
Meier, J.S. 137
memory-based education 58
mental health
  adverse childhood experiences 125
  burnout/stress 80, 85, 87–88, 102, 114, 125
  depression 4, 18, 65, 66, 127, 138–139
  deterioration of 138–139
  grief 15, 16–18, 24–25, 73–82
  managing the mind 105–116
  and the neo-liberal university 5
  panic attacks 18
  statistics 3, 4
  student support services 126
  suicidal thoughts 18, 27, 128, 135, 139, 140
  supporting students' 140
  of your whole family 97
  see also grief

mental preparation 30–31
mentors 23, 37, 40, 80, 91, 182, 203, 210
methodologies 40–41, 145, 147, 156–168
Milicev, J. 3
mind management 105–116
mindfulness 80
mistakes, making 52, 113
monographs 175, 181
moral purpose 196
motivation, keeping up 94, 102, 214
moving countries 45–56, 205
moving house 180
MPhil degrees 49, 51, 52, 53–54, 61, 63–64

N

narrowing topic choices 36, 42–43, 44
National Student Survey 192, 197
negative feedback, receiving 41–42, 48, 63, 90
neoliberalism
  academic capitalism 197, 198, 199
  effect on supervisory relationships 212
  equality, diversity and inclusion (EDI) 123
  imposter syndrome 192
  individualism 125, 134, 166, 167
  marketisation of universities 4, 5, 198, 211, 213, 219
  neo-liberalisation of academia 4
  structural conditions 161–164, 168, 181
  trauma-informed approaches 124–125, 127
  workloads 218
  see also competition/competitiveness
nervousness 31
neurodiversity 107–113, 142
Newsome, L.K. 48
'no', learning to say 85
non-academic outputs 183
Nori, H. 141
Nuytiens, A. 148

O

Oakley, A. 147
Oberg, K. 45, 47
observant participation 151–152
online platforms 126, 140, 176–177, 197, 207–208
online research 141
original knowledge 26–28, 30, 50, 211, 213

P

paid employment 84
  see also part-time work; teaching roles
panic attacks 18
parenthood 74, 75, 93–104, 111–112, 137–138, 205
  single parenthood 74, 93, 99–100, 115, 137

Index

parents
  death of 15–25, 75–76
  influence of 77–78
  leaving to move abroad 46
  pride 74, 77
  support from 18, 27
partially-funded PhDs 66, 83, 84, 136
participant-observer status 147, 150–151, 163
participatory action research 158–159, 161–162, 165–167
partners
  moving because of 205
  moving countries 46–48
  relationship breakdowns 138, 206
  sharing domestic labour 99
  support from 65
part-time study 3, 23, 78–79, 94–95, 175
part-time teaching roles 143
part-time work
  balancing 75, 79, 137, 143, 207
  cost-of-living crisis 84
  international students 51, 64, 65
  as means to gain relevant experience 201
  self-funding 96
pass rates 3
passion 23, 29, 31, 38, 65, 74
peer comparisons 50
peer support 48, 52, 133, 143
perfectionism 86–87, 127–128
'performance reviews' 197
personal development/change 49, 50
personal safety 47
personal statements 28–29, 61, 63
plagiarism 58, 60
Polyvagal Theory 126
Porges, S. 126
positive affirmations 80, 81
post-doctoral studies 180
practical research skills 58, 59
precarious work 4, 143, 156, 180, 218
'pre-defined' PhD programmes 37
Prince, S. 141
procrastination 79–80, 101
professional development 50
professional networks
  academic job markets 179, 181, 182–183, 185
  balancing family life 99–100, 143
  and choice of location for PhD 61, 62
  choosing a PhD topic 39, 41–42
  managing the mind 115
  moving countries 49, 52–53, 62–63
professorships 205
promotions 198, 204
'protective mission' of universities 213
public speaking 31, 128, 185, 194

publication
  journal articles 181
  as metric 208
  MPhil research 64
  'publish or perish' mentality 88, 125, 208
  publishable quality work 213
  publishing plans 181
  publishing your PhD data 181
  reaching required standards for 60
  seeking opportunities for 63
purpose 5, 21, 38, 94, 118, 196–209

Q

quitting 80
  see also dropping out

R

racism 200
Raymen, T. 5
Reader roles 204
'Reading Clubs' 49
reasonable adjustments 128
references 62, 63
refining a topic 40–42
rejections, handling 27, 33, 62–63, 65, 66
relaxation, timetabling 86, 102
relocation
  costs 46
  moving countries 45–56, 57–68
  moving institution 49–55
remote working 125–127, 140
research assistant roles 65, 96, 180, 182, 201–202, 205
research clusters 183
Research Excellence Framework (REF) 4, 181, 192
research experience, gaining 32, 63, 67, 201
research participants, building relationships with 54, 145–155
research portfolio, building 180, 182
research proposals
  constructing 29–30
  draft stages 39, 40
  originality and innovation 26–28, 50
  presenting 31–32
  soliciting feedback on 62
research question, conceptualising 35–36
research skills guidance 58
researcher identity 84, 149
researcher positioning 30, 31, 145–155, 158, 163
resilience 44, 67, 218
rest and relaxation 86, 88, 95
ringfencing your PhD time 100–101

S

sabbaticals 141
safe spaces 132

SAMHSA (Substance Abuse and Mental Health Services Administration) 129, 130, 134
scheduling in times to work on your PhD 100–101
Scheirs, V. 148
scholarships 62
  see also funded PhDs
school underachievement 17, 27, 36, 73–74, 106, 188, 201
Seim, J. 146, 150
self-belief 23, 30, 64, 114, 179, 192
self-care 80, 81
self-criticism 22
self-discovery 43
self-doubt
  about doing a PhD 22
  balancing full-time lecturing and PhD 90–91
  embarking on a PhD 23
  exploited PhD students 135, 157
  international students 63
  managing the mind 114
  pervasive after PhD 185–195
  re-entering academia 20
  strategies to overcome 80
  and supervisors 215, 217
  when applications are rejected 27
  see also imposter syndrome
self-funding
  and academic freedom 37, 207–208
  application processes 65–66
  expectations of supervisors 219
  loans 66
  pros and cons 23
  socioeconomic disadvantage 84
  student loans 74
self-sabotage 20, 96
shared decision-making 132
Shedd, J.A. 52
Siegal, D. 125
single parenthood 74, 93, 99–100, 115, 137
situated cognition 150–151
small progress, making 100
social media 135, 138, 143, 182, 199, 204, 206
socialising 47, 51
  see also friends
socioeconomic disadvantage 3, 28, 83–84, 123–124, 129, 130
spatial identity 55
spotlight effect 128
Starr, K. 137
stipends 95
stress and burnout 5, 80, 85, 87–88, 102, 114, 125
structural conditions, incorporating 166, 167

'student' identity 149
student loans 4, 66
student support services 126
study abroad 45–56
study skills sessions 52
submission 87, 90–91
Sufrin, C. 151
suicidal thoughts 18, 27, 128, 135, 139, 140
supervision
  changing methodology 165, 217
  changing topic 157
  collaborative reflection on 210–221
  critical friends 215
  emotional support 50
  emotional support from supervisors 50, 54
  encouraging not quitting 80
  ethics 154
  finding supervisors 42–43
  mock Vivas 178
  quality of 165
  'red flags' 214–220
  relationship with supervisor 50, 53–54, 59, 64, 212–213, 215
  setting boundaries 85
  trauma-informed supervision 131–134
  trust and transparency 133
  unpaid work for 59
  and Vivas 179
support
  from academic community 50
  academic writing skills 48
  building networks of 52–53
  encouraging not quitting 80
  from friends 18, 20, 24
  importance of academic supporters 22
  importance of support network 87–89, 167
  institutional 31
  personal support networks 52–53
  postgraduate student community 51
  student support services 126
  see also professional networks
symposia 183

T

teaching assistant roles 95
Teaching Excellence Framework 192
teaching roles
  academic capitalism 197, 203–204, 206
  balancing with PhD 95–96
  career paths 23, 179, 180
  emotional labour 140
  exploitation 139
  gaining teaching experience before applying 32
  partially-funded PhDs 136
  purpose 21–22

therapy 18
time management 84–86, 94, 96
time off 85, 88
  see also rest and relaxation
time taken to complete 87, 211
timeline planning 165
Toffoletti, K. 137
topics
  changing topic 157
  conceptualising a PhD topic 35–44
  finalising topic after enrolment 42–43
  gaps in the literature, finding 39–40, 42, 53
  mentors 37, 40
  narrowing topic choices 36, 42–43, 44
  refining a topic 40–42
  time pressures to choose 38, 40–41
Townson, S. 215
toxic academic work cultures 87–88
trauma 18, 19, 28, 30–31, 76, 79, 123–134
trauma-informed approaches 123–124, 128–129, 151, 153
'trigger warnings' 130
tuition fees 4, 83, 84, 199, 212
Tyler, I. 142

U

university accommodation 51
unknown, stepping into 2, 21, 50
US 129

V

validation, seeking external 192–193, 194
'verstehen' 147
visiting lecturer roles 21, 32
Viva 175–184, 211
volunteer roles 148–149, 154, 190
volunteerism 161–162

W

Wacquant, L. 150–151
waivers 203
walking breaks 80
Weber, M. 147
Weller, M. 140
'why,' figuring out your 94, 102
'window of tolerance' 125, 128
Winlow, S. 179, 192, 211, 212, 213
word counts 35–36
work and non-work distinction 88–89
working class academics 77–78, 83–92, 142–143
working from home 88, 97
working hours 88–89
work-life balance
  balancing a family 93–104, 136–138
  balancing full-time lecturing and PhD 87–89
  grief 75
  Indian education system 59
  normalisation of unsustainable 87–88
  supervisors' 215
workloads
  excessive 51–52, 135–144, 197
  increased during COVID-19 140
  normalisation of unsustainable 87–88
  prioritisation 84–86
  supervisors' 217
writer's block 80, 101
writing goals, setting 89
writing retreats 86
writing up period 86

Y

youth-led participatory action research methodology (YPAR) 157, 158, 166

www.ingramcontent.com/pod-product-compliance
Lightning Source LLC
Chambersburg PA
CBHW071154070526
44584CB00019B/2786